The Complete Guide to
Public Safety
Cycling SECOND EDITION

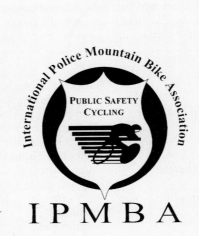

International Police Mountain Bike Association

Baltimore, Maryland

JONES AND BARTLETT PUBLISHERS
Sudbury, Massachusetts
BOSTON   TORONTO   LONDON   SINGAPORE

World Headquarters
Jones and Bartlett Publishers
40 Tall Pine Drive
Sudbury, MA 01776
978-443-5000
info@jbpub.com
www.jbpub.com

Jones and Bartlett Publishers Canada
6339 Ormindale Way
Mississauga, Ontario L5V 1J2
Canada

Jones and Bartlett Publishers
International
Barb House, Barb Mews
London W6 7PA
United Kingdom

I P M B A
International Police Mountain Bike Association
583 Frederick Road, Suite 5B
Baltimore, MD 21228
410-744-2400
www.ipmba.org

Jones and Bartlett's books and products are available through most bookstores and online booksellers. To contact Jones and Bartlett Publishers directly, call 800-832-0034, fax 978-443-8000, or visit our website www.jbpub.com.

Substantial discounts on bulk quantities of Jones and Bartlett's publications are available to corporations, professional associations, and other qualified organizations. For details and specific discount information, contact the special sales department at Jones and Bartlett via the above contact information or send an email to specialsales@jbpub.com.

Production Credits

Chief Executive Officer: Clayton Jones
Chief Operating Officer: Don W. Jones, Jr.
President, Higher Education and Professional Publishing: Robert W. Holland, Jr.
V.P., Sales and Marketing: William J. Kane
V.P., Design and Production: Anne Spencer
V.P., Manufacturing and Inventory Control: Therese Connell
Publisher—Public Safety Group: Kimberly Brophy
Acquisitions Editor: Jeremy Spiegel
Associate Managing Editor: Janet Morris
Production Editor: Karen C. Ferreira

Director of Marketing: Alisha Weisman
Manufacturing Buyer: Therese Connell
Composition: Modern Graphics, Inc.
Text and Cover Design: Anne Spencer
Photo Researcher and Photographer: Kimberly Potvin
Associate Photo Researcher and Photographer: Lee Michelson
Top left cover image courtesy of Kathleen Vonk; bottom cover images © Jones and Bartlett Publishers, courtesy of MIEMSS.
Printing and Binding: Courier Kendallville
Cover Printing: Courier Kendallville

Library of Congress Cataloging-in-Publication Data

The complete guide to public safety cycling / International Police Mountain Bike Association. — 2nd ed.
   p. cm.
   Includes index.
   ISBN-13: 978-0-7637-4433-5
   ISBN-10: 0-7637-4433-6
  1. Police patrol—Specialized units.   2. Bicycles.   3. All terrain bicycles.   I. International Police Mountain Bike Association.
   HV8019.C66 2007
   363.2'32—dc22

6048
                                                   2007007225
Printed in the United States of America
16 15 14   10 9 8 7 6 5

Additional credits appear on page 254, which constitutes a continuation of the copyright page.

Brief Contents

Contents

Preface

The Complete Guide to Public Safety Cycling, Second Edition, is the latest version of the *Complete Guide to Police Cycling.* The name and the content have been updated to reflect the expansion of the field of public safety cycling to include emergency medical services (EMS) and private security personnel.

Quiet, cost efficient, and amazingly effective, mountain bikes are able to bridge the gap between automobiles and foot patrol. Both police and security cyclists are able to use all of their senses, including smell and hearing, to detect and address crime. They can choose to operate with stealth, approaching suspects virtually unnoticed, or to be highly visible, enhancing the perceived safety of an area.

The mobility of an EMS provider on a bike can mean the difference between life or death in congested or crowded conditions. Emergency medical providers on bikes are deployed in tourist areas and pedestrian zones, during special events, in amusement parks and sports arenas, on college campuses, and in airports, train stations, and other transportation hubs. They are also indispensable in urban and wilderness search and rescue and mass casualty situations.

While many officers and EMS providers know how to ride bikes, far fewer know how to cycle and survive in complex traffic. Unlike recreational cyclists who can choose routes that are convenient

and safe, public safety cyclists have to ride where they are needed. That may mean they have to ride in extremely heavy and/or complicated traffic. They need to know how to brake safely with maximum effectiveness and control, and perform emergency maneuvers if a car or object suddenly appears in their path. Public safety cyclists need the skills to ascend and descend curbs, stairs, and other environmental obstacles. Police cyclists must know what tactics to use in a pursuit and how to quickly, but safely, dismount and perform an arrest or fire their sidearm. EMS cyclists must know how to cycle with a heavy load, select and pack medical equipment, and position a bike at a scene in such a way that it blocks curious onlookers yet does not hamper access to their medical equipment. Security cyclists need to know how to operate their bikes in a manner that maximizes the safety of their patrol area.

This book is designed to assist public safety cyclists of all types to operate a bicycle safely, effectively, and as an essential tool for service delivery. However, it is only one part of the process. Motor skills cannot be learned from a book; they must be demonstrated and practiced. In order to achieve this goal, aspiring public safety cyclists must use the information in this book to supplement the techniques they learn in an IPMBA Police, EMS, or Security Cyclist Course.

Acknowledgements

Editors

Maureen Becker, Executive Director, International Police Mountain Bike Association

Jim Bowell, EMSCI #001T/PCI #567T, Troy Fire Department

Contributors

Kirby Beck, PCI #002T/EMSCI #017T, Coon Rapids Police Department (retired)

Neil Blackington, EMSCI #031/PCI #902, Boston EMS

Marvin Boluyt, Ph.D Assistant Professor, University of Michigan Laboratory of Molecular Kinesiology

Lamar Booker, Columbus Police Department

John Brandt, PCI #204/EMSCI #055, University of Maryland Police Department

Jeffrey Brown, PCI #487/EMSCI #064, Dayton Police Department

Christopher Bryant, PCI #604, Nashville Police Department

Ron Burkitt, PCI #488, Hilliard Police Department

Justin Coleman, Columbus Police Department

Paul Conner, PCI #627, Anne Arundel County Police Department

Eddy Croissant, PCI #366/EMSCI #086, Tampa Police Department

Christopher Davala, PCI #490/EMSCI #056, Maryland State Police

Steve Denny, EMSCI #040, Franklin Fire Department

Eva Dexter

Patrick Donovan, EMSCI #025, Puyallup Fire Department

Michael Emmons, Kettering Medical Center Security

Donald Erb, PCI #205/EMSCI #018, Lancaster Police Department

Doug Evans, PCI #797, Sugarcreek Township Police Department

Kurt Feavel, PCI #539, University of Wisconsin Police Department

Steve Forbes, PCI #743, University of Guelph Police Department

Dan Ganzel, PCI #097, Palm Beach County Sheriffs Office

Nick Gatlin, EMSCI #036, Williamson Medical Center EMS

Sean Genest, Anne Arundel County Police Department

Michael Goetz, PCI #063T/EMSCI #003T, Seattle Police Department (retired)

Lou Ann Hamblin, PCI #306/EMSCI #062, Van Buren Township Police Department

Robert Hatcher PCI #629/EMSCI #103, Delaware Police Department

David Hildebrand, PCI #404T/EMSCI #118T, Denton Police Department

Nancy Hill McClary, Assistant Director, Ohio State University Center for the Study and Teaching of Writing

Doug Johnson, PCI #377/EMSCI #163, Indianapolis Metropolitan Police Department

Michael Johnston, PCI #107, Utah's Hogle Zoo

Al Jones, Tri-State Regional Community Policing Institute

Thomas Lynch, MBE, EMSCI #149, London Ambulance Service

Chris Menton Associate Professor, Roger Williams University School of Justice Studies

Monte May, PCI #262T/EMSCI #009T, Kansas City Police Department

Shawn McMaken, Troy Fire Department

Michael Murphy, PCI #385, Warminster Police Department

Don Pemberton, Troy Fire Department

Karen Pemberton

Ross Petty, Professor of Marketing Law, Babson College

Donald Reed, PCI #195T/EMSCI #038T, Denver Police Department

Jody Reid, Director, Chinook Centre Security

Robert Ricciardi, PCI #282T/EMSCI #078T, Palm Beach County Sheriffs Office

Thomas J. Richardson, PCI #139T/EMSCI #010T, San Antonio Police Department (retired)

James Roy, PCI #175, Topeka Police Department

Loren Ryerson, PCI #413/EMSCI #140, Aspen Police Department

Jason Schiffer, PCI #483, Bethlehem Police Department

Tim Schurr, Instructor, United Bicycle Institute

Alan Simpson, PCI #165T/EMSCI #005T, Pompano Beach Police Department (retired)

David Simpson, PCI #115/EMSCI #011, Cincinnati Police Division

Thomas Sipin, PCI #254, West Allis Police Department

Matthew Sledgeski, PCI #634, Anne Arundel County Police Department

Mitchell Trujillo, PCI #244T, Boulder Police Department

Tony Valdes, PCI #256/EMSCI #012, Miami-Dade Police Department

Kenneth Viehmann, PCI #623, Tacoma Police Department

Kathleen Vonk, PCI #042T/EMSCI #063T, Ann Arbor Police Department

Dexter Wade, Troy Fire Department

John F. Washington, Jr., PCI #461T/EMSCI #037T, University of Pennsylvania Police Department

Christopher Whaley, PCI #706/EMSCI #116, Ontario Provincial Police

Barbara Winstead, PCI #731/EMSCI #132, Cincinnati Police Division

Thomas Woods, PCI #010T/117T, Denton Police Department

Marc Zingarelli, EMSCI #179, Circleville Fire Department

Public Safety Cycling

A Brief History of Public Safety Cycling

Introduction

Many believe that the Seattle Police Department introduced the concept of public safety cycling in the late 1980s. However, police departments employed bicycles as early as the 1860s, and bikes remained popular until they were replaced by motor vehicles. Seattle's recognition of the tactical advantages offered by mountain bike technology ushered in a new era, one in which the bike would gain widespread use in all branches of public safety cycling–police, security, and emergency medical services.

Police Cycling

England pioneered the use of police patrols in 1818, and in 1829, Sir Robert Peel introduced the Metropolitan Police Act, which established police districts staffed by paid constables. These constables patrolled 14 to 17 hours per day, covering up to 20 miles per day on foot. They were required to leave a ticket at a designated home at the far end of their beat as evidence that they were not shirking their duty. As American cities formed police departments from the 1830s through the 1850s, police sought alternatives to walking, and many departments turned to the newest transportation technology—the bicycle.

Connecticut bike officer, circa 1914.

In the 1860s, the earliest pedal bicycles, called "boneshakers," were introduced. The earliest use of the bicycle by police is reported to have been in Illinois in 1869, but the bikes were heavy, uncomfortable, and expensive. By 1893, the bicycle had evolved to its modern form, and by 1894, Philadelphia, Brooklyn, Cincinnati, and Chicago all had active bicycle police patrols, as did the Canadian cities of Ottawa and Winnipeg. New York City started its bicycle unit in December 1895 with two bicycle policemen. These bike officers proved effective in controlling scorchers (speeders on bicycles) and runaway horses, so Police Commissioner Theodore Roosevelt expanded the so-called "scorcher squad." Within its first year of service, the 29-man bicycle squad was responsible for 1366 arrests. Their success was echoed in cities such as Denver and Grand Forks, MN, which established bike squads in 1896 to control scorchers and sidewalk cyclists. Other cities adopting bike patrols during this era included St. Paul, MN, and Fargo, ND.

Police departments increased their use of bikes for patrol purposes into the early 20th century (FIGURE 1-1). In 1907, Indianapolis' 10-person bike squad made more arrests than any other police branch; and of 11,000 arrests made in 1908, the now 12-member bike squad claimed credit for more than 2500. In 1917, a bicycle trade publication reported that New York City had 1200 bike officers.

After World War I, however, the introduction of new technologies helped hasten the demise of the bicycle squads. The use of motor vehicles increased, while telephones and radios enabled the shift from patrols to call-driven responses. New Haven terminated its bike patrol in 1925, and by 1929, even New York City no longer had a bike squad.

The trend towards motor vehicle use and radio dispatch continued throughout the post World War II era, and the use of bicycles by police was rare, although not nonexistent. For instance, in the 1960s, bikes were used in Hennepin County, MN, and the New York City police department deployed undercover officers on bikes to combat criminals who targeted joggers and cyclists. It was also during this period that the isolation of police from their communities was highlighted by clashes between demonstrators and police officers. A complex series of events led to the return to the roots of modern policing—police patrolling neighborhoods and interacting with citizens—in a movement known as Community Oriented Policing.

Although the return to community policing signaled the re-establishment of foot patrols in most places, many departments recognized that the principles of community policing could also be supported by the bicycle. Lindsay, CA, established a bike patrol in 1970; Baltimore followed suit in 1972 in a successful attempt to police the city's crime-ridden alleys. Richmond re-established its bike patrol in 1973; Madison, WI, formed a bike unit in 1978; and San Jose did so in 1979. Some of these bike units were a byproduct of the gasoline shortage of the early 1970s.

The trend continued into the 1980s, with the creation of bike units in Dallas, Fort Lauderdale, San Diego, Los Angeles, and Englewood, NJ, among others. Cincinnati revived its bike patrol in 1982.

The renaissance of police cycling gained momentum beginning in 1987, with the Seattle Police Department's bike squad (FIGURE 1-2). Frustrated

FIGURE 1-2 In 1987, the Seattle Police Department sparked the modern renaissance of police bike patrol.

by traffic congestion in the rapidly growing city, police officers Paul Grady and Mike Miller, both bike enthusiasts, hopped on their mountain bikes and pedaled into history. High arrest rates, positive public opinion, and widespread deployment of bicycles became hallmarks of the Seattle bike squad, and they did not hesitate to publicize their success. From 1991 to 1992, the bike squad received more than 600 inquiries from other agencies, and by 1993, they had 70 officers on bikes (Petty 2005).

Police bicycle use continued to increase (see TABLE 1-1). In 2000, according to the U.S. Bureau of Justice Statistics *Reports on Local Police Departments 2000* (NCJ 196534) and *Sheriff's Offices 2000* (NCJ 196002), approximately 5600 (43%) of all local police departments reported using bike patrol on a routine basis, including 90% of departments serving at least 100,000 residents and 98% of departments serving at least 250,000 residents (*Police Departments in Large Cities, 1990-2000 – NCJ 175703*). Approximately 390 (13%) of all sheriffs' departments, including about 50% of those serving 500,000 residents or more, also employed officers on bikes. This number declined somewhat by 2003, to about 38% of local police departments, although that number still included more than 80% of departments serving at least 100,000 residents and 60% of departments serving between 10,000 and 99,999 residents. Adding those departments using bikes on a non-routine basis brought the totals to

45% of police departments and 16% of sheriffs' offices, and an estimated 32,000 bicycles.

In the 21st century, police departments use bikes for a variety of operations, including routine patrol, drug enforcement, community policing, directed patrol, crowd management and control, and a wide variety of special events. Police personnel frequently use bikes in tourist areas, downtown business districts, low-income housing districts, high-crime areas, airports, and parks.

Bikes are employed not only by police officers, but also by non-sworn patrol personnel. The growth in private security following September 11, 2001, led to an increase in the use of bikes by security officers. The private sector has embraced the bicycle due to its practicality for patrolling facilities such as campgrounds, hospitals, corporate and academic campuses, gated communities, theme parks and resorts, shopping malls, and casinos. This widespread use suggests that bike patrols in the security industry will continue to grow.

EMS Bike Operations

The success of police on bikes did not escape the notice of emergency medical services (EMS) providers. It quickly became apparent that some of same qualities—such as speed and maneuverability—that contributed to the effectiveness of the bike officer could also benefit medics (FIGURE 1-3). Although the history of medics on bikes is less well-documented than that of police on bikes, it is likely that bike medics were first deployed during special events as an alternative to walking, and were an equally effective means of overcoming the crowds and traffic that inhibited timely response to medical emergencies.

Several colleges and universities began using bikes in 1980s, but mostly for basic transportation. Members of the Indianapolis Fire Department likewise started using their own bikes at special events, because, according to a former member, they "got tired of walking." The department purchased their first bikes in about 1984, and a bike team was in operation by 1989. Denver Health Paramedic founded one of the first officially organized EMS bike teams in 1991.

Some of the pioneers of EMS cycling were touring cyclists who replaced the camping gear in their panniers (saddlebags) with medical equipment and set out to save lives. Before the creation of the International Police Mountain Bike

TABLE 1-1 Growth in the Use of Bicycle Patrol by Local Police Departments and Sheriffs' Offices		
Year	Local Police Departments	Sheriffs' Offices
1993	No mention	No mention
1997	28% use bike patrol routinely; 8% for special events only	6% use bike patrol routinely
1999	34% use bike patrol routinely	9% use bike patrol routinely
2000	43% use bike patrol routinely	17% use bike patrol routinely
2003	38% use bike patrol routinely	10% use bike patrol routinely
	7% use bike patrol occasionally	6% use bike patrol occasionally

Source: U.S. Bureau of Justice Statistics, *Reports on Local Police Departments* and *Reports on Sheriffs' Offices, 1993, 1997, 1999, 2000, 2003.*

FIGURE 1-3 EMS cyclists in action.

FIGURE 1-4 British Columbia Ambulance Service Advanced Life Support Bike Squad, 1993.

Association (IPMBA) course for EMS cyclists, some bike medics enrolled in the IPMBA Police Cyclist program to learn how to handle their bicycles with precision while carrying 30 to 50 pounds of lifesaving equipment.

British Columbia Ambulance Service implemented the Advanced Life Support Bike Squad in 1993, a program which quickly expanded through the province (**FIGURE 1-4**). It was used as a model by the Troy (OH) Fire Department, which formed a team in 1994. In Troy, two paramedics staffed mountain bikes carrying both BLS and ALS equipment, an abbreviated drug bag, intubation supplies, and a cardiac monitor, split between the two bikes. The bicycles were owned by the riders, but the fire department and local hospital furnished all other equipment. In 1996, the Lebanon, OH, fire division established a bike medic team for Applefest; Fremont, CA, launched an EMS bike unit for the Fourth of July and both Boston and Toronto began bike operations. By 1997, EMS bike units could be found in Alexandria, VA, Gaston County, NC, and Lakewood, CO, among many other places.

Although most medical bike units in the United States are still used primarily for special events, some have been deployed on a more routine basis.

In 1997, the Nashville Fire Department began assigning bike medics to patrol the Second Avenue/ Printer's Alley district on Thursday, Friday, and Saturday nights, in response to an incident in which it took the ambulance 25 minutes to penetrate the crowds and reach a person suffering a heart attack. In 2000, the Orlando, FL, medical bike unit (BLS) was introduced for special events, but soon began patrolling the entertainment district from 9 p.m. to 3 a.m. on Fridays, Saturdays, and holidays. For the first two years after its founding in 1996, Boston EMS bike medics were deployed on every shift. In later years, they patrolled on a less frequent basis, focusing more on such events as the Boston Marathon, First Night Boston, and St. Patrick's Day.

In 2000, a pilot project launched by the London (UK) ambulance service deployed four paramedics on a 10-hour day, 7-day-a-week shift pattern in a five-kilometer area in the heart of the city. After 6 months, the ambulance service noted that the bike team responded to an average of 46 calls per week (35% of area calls). The average response time for the bike team was 6 minutes, and the team's efforts saved over 250 hours of front-line ambulance time. Each bicycle logged about 170 miles per week, or approximately 4500 miles over 6 months. The team saved the ambulance service approximately £80,000 (U.S. $160,000 in 2007) in ambulance non-dispatch/attendance and £2000 (U.S. $4,000 in 2007) in fuel. The overwhelming success of the venture resulted in the establishment of a full-time cycle response unit.

Medics on bikes have also found a niche within the airport environment. EMS personnel in airports face the challenges of crowded terminals as well as the difficulty of deploying emergency vehicles across heavily trafficked airfields. As early as 1998, Eau Claire Airport in Wisconsin and Vancouver (BC) International Airport used medics on bikes. Nashville International Airport began deploying cross-trained first responders (police officers trained in emergency first aid) in 2000. In 2004, London Ambulance Service began Cycle Response Unit service in Heathrow Airport, and paramedics took to their bikes at the Calgary airport. Several airports in the United States followed suit, including Fort Lauderdale International Airport in 2005 and Los Angeles (LAX) in 2007.

The use of bikes by medics has continued to increase, and EMS services deploy personnel on bikes in tourist areas, during special events, in amusement parks and sports arenas, on college campuses, and in airports, train stations, and other transportation hubs. EMS cyclists are also indispensable in urban and wilderness search-and-rescue and mass casualty situations. In 2000, the *Journal of Emergency Medical Services'* (JEMS) 200-city survey reported that more than 300 bike medic teams were in operation across the United States and that 52% of EMS agencies in the nation's largest 200 cities deployed a bike medic team.

International Police Mountain Bike Association (IPMBA)

The resurgence of policing by bike created a demand for information. In 1991, the League of American Wheelmen (now known as the League of American Bicyclists, or the League) organized the First National Conference of Bicycle-Mounted Police in Tucson, AZ. Attendees at this gathering realized that police cyclists could benefit from an association that would facilitate information sharing and establish training and equipment standards. The following year, at the League's Second Annual Police on Bikes Conference in Las Vegas, NV, the International Police Mountain Bike Association (IPMBA) was formed as a division of the League. Members elected the first governing board (see TABLE 1-2), launched the *IPMBA News*, and designated League staff member Susie Jones as program director for IPMBA.

At that time, the League operated an educational program based on John Forester's book, *Effective Cycling*. This program, delivered by certified *Effective Cycling* instructors, was designed to teach cyclists how to safely, legally, and efficiently operate bicycles as a mode of transportation. Officer Allan Howard, of the Dayton, OH, Police Department and Officer Kirby Beck of the Coon Rapids, MN, Police Department, both *Effective Cycling* Instructors, were among IPMBA's founders. They realized that one of the most important services IPMBA could offer was a program tailored to the needs of police cyclists. They launched a collaborative effort involving bike officers from around the country, who combined their knowledge and experience of cycling with police tactics to create what would become the first standardized training program for police cyclists. In late 1992, the League's board approved the Police Cyclist Certification. In April 1993, 10 instructors from across the United States gathered in Ft. Lauderdale, FL, to present the first, 4-day IPMBA Police Cyclist (PC) Course to 90 officers from the United States and Canada (TABLE 1-3). The curriculum

TABLE 1-2 First IPMBA Governing Board			
Allan Howard	President	Dayton Police Department (OH)	1992–1997
Jessica Cummins	Vice President	Oklahoma City Police Department (OK)	1992–1992
Tom Woods	Secretary	Denton Police Department (TX)	1992–1998
Gary McLaughlin	Newsletter Editor	Sacramento Police Department (CA)	1992–1999
Gary Gallinot	At-Large	Santa Monica Police Department (CA)	1992–1995
Paul Grady	At-Large	Seattle PD (WA)	1992–1993
Scott Virden	At-Large	Bel Air Police Department (MD)	1992–1993
Ray Wittmier	At-Large	Univ of WA Police Department (WA)	1992–1993

TABLE 1-3	The First IPMBA Instructor Cadre	
Allan Howard	Dayton Police Department	PCI #001
Kirby Beck	Coon Rapids Police Department	PCI #002
Stuart Bracken	Tacoma Police Department	PCI #003
Gary Gallinot	Santa Monica Police Department	PCI #004
Gary McLaughlin	Sacramento Police Department	PCI #005
Joseph Martin	Hayward Police Department	PCI #006
Gene Miller	Tacoma Police Department	PCI #007
Scott Virden	Bel Air Police Department	PCI #008
Brad Welton	West Hartford Police Department	PCI #009
Tom Woods	Denton Police Department	PCI #010

included not only bike handling and vehicular cycling techniques, but also patrol procedures, police tactics, basic maintenance, emergency skills, and legal issues.

The Third Annual Police on Bikes Conference was held immediately after the first Police Cyclist course. More than 250 North American police officers attended 3 days of workshops and exhibits on such topics as citizen patrol groups, storefront operations, community policing, officer selection, bicycle maintenance, and patrol tactics. The first IPMBA competition was an exciting addition to the program. During that conference, IPMBA formed an Education Committee and named Gene Miller of the Tacoma Police as its first chair. Robin Miller (no relation to Gene) became IPMBA's new program director.

In 1994, the conference was held in San Antonio. Later that year, IPMBA became the first American police training organization to establish, equip, and train a bike team for a former Soviet police department. As part of Project Harmony, the first Russian police bike squad, consisting of six SWAT team members, was established in the city of Petrozavodsk, Republic of Karelia. This event set the stage for many future international training opportunities and collaborations.

In 1995, Jennifer Horan took over the position of program director, and the Fifth Annual Police on Bikes Conference was held in Milwaukee, WI. The organization added the IPMBA Police Cyclist Instructor Development Course

(PCID) to its offerings and provided the course prior to the conference. This course introduced certified Police Cyclist Instructors to different methods of instruction and demonstrated varied approaches to difficult teaching situations. The instructors also learned about the emerging field of bike-specific firearms instruction.

The Sixth Annual Police on Bikes Conference, in Rochester, NY, featured the debut of the IPMBA Maintenance Officer Certification Course (MOCC). The MOCC provided mechanically adept bike personnel with the skills to maintain the department fleet. The crowning achievement of 1996, however, was the publication of the first edition of the *Complete Guide to Police Cycling*, which would become the definitive work on the subject.

The 1997 conference was held in Nashville, TN. The new IPMBA EMS Cyclist Course (EMSC) drew 12 attendees from 7 states and ushered in a new category of public safety cycling. In 1998, the Tacoma Police Department hosted the conference, where the organization introduced the IPMBA Police Cyclist Advanced Course. This course combined cutting-edge police training techniques with highly technical cycling skills.

In late 1998, IPMBA separated from the League of American Bicyclists and was reborn as Police on Bikes, Inc., although the organization continued to be known as IPMBA. The independent IPMBA's first priority was the ninth annual conference, held in 1999, in Chicago.

The 10th anniversary of the conference was celebrated in 2000, in Tucson, AZ, host of the first conference. The organization elected its first EMS professional to the board of directors, which was further evidence of IPMBA's commitment to medics on bikes; and replaced the practice-teach method of becoming an IPMBA instructor and the PCID with the standardized, 40-hour IPMBA Instructor Course (IC). Also in 2000, Maureen Becker replaced Jennifer Horan, who had been Executive Director since IPMBA's separation from the League.

At the 2002 conference in Ogden, UT, IPMBA introduced IPMBA Bicycle Rapid Response Team Training (BRRT). In 2003, at the annual conference in Charleston, WV, the organization debuted the IPMBA Intermediate Police Cyclist Course (IPC), an intense course that focused on bicycle operations and practical policing. Shortly after the conference, IPMBA participated in the first annual Emergency Services Cycling Seminar, hosted by the North Yorkshire Police Force in York, England.

Held in conjunction with the Cycle Touring Club's Annual York Rally, Britain's largest single gathering of cyclists, it marked IPMBA's first formal participation in the international scene.

In 2004, IPMBA revisited San Antonio. The newest addition to the menu of course offerings was the 24-hour IPMBA Security Cyclist Course (SC), designed to meet the needs of non-sworn patrol personnel. The organization changed the name of the Police Cyclist Advanced Course to IPMBA Survival Tactics and Riding Skills Course (STARS). IPMBA once again participated in the York Rally and Emergency Services Cycling Seminar in York, England, and participated in a steering committee meeting at New Scotland Yard. Also in 2004, IPMBA authored model bike patrol policies for the National Law Enforcement Policy Center of the International Association of Chiefs of Police (IACP).

In 2005, at the conference in Scottsdale, AZ, the IPMBA Intermediate Police Cyclist Course was reinvented as the IPMBA Public Safety Cyclist II Course (PSC II), broadening its scope to include EMS and security cyclists and emphasizing the frequent collaboration among the various branches of public safety cycling **FIGURE 1-5** . IPMBA continued its involvement in the United Kingdom by participating in the third Emergency Services Cycling Seminar, once again held in York, England, and conducting the first IPMBA Instructor Course held outside the United States.

The 2006 IPMBA conference brought IPMBA to Dayton, OH, as a tribute to founding member Allan Howard, PCI #001. In a move symbolic of the unifying force of the bicycle, the IPMBA Board of Directors elected an EMS professional to the position of president. Firefighter/paramedic Jim Bowell, EMSCI #001, of the Troy, OH, Fire Department, ushered the organization into a future in which an EMS agency hosted the annual IPMBA conference for the first time (East Baton Rouge EMS in 2007), and the name of the *Complete Guide to Police Cycling* was changed to the *Complete Guide to Public Safety Cycling*.

With publication of the second edition of the *Complete Guide* more than a decade after the first, IPMBA continues to write its history. It faces many challenges, such as the ongoing effort to prove the effectiveness of bike patrol, the lingering resistance to the notion of training for bike personnel, the challenges of globalization, and the introduction of new technologies. Despite these challenges, there is no doubt that public safety bicycles are here to stay!

References

Lynch, Tom (2003). London's Life-Saving Team. *IPMBA News,* Fall, pages 6–7.

Petty, Ross (2006). Transportation Technologies for Community Policing: A Comparision. *International Journal of Police Science and Management,* Vol 18(3):165–175.

FIGURE 1-5 The IPMBA Conference attracts public safety cyclists from throughout the United States and beyond its borders.

The Public Safety Bike Unit

Introduction

Since the modern renaissance of police cycling, the value of mountain bikes to the mission of public safety has continued to expand. A wide range of public safety personnel use bicycles for a variety of purposes. The bike has evolved from a simple mode of transportation into a versatile tool that is ideal for use by police, EMS personnel, private security, and other patrol personnel. When integrated into departmental operations, bikes can enhance an agency's ability to serve the members of its community.

Benefits of Bikes in Public Safety

Bikes offer many benefits. As a result, the growth of bike use by public safety agencies has been rapid and sustained.

Access and maneuverability

Cyclists' ability to move through gridlocked traffic by using sidewalks, alleys, bike paths and trails enables faster response in congested or urban areas (FIGURE 2-1). Cyclists can ride into or

FIGURE 2-1 Bikes can easily patrol areas inaccessible to motor vehicles.

through buildings, if necessary. With proper training, they can move deftly into, through, and around crowds. Bike patrol personnel function much like foot patrol personnel, but are able to cover a much larger area, and do so more quickly and efficiently.

These characteristics can be advantageous in pursuit situations. Foot pursuits become almost unnecessary when the bike can go nearly anywhere a criminal can run. The mountain bike's wide range of gears gives the cyclist a mechanical advantage; the cycling officer does not tire as easily as the fleeing suspect. Many offenders will not even try to run if they see an officer on a bicycle.

The bicycle's maneuverability also creates a stealth advantage. Police and security cyclists can be swift and silent when approaching crimes in progress and use cover or concealment while observing suspects or activity. Because they can gain access to areas not normally patrolled by officers who are in vehicles or on foot, they can approach from unexpected directions and locations.

■ Awareness

Public safety cyclists are able to use all of their senses to detect crime, public disorder or calls for help. Because cyclists are exposed to the environment, they are better able to use their sight, hearing, and smell to detect situations that might be overlooked by personnel in motor vehicles.

■ Public Contact

Studies have shown that bike officers have significantly more contact with the public than those in cars. A 2005 study compared bike patrol to motor vehicle patrol in five cities with populations of more than 100,000. The researcher "rode along" with each type of patrol officer for 110-115 hours over 16 shifts each. He counted all public contacts, recording the number of persons, the seriousness of the contact, and the nature of the contact, as well as the origin. His findings indicated that for serious and somewhat serious activity, bicycle patrols were comparable to squad car patrol, but for positive and non-serious contacts and overall number of contacts, bikes were far superior (TABLE 2-1).

Similar statistics comparing the activities of officers in cars with those on bikes by the Cincinnati Police Division appear in (TABLE 2-2). These figures were collected during the 1993 pilot study which resulted in the implementation of a department-wide bicycle unit. That same year, during a two-week Holiday Task Force, the number of robberies in the targeted areas decreased from 24 to four, while thefts decreased from 62 to 27 from the previous year.

People often do not feel comfortable knocking on the window of a patrol vehicle or ambulance, but they will not hesitate to approach a public safety cyclist. The bike removes barriers to, and may help open lines of, communication. All types of public safety cyclists can use their approachability to engage youth, educate community members, and serve as positive role models (FIGURE 2-2). The accessibility of a public safety cyclist facilitates positive relationships with community members.

■ Positive Public Image

The bicycle can be an excellent tool for public relations. Members of the public often view bicycles as wholesome and friendly, and personnel on bikes can greatly enhance an agency's image. Bikes encourage positive interaction. Personnel seem friendlier, and, in the case of police, less intimidating. Cyclists are also typically more athletic, fit, or healthy, which may inspire confidence in their ability to respond quickly and perform their jobs well. In 2002, Nick Gatlin of Williamson Medical Center in Franklin, TN, calculated the public relations value of their EMS bike team. Team members attended events to provide medical care and also to distribute educational brochures, offer bike safety training to children, and engage in similar activities. He estimated that in the course of a year, the hospital would have spent $70,000 advertising dollars to reach the 600,000 persons with whom the bike medics interacted. In addition, he determined that contracting for display booths at local events could cost upwards of $10,000—significantly more than the cost of deploying bike medics to work the event.

Community Relationships

The bike removes barriers to, and may help open lines of, communication. The accessibility of a public safety cyclist facilitates positive relationships with community members.

TABLE 2-1   Comparison of Bicycle Patrols and Motor Vehicle Patrols

	Bicycle Patrol	Motor Vehicle Patrol
Avg. number of contacts per hour	7.3	3.3
Avg. number of people in contacts per hour	22.82	10.54
Positive/Negative/Neutral Encounters (note: positive = 1; negative = −1; neutral = 0)	Mean: .42	Mean: .051
Seriousness (note: serious = 1; not serious = −1; somewhat serious = 0)	Mean: −0.601	Mean: −0.241
Type of Encounter per Hour	Serious: .333 Somewhat Serious: 1.87 Non-Serious: 5.097	Serious: .467 Somewhat Serious: 1.373 Non-Serious: 1.46

Source: Menton, Chris. Proving the Effectiveness of Police Bicycle Patrols. 2007 IPMBA Conference, April, Baton Rouge LA.

TABLE 2.2 Activities of Officers in Cars Compared to Officers on Bikes		
Officers' Weekly Average	Officer in Car	Officer on Bike
Hours on duty	40.00	40.00
Arrest – Felony	01.00	02.25
Arrest – Misdemeanor	02.98	09.49
Juvenile arrests & referrals	00.88	02.11
Field Interview Report (FIR)	00.23	01.69
Vice incidents	00.48	04.67
Property recovery incidents	01.22	02.87
Warrants served	04.86	09.74
Crimes discovered	00.44	01.55
Misdemeanor cleared/follow-up	00.51	02.55
Parking violation	02.80	09.78
Motorist assists	00.64	06.57

Source: Simpson, David. Cincinnati Pilot Study Flies. *IPMBA News*, Fall 2002, page 11.

■ Cost Efficiency

A department can equip 7 to 10 bike team members with bikes and full uniforms for less than the price of one patrol car, or about the same cost as a fully equipped motorized ambulance cart. In addition, physically fit personnel have less absenteeism resulting from injuries and illness. Morale among bike personnel is usually quite high, which translates into more proactive and effective behavior. Finally, bicycles do not require fuel to operate, which can offer substantial savings. In 2003, Tom Lynch of London Ambulance Service calculated a fuel savings of £2000 (U.S. $4000 in 2007) over the course of six months as a result of using bicycles rather than ambulances on some calls.

■ Environmental Benefits

Bicycles do not create air or noise pollution and thus contribute to improved air quality. Several bike units, including the Victor Valley Community College (CA) Police Department, have received grants

FIGURE 2-2 Public safety cyclists can use their approachability to engage youth, educate community members, and serve as positive role models.

through air quality improvement funds and/or donations of bicycles from local businesses interested in reducing emissions. Bicycles do not add to traffic congestion, and they take up few or no parking spaces. They can be carried on bike racks and used to supplement motorized vehicles, reducing the amount of shift-time that the car engine is running and emitting pollutants.

■ Versatility

The most important reason to establish a bike unit is its versatility. The applications are nearly unlimited, as demonstrated by the creative ways bicycles have been integrated into everyday operations. Many different types of agencies use bikes—including state and municipal police, university public safety departments, park rangers, border patrol, sheriff's departments, fire departments, private and third-service EMS agencies, contract and proprietary security providers, and downtown ambassadors.

Agencies that have embraced the bicycle have found many ways to use it to their advantage. A few applications of the bicycle are described in this section.

Emergency Medical Services (EMS)

The proliferation of special events of all kinds has spurred the growth of EMS cycling. Bicycles provide an extremely effective means of providing EMS services among throngs of people in confined areas. Bike medics can provide services during sporting events, fairs and festivals, parades, running and cycling events, golf tournaments, and more (FIGURE 2-3). Bike medics can respond rapidly, provide patient care, and determine whether patients require further assistance or transport.

Bike medics can also be effective on patrol. Entertainment districts, shopping malls, airports, and pedestrian-only zones are just a few examples of areas in which bike medics can provide vital lifesaving service.

FIGURE 2-3 Bike medics can deliver efficient and effective care during such large-scale events as this parade in Los Angeles' Chinatown.

Community-Oriented Policing

Bicycles are an ideal way to apply the principles of community-oriented policing in a variety of situations. Many bike patrol officers have learned that it is nearly impossible to ride through a community in uniform without encouraging the kind of communication and interaction community policing requires.

Reactive Policing

Police officers on bicycles can and should do reactive policing. Bike cops can perform the everyday functions of police work, such as investigating burglaries, handling suspects, and responding to requests for support from EMS personnel; the only difference is that they arrive on the scene on bikes instead of in cars. If an officer cannot ride a bicycle for his or her entire shift—perhaps because the geographical area is too large—the officer can mount a bike rack on the patrol car and use the bicycle for part of the patrol shift.

Surveillance

Bike officers can also perform surveillance. They can follow and observe suspects, even while wearing police bicycle uniforms. Police cyclists can also wear plain clothes and ride bicycles with no visible police markings. Bike cops can use parking structures, alleys, walls, fences, trees, dumpsters, shrubbery, landscaping, and buildings to conceal themselves from targeted persons (FIGURE 2-4).

Night Operations

Working at night poses different challenges to the Public Safety cyclist, but it also offers additional advantages. A bike cop is even more stealthy under the cover of darkness. The police cyclist working at night can use shadows, parked cars, building corners, and many other objects to conceal his or her position or from which to approach scenes.

Traffic Enforcement

Bikes can be very effective in traffic enforcement in certain settings, such as downtown areas where congestion is high and speeds are low. Officers can ride between lines of bumper-to-bumper traffic easily, looking down into the passenger compartment of the stopped vehicles they pass. Resulting traffic stops often lead to charges such as driving with a suspended license, open warrants, and drugs.

Bicycle-mounted officers are also useful in residential areas, where speeding and stop sign violations may be rampant. Officers frequently use a

FIGURE 2-4 Bike cops can use parking structures, alleys, walls, fences, trees, dumpsters, shrubbery, landscaping, and buildings to conceal themselves.

team approach for such types of enforcement. One officer is stationed in an inconspicuous location with a hand-held, battery-operated laser or radar unit. This officer reports speeds and descriptions to his partner(s), stationed a short distance up the street, ready to hand-stop the vehicle, or waiting near the next stop sign to initiate contact.

Public Order

In the early 2000s, police discovered that bicycles could enhance their ability to deal with crowds and rioters. Bike officers clad in riot gear are able to move faster than normal response teams and are often able to head off groups of troublemakers before they have time to act. Their approachability and the ease with which they interact with crowds often defuse situations before they get out of control. With their effectiveness honed and highlighted at national political conventions, football matches in England, and various politically charged events, bicycle response teams are in-

FIGURE 2-5 Bike-mounted security officers provide an effective means of patrol in and around shopping centers and malls.

creasing in number, improving their tactics and equipment, and gaining the respect of administrators and anarchists alike.

Search and Rescue and Disaster Response

Bicycles can be integrated into search and rescue (SAR) operations. Trail patrollers apply the principles of SAR during volunteer patrols of recreational trails. When natural disasters like tornados, earthquakes, or hurricanes strike an urban area and normal transportation and communications systems are disrupted, bikes provide the fastest alternative means of transportation for emergency workers conducting SAR and security operations in the affected area. This application has also proven invaluable during manmade disasters, as demonstrated by the use of bikes by Pentagon police and the valuable service provided by bike messengers delivering blood and other supplies to rescue workers in the aftermath of September 11, 2001.

Private Security

The benefits that the police have enjoyed are of value to private security as well. Patrolling properties with defined boundaries, parking lots, alleyways, and parking ramps is often quicker, easier, and more economical on a bicycle than in any other type of patrol vehicle. Security personnel in shopping malls, amusement parks and casinos, hospitals, sports and entertainment complexes, campgrounds, gated communities, corporate campuses, and many other venues frequently use bikes (FIGURE 2-5).

Limitations of Bike Patrol

Like anything else, bike patrol is not without its disadvantages. An awareness of the limitations and risks can help an agency deploy bicycles more effectively and safely. Sometimes a factor that is an advantage in one situation can be a disadvantage in another. There may be times when a bike officer has too much stealth, for example, riding up upon a crime in progress and not immediately recognizing the nature of the situation. Because bicycles don't have reverse gear, a tactical retreat can be difficult. Additional issues are discussed in this section and throughout this book.

■ Accidents and Injury

Bike personnel are exposed to a different set of risks than their motorized counterparts. A crash, fall, or collision can result in injury, as can over-exertion, improper riding technique, or inferior equipment. Public safety cyclists who enter high-risk areas or situations are more vulnerable to attack due to their lack of cover. These risks can be minimized through proper training and equipment.

■ Misidentification

Misidentification due to modified uniforms and perceptions is not uncommon. People in some areas are not accustomed to seeing public safety personnel on bicycles. Even in uniform, personnel may not be recognized as public safety personnel. This may result in people questioning an officer's authority when making arrests or using force, or claiming in court that the officer's identity was not obvious. Bike personnel must be sure to identify themselves clearly as police or EMS upon arrival on a scene. In addition, the similarity in attire between police and EMS may cause confusion if EMS personnel are mistaken for police, and vice versa. This can be overcome by the selection of distinctive, clearly marked uniforms.

■ Weather

Weather conditions affect the ability of a public safety cyclist to operate. Departments must establish policies dictating conditions under which personnel should not ride. Riding in extreme temperatures, storms, heavy winds, and when road conditions are otherwise dangerous is not advisable, although cyclists can withstand a wide range of weather conditions if they are outfitted and equipped properly.

Weather conditions and exposure to the elements may cause slower response times; with proper planning, this can be anticipated and compensated for. Bike personnel are frequently exposed to cold, rain, wind, and heat, making quality uniforms essential for both comfort and well-being.

■ Cargo Limitations

There are limitations on what can be carried on the bike. Most public safety cyclists do not carry the same equipment on a bike as they do in a motorized vehicle. Equipment is limited to what can fit inside a rack bag or panniers. Most medical bike units assess their needs based on patient care history and plan accordingly; some are strictly BLS (Basic Life Support), while others are equipped with trauma kits and for ALS (Advanced Life Support). They often ride in pairs, with the equipment split between the two bikes. Public safety cyclists are unable to transport prisoners or patients, which requires careful planning to ensure that a vehicle and driver are available for support.

■ Communications

Communications limitations may hamper public safety cyclists. Without an automobile, radio and computer equipment may be limited to lower-powered, handheld units. However, emerging technologies continue to enhance handheld communications devices, which are expected to enable bike personnel to remain connected and have access to as much data as their counterparts in cars.

■ Misperception

Bikes are still often not seen as part of the traditional police, EMS, and security paradigm, and administrators may not know how best to use them or may not take them seriously. Bike personnel are often more proactive than reactive, and therefore may not be assigned calls for service. They may be seen merely as a public relations tool or just another program to appease the community, and some may think that bike personnel are just out there to have fun. These perceptions are usually overcome by presenting statistics that demonstrate the effectiveness of bikes for public safety and by striving to integrate bikes into everyday operations.

Conclusion

Bicycles will never replace motor vehicles for public safety use, but that was never the intention of advocates for bicycle use in public safety. With proper planning and deployment, bicycles can enhance most emergency services operations. Through training and experience, public safety bicycle patrol personnel soon learn to work around the limitations and perceived disadvantages. They learn to maximize the advantages. They soon realize that a bicycle is more than merely a method of transportation. Properly used, a bike is a very effective tool for public safety personnel working in a complex and ever-changing society.

References

Gatlin, Nick (2002). What's a Bike Team Worth? *IPMBA News*, Fall, pages 13–14.

Lynch, Tom (2003). London's Life-Saving Team. *IPMBA News*, Fall, pages 6–7.

Menton, Chris. Proving the Effectiveness of Police Bicycle Patrols. 2007 IPMBA Conference. April, Baton Rouge LA.

Simpson, David (2002). Cincinnati Pilot Study Flies. *IPMBA News*, Fall, page 11.

Vonk, Kathy (2002). Beyond Community Policing: The Crime-Fighting Effectiveness of the Police Cyclist. *Law & Order Magazine*, April, pages 92–96.

3

Bicycles

Introduction

Bicycles come in several types, many styles, and a wide range of prices. Most states in the United States regard bicycles as vehicles and, like other vehicles, require that they be in good working order. IPMBA advocates that the public safety bikes not only should be in good working order, but also should be high-quality bicycles that are built to withstand the rigors of public safety cycling.

The Dayton Police Bicycle Patrol was given several low-quality bicycles when it first started. Those gifts cost more to maintain than it would have cost to purchase several better bikes. More importantly, they all failed in one way or another, some while being ridden on patrol. Modern gearing ranges give even a marginally fit rider the ability to propel himself or herself at speeds that, in the event of catastrophic frame or wheel failure, can cause serious injury or death. This type of failure occurs more frequently in bikes not sold by reputable bicycle retailers. The bikes used in public safety applications are often pushed to their design limits. Public safety cyclists carry more and heavier equipment than the average cy-

clist. The public safety cyclist's life—or someone else's—may depend on the reliability of the transportation, so this is not an area to cut costs.

Bicycle Types

There are four basic types of bicycles on the market today: the road bike, the mountain bike, the hybrid, and the cruiser.

The road bike is what many people still call a ten-speed. It has turned-down handlebars, narrow tires, and lightweight rims. The road bike is designed to increase speed through improved aerodynamics and reduced weight. Road bikes are built for speed on pavement, and unless designed for touring, are generally too fragile for heavy loads or riding on rugged surfaces. The turned-down, or racing style, handlebars force the rider into a position that is less than ideal for observing the surroundings. In addition, the gearing on a road bike is usually too high (except on touring models), and the wheels are not durable enough for anything but smooth pavement (**FIGURE 3-1A**).

The mountain bike was developed specifically for off-road use on rugged terrain. The high-quality mountain bike has no rival when it comes to overall strength, durability, and usefulness. Its durability is the result of the combination of strong yet light materials, close tolerances in the components, and a frame made of tubing specifically designed to endure the physical stresses of aggressive off-road riding, while keeping the overall weight low. With up to 27 gears, the modern mountain bike enables the rider to negotiate most terrain effectively and efficiently (**FIGURE 3-1B**).

The hybrid bicycle combines aspects of the mountain bike (frame, drive train, brakes) with aspects of the road bike (tires and wheels). The hybrid is a lightweight version of a mountain bike. The tires, rims, and frame are all narrower than those of a standard mountain bike and generally are not sufficient for public safety use (**FIGURE 3-1C**).

The cruiser bike is a remake of the bicycles from the 1950s. They are simple bicycles, usually with only a few gears—often only one. Their major flaws are, first, an inability to accelerate and brake quickly due to a lack of gears, and, second, excess weight. They are designed to appeal to a broad spectrum of cyclists, but mainly those who are seeking a comfortable, casual bike to ride for fun or basic transportation. They are not built to absorb the rigors of public safety use (**FIGURE 3-1D**).

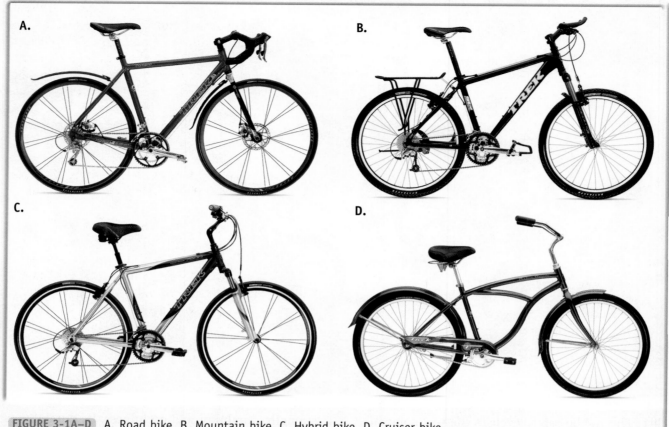

FIGURE 3-1A–D A. Road bike. B. Mountain bike. C. Hybrid bike. D. Cruiser bike.

■ Reasons for Using a Mountain Bike

The mountain bike is the most practical bicycle for public safety use for a number of reasons. Specifically, the tires, gear range, riding position, and the ability to carry equipment make the mountain bike the preferred vehicle.

The mountain bike's wheel rims are smaller in diameter than its road and hybrid counterparts, but are also wider, which enables a wider tire to be mounted. Larger tires hold a larger volume of air, which can better absorb shock. They can also prevent pinch flats, which occur when an under-inflated tire hits a hard edge, compressing the tire and pinching the tube against the inside of the rim. Larger tires also get slightly better traction, although they cause more rolling resistance.

The range of gearing on the modern mountain bike allows most riders to climb the steepest of hills while also providing the gear combinations needed for high-speed call responses or pursuits. The gearing can also be tailored to match the special needs of specific patrol areas. The industry describes gearing by counting the teeth on the gears. A general rule for gearing is that a combination of a small chain ring in the front and large cogs in the back will allow a rider to climb steep hills; a large chain ring in the front with small cogs in the rear will allow a higher top speed. Mountain bikes generally carry the broadest variations of gearing, which is useful to public safety cyclists.

The riding position of most mountain bikes is well-suited for long hours in the saddle. The body position biases the body weight towards the saddle and the buttocks, instead of the arms and hands. This upright position helps prevent arm fatigue, reduces neck cramps, and allows freer breathing. Of course, this holds true only when the frame size is correct for the rider and the saddle and stem are adjusted properly.

Modern mountain bikes are designed to be used off-road in remote areas. They include braze-ons that facilitate carrying extra gear. These threaded tabs are welded to the frame and allow for the attachment of water bottle cages, racks, and fenders. Although most public safety cyclists do not ride in remote areas, the ability to carry significant amounts of equipment is essential to the performance of their duties. This equipment may add an additional 10 to 50 pounds to the bike and is another reason to select a stronger, lighter, mid-level to high-end mountain bike.

FIGURE 3-2 shows a diagram of a bicycle and its components.

Bicycle Frames

The frame is the very heart of the bicycle; therefore, it is essential to purchase a bike with a high-quality frame that fits the rider. If the frame is low-quality, no matter what components are attached to it, it will still be an inferior bike.

A number of different materials are used for bike frames. The cheapest are of very low quality and very heavy weight. Generally, as the price rises, the weight drops. The most common frame materials are plain steel (often called high-tensile steel), chromoly steel (a steel alloy), aluminum, titanium, and carbon fiber. There are other materials as well, but they are less common and often very expensive.

Plain steel is relatively inexpensive, heavy, and weaker than steel alloys. Inexpensive bicycles made of plain steel can weigh 30 to 40 pounds; they are heavier than the average mountain bike, yet even small stresses can bend or crack the frame. Therefore, plain steel is undesirable for use by public safety cyclists.

Chromoly steel is a strong alloy of steel, chromium, and molybdenum, which is vastly stronger, more flexible, and lighter than plain steel but generally heavier than aluminum. Many mid- and high-grade mountain bikes are made of this material. Because it is fairly flexible, it absorbs some road shock but does not transfer power from the rider to the pedals as efficiently as do stiffer frames.

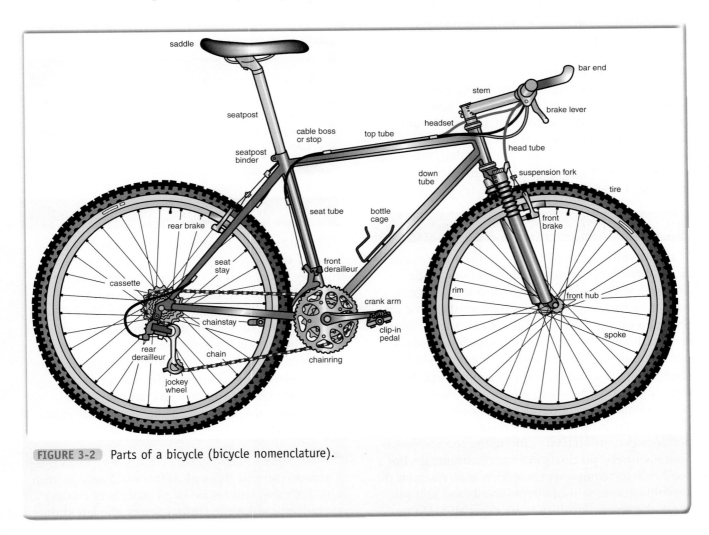

FIGURE 3-2 Parts of a bicycle (bicycle nomenclature).

Aluminum can be significantly lighter and stiffer than steel, making it an ideal material for bikes designed to carry extra weight. Stiff aluminum frames transfer power better but do not absorb shock as well, so suspensions (front, rear, and/or seat post) are often added. Aluminum's greatest drawback is that it is very difficult to repair. Although it is durable, when it breaks, it is often a total loss.

Titanium and carbon fiber are costly materials on the cutting edge of technology, but the benefits gained for the extra cost are slight. Titanium and carbon fiber materials are used in component construction because of their strength and low weight, but most budgets do not allow for the purchase of titanium or carbon fiber frames.

Each of these materials can be used to build a bike frame and each can be assembled or joined together in a number of ways. Frame tubes can be welded, bonded, glued, or lugged and brazed. A discussion of these construction methods is beyond the scope of this book, but in general, all mid- to upper-priced mountain bikes from reputable companies are manufactured with strong materials using a stringent assembly process, resulting in a high-quality product. Frame failure is rare with reasonable use and proper care.

The pros and cons of each frame material are hotly debated by bicycle enthusiasts, but most public safety cyclists agree that the ideal frame is sturdy yet lightweight, and not too expensive. As of the writing of this book, most public safety bicycles are constructed of aluminum because it meets all these criteria.

Bicycle Components

"Components" generally refers to the mechanical parts of the bicycle, including the crankset, derailleurs, shifters, and brakes. Most mid-range mountain bikes use components manufactured by Shimano or SRAM. Each of these companies offers several different grades of mountain bike component groups. Higher-grade components are lighter, stronger, more durable, and more expensive. However, it is not necessary to purchase the most expensive component group for public safety use; there may be little or no discernable difference in performance or longevity among the top few levels. Manufacturers' products change continuously, but a good rule for component selection is to research the available grades within a reputable brand and purchase the second or third most expensive. Do not

try this from the bottom up; there are many inexpensive, low-quality components on the market. The components make the bike work, and higher-grade components, if properly cared for, work better and last longer.

Bicycle manufacturers typically install or "spec" (specify) components as a complete group of parts designed to work compatibly with each other. It is typically more cost effective to buy a bike in the middle to upper price range with a complete group of parts than to special-order a bicycle with mixed parts. However, a knowledgeable rider can carefully mix and match components from different quality levels; this can be an effective way to save money while still obtaining a good bicycle.

Regardless of the level of component, if the rider does not keep the bicycle clean and properly lubed, it will wear out quickly. While bicycle chains and gears will eventually wear out, dirty components accelerate the process. Buy good components and take good care of them.

Component Care

Regardless of the level of component, if the rider does not keep the bicycle clean and properly lubed, it will wear out quickly. Buy good components and take good care of them.

The Drive Train

There are several kinds of gear systems, but the type of multi-speed gear system found on most modern bikes, and virtually all mountain bikes, is the derailleur system. A derailleur is a gear-changing device that allows a rider to "de-rail" the chain and move it from one chain ring to another while the bicycle is in motion. The drive train of a derailleur bike consists of the shifters, the cassette (cluster of gear cogs at the rear axle); the front and rear derailleurs; the crank set (pedals, crank arms, and front chain rings), and the chain (FIGURE 3-3).

■ Shifters

There are several types of shifter mechanisms available for mountain bikes. In all models of shifters manufactured for the United States, the left shifter

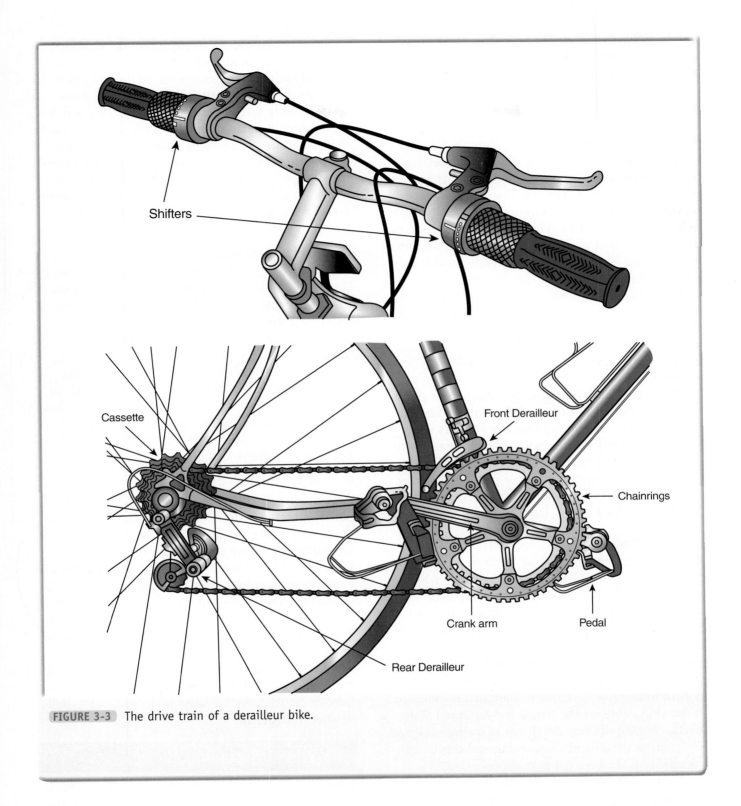

Shifters

Cassette

Front Derailleur

Chainrings

Crank arm

Pedal

Rear Derailleur

FIGURE 3-3 The drive train of a derailleur bike.

controls the front derailleur and the right controls the rear derailleur; in some markets outside the United States, this orientation is reversed.

Modern derailleur systems use indexed shifting. Indexed shifting means that moving the shifter or pushing the shifter button moves the derailleur a precise, preset distance to the desired cog. One click moves it one cog, two clicks move it two cogs, and so on. This accurate alignment ensures smooth shifting and prevents premature wear of the chain, chain rings, and cassette cogs. The decision about which shifter to use is dictated by preference or by which shifter comes on the bike. Two variations of shifting mechanisms are available on mountain bikes; one is operated by actuating levers with the thumb and forefinger, and the other by twisting the handlebar grip forward or back.

■ Derailleurs

Mountain bikes, like most multi-speed bikes, have two derailleurs, one at the crank set (front) and one at the cassette (rear). Though a derailleur can be moved while the bike is stationary or coasting, it cannot derail the chain. The chain must be moving forward for a tooth to catch the chain and the shift to take place. With a derailleur pushing it sideways and the chain ring moving forward, the chain climbs or drops to another cog. Not all of the teeth on the front chain rings are the same size. Some are shorter than others to allow the chain to climb on to the ring when shifting to higher gears in the front. Even so, the cyclist must be pedaling to change gears.

Mountain bikes typically have three front chain rings of 22, 32, and 44 teeth, and a rear cassette, or cog set, with gears ranging between 11 to 34 teeth. Shifting these gears creates various combinations of the chain rings and cassette cogs to produce gear ratios that facilitate speed or enable pedaling leverage for climbing hills or traversing rough terrain. This setup is ideal for a public safety mountain bike.

The Rear Derailleur

The rear derailleur consists of a pair of hinged plates forming a parallelogram, attached to which is a jockey wheel cage housing two small plastic wheels that help guide the chain onto individual cassette cogs when shifting. The whole assembly is attached to the frame just below the cassette cogs. The derailleur body is spring-loaded to take slack out of the chain when shifted to a smaller cog. To shift from cog to cog, tension is applied or released to the shift cable via the handlebar-mounted shift levers, causing the rear derailleur to swing back and forth across the axis of the cassette and centering the chain on the selected gear.

Many cyclists err in assuming the two small screws found on the derailleur body are for fine-tuning; however, these screws are set by the manufacturer to control the inward and outward travel limits of the derailleur and should not be adjusted. Unless components in the drive train are damaged, most shifting problems can be corrected by turning the barrel adjusters mounted either on the shifter or

where the cable passes through the rear derailleur, as described in Chapter 12. The barrel adjusters gradually add or release tension to the shift cable to position the chain on the selected gear.

Generally speaking, rear derailleurs are much more prone to malfunction than front ones, because their position on the frame is usually unprotected, leaving them vulnerable to damage from falls onto the drive side of the bike or from being struck by objects or obstacles. However, damage can be minimized with the addition of a removable derailleur guard.

The Front Derailleur

The front derailleur consists of a simple pivoting spring-loaded cage through which the chain is routed. Engaging the shifter causes the cage to move sideways and at an angle, pushing or pulling the chain toward the next chain ring. When adjusted properly, the front derailleur is never in contact with the chain except during shifting. The front derailleur is more difficult to adjust than the rear one; like the rear one, it has stop limit screws, but it has no barrel adjuster. The barrel adjuster on the front shifter is used to fine-tune the front derailleur.

■ Crank Arms

Crank arms are the arms or levers to which the pedals are attached and that hold the front chain rings. The complete crank set assembly is attached to the frame at, and rotates around, the bottom bracket. Various lengths of crank arms are available to accommodate different leg lengths, facilitating a more efficient use of power through leverage. Crank arm length is measured center-to-center from the pedal spindle hole to the bottom bracket spindle. Bikes with 16.5-inch frames or smaller are usually equipped with 170-mm crank arms, and larger frames use 175-mm cranks. Longer crank arms for very tall riders can usually be special ordered.

Wheel Assembly

Wheels used on public safety bikes should be built for strength. The wheel assembly is comprised of four parts: hub, rim, spokes, and tire (**FIGURE 3-4**).

■ Rims

The rim is the outer metal hoop of a bicycle wheel. Modern rims are made of extruded aluminum; semi-molten aluminum is squeezed out of specially

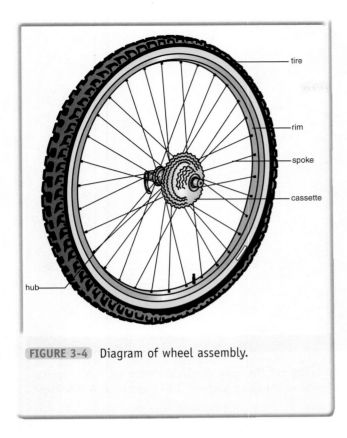

FIGURE 3-4 Diagram of wheel assembly.

shaped openings that determine the cross-section of the rim. The extrusions are formed into hoops, then joined either by welding or by inserting a filler piece into the hollows at each end of the rim. Mountain bike tires are generally quite wide, ranging from 1.9 to 2.35 inches, so they require a fairly wide rim. Using a wide tire with a narrow rim risks poor tire performance. During braking, narrow rims may cause brake pads to contact the sidewall of the bulging tire, resulting in damage or a blow-out flat. On the other hand, using a wide rim with a narrow tire could cause rim damage because the tire will flatten out trying to span the width of the rim. The resulting lower sidewall height offers less protection from contact between the rim and the road or obstacles. For public safety cycling, it is preferable to use rims at least 22 mm wide and at least a 1.9-inch tire; wider is generally better.

■ Spokes

Wheels with 36 spokes are highly recommended, because more spokes translate into a stronger wheel and reduce the need to true (straighten) the wheel. Stainless steel is the best choice for spokes because it is strong and will not rust. Inexpensive wheels are built with chrome-plated (UCP) or zinc-plated (galvanized) carbon-steel

spokes, which are not as strong and are prone to rust. Spokes should be straight 14 gauge. Unlike butted spokes, which are thicker on the ends and thinner in the middle to save weight, straight gauge spokes are the same thickness throughout the length of the spoke and are therefore stronger.

■ Hubs

All modern hubs of decent quality are made of aluminum alloy using ball bearings around the axle that can be adjusted, maintained, and rebuilt. Better-quality hubs might use sealed cartridge bearings that require less maintenance and have greater load-bearing capabilities.

■ Tires, Inner Tubes, and Puncture Prevention

A typical mountain bike comes equipped with aggressive, knobby tires (**FIGURE 3-5A**). This is beneficial for recreational mountain bikers as well as public safety cyclists such as park rangers or conservation officers who patrol off the road or on especially rough terrain. However, for most public safety cyclists, this style of tread pattern is not recommended. The knobs reduce the amount of tire surface that contacts the ground, especially on paved or smooth surfaces. This lack of contact can create a yawing effect, resulting in the tire sliding out from under the rider, especially during cornering. Knobby tires can also create a noise signature, which might reduce a stealth advantage.

Tires

The duty assignment and riding environment dictate the choice of tires for public safety bicycles. There are various tire tread pattern designs available, but the most practical choice for public safety cyclists operating in the typical urban or suburban setting is a combination tread pattern (**FIGURE 3-5B**). These tires combine the features of a mountain bike tire with those of a street tire (**FIGURE 3-5C**), i.e., some knobs for traction on the edge of the tire, with a slick or slightly grooved surface on the main body of the tire that contacts the road surface. This type of tire provides traction over a wide range of surfaces and can be purchased with Kevlar belts and sidewalls for added puncture resistance. Studded tires are available for those who patrol in the snow.

When evaluating a tire, first determine the width of the tire (imprinted on the sidewall) that

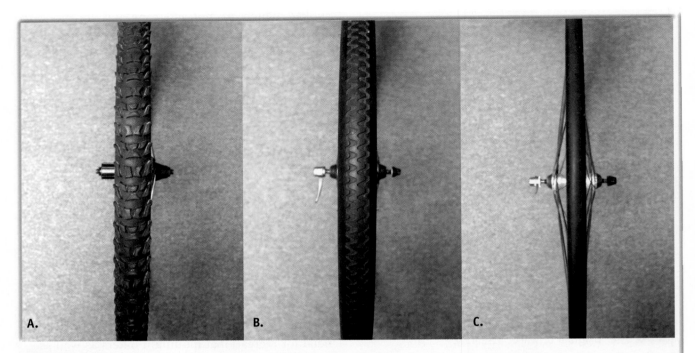

FIGURE 3-5A–C There are various tire tread pattern designs available, but the most practical choice for public safety cyclists operating in the typical urban or suburban setting is a combination tread pattern. Tread patterns: A. Knobby, B. Combination, C. Road.

suits the riding environment and load to be carried. Tires suitable for public safety cycling range from 1.25 to 2.5 inches wide. Wider tires have more air volume, offer more shock absorbtion, are less subject to pinch flats, and support heavy loads, but are slightly heavier and create more rolling resistance than narrower tires. For public safety cycling, a minimum of 1.9-inch tire is recommended.

The inflation range, also found on the sidewall, will generally depend on the width of the tire. The wider the tire, the less air pressure is required to support a given load, while a narrow tire will require higher pressures to support that same load. For public safety cycling, tires should be inflated to within 5 pounds per square inch (psi) of the maximum recommended tire pressure.

Inner Tubes
Inner tube valve stems are of two types: Schrader and Presta. Schrader valves, the standard valve stem found on passenger vehicles, are held shut by a spring (**FIGURE 3-6**). Presta valve stems are thinner, screw shut, and are held closed by air pressure (**FIGURE 3-7**). Prestas require a smaller hole in the rim than do Schraders, and a rim with a smaller hole will always be stronger. Prestas can be inconvenient because they require an adaptor for stan-

FIGURE 3-6 Schrader valves, the standard valve stem found on passenger vehicles, are held shut by a spring.

dard air sources like automobile air compressors and some floor pumps. However, many good-quality frame-mounted and floor pumps have dual heads to accommodate both types of valve stems.

Puncture Prevention
There are a number of products available to help prevent inner tube punctures. Tire inserts, which

FIGURE 3-7 Presta valve stems are thinner, screw shut, and are held closed by air pressure.

come in different thicknesses, are designed for placement between the inner side of the tire and the outer circumference of the inner tube. Thorn-proof tubes are constructed of thicker material than standard inner tubes and are a good choice for riding in areas with surface hazards like glass, grass burrs, thorns, and other sharp objects. Both inserts and tubes take up space inside the tire; therefore, it is important to know the dimensions of the tire and the type of valve stem when selecting spare inner tubes. Liquid or gel inner tube additives repair punctures by quickly filling the hole with fibers and a congealing agent that form a clot to prevent all of the air from escaping until the tube can be patched or replaced.

These three puncture-preventing products add weight to the wheels and therefore the bike. The thorn-proof tubes are the heaviest, although it is not uncommon to find public safety bikes that use both thorn-proof tubes and liquid sealer.

Brake Systems

The braking capacity of a public safety bicycle is extremely important, especially when the bike is operated in emergency response mode. The ability to perform maximum braking procedures effectively depends on both the type of braking system and the rider's techniques and skill.

■ Rim Brakes

Rim brakes work by applying pressure on both sides of the wheel rim. They slow or stop the rotation of the tire by the contact of the brake pads

with the rim. Front brakes are mounted on the front side of the fork legs and rear brakes are mounted on the seat stays; both are aligned with the braking surface of the rims.

There are several types of rim brakes in common use. Side-pull caliper and center-pull braking systems are generally not found on better quality mountain bikes because of the longer stopping distance they require. Linear-pull, or V-brake, systems have become the norm because their design provides better stopping power via the increased leverage exerted on the brakes pads against the rim (FIGURE 3-8).

Brake pads are an essential component of rim brakes, as the pads are applied to the wheel rims to stop the bicycle. They are generally composed of carbon rubber and have small grooves, or wear marks, through the face of the pad to help indicate the amount of wear. Brake pads need to be replaced when they are worn down, have hardened with age, or have accumulated debris and aluminum from the braking surface of the rim, all of which render them ineffective.

Brake pads can be either post pad units or cartridge units. On post pad units, the rubber pad is attached permanently to a threaded or unthreaded post that is mounted to the brake arm by nut or bolt; the entire post pad assembly must be replaced when worn. Cartridge-style pads are mounted to the brake arm like the post pads, but the rubber pad material is held into the holder by a small cotter pin. Removing the pin allows the worn pad to slide out of the holder for replacement without removing the assembly from

FIGURE 3-8 Linear pull, or V-brake, system.

the brake arm. These are easier to replace than post pads.

■ Disc Brakes

Disc brake systems, previously used mostly on tandems, are becoming more readily available on public safety bicycles. Better-quality mountain bike frames, even if not initially equipped with disc brakes, usually have braze-ons capable of accepting both front and rear disc-brake systems.

Disc brakes consist of a caliper and rotor, mounted on the front fork and on the rear where the chain-stay and seat-stay converge, near the hub of the wheel assembly (FIGURE 3-9). They are operated by an actuating system of an internal piston, either mechanical or hydraulic. They work by overcoming centripetal force at the center of the wheel, which generally requires less force than that required for stopping centrifugal force at the outside of the rim, i.e., they are more effective at slowing the wheel's rotation than are rim brakes.

Since the disc brake system provides more powerful and efficient braking than the V-brake system, the cyclist must use caution when braking hard to prevent an over-the-handlebar crash, or "endo." It takes time to grow accustomed to the modulation sensation felt when applying the disc brakes as compared to less powerful linear pull brakes.

If a hydraulic disc brake system is used, it is essential to make sure that the appropriate hydraulic fluid is used. The fluid can be glycol, phosphate-ester, or mineral-oil-based, and they are not all compatible with each other. The hydraulic fluid needs to be changed periodically; and the rotors

FIGURE 3-9 Disc brakes.

and calipers must be inspected and adjusted to ensure optimal performance.

■ Suspension

Most mountain bikes are equipped with front-only or front and rear suspension. A bike with front suspension only is sometimes referred to as a hardtail. A bike with both front and rear suspension is generally called a dual suspension or full suspension bike. In most instances, a full suspension bicycle is not required for public safety use; a good quality hardtail is usually sufficient and less expensive.

■ Front Suspension

Front suspension is provided by means of a suspension fork. A good suspension fork can relieve fatigue in the hands, wrists, arms, and shoulders. To be effective, the suspension fork must be adequate to support the weight of the rider. A rider weighing 200 lbs or more (not uncommon for a fully equipped bike officer or a fully loaded EMS bike) could bottom out an entry-level suspension fork. In this situation, the fork is ineffective and potentially dangerous, in that it could pitch the rider's weight too far forward during maximum braking or when negotiating obstacles, resulting in a crash. Similarly, a high-end cross-country racing fork could be so lightweight that it could flex under lateral stress, bending or causing imprecise steering.

Most suspension fork manufacturers make heavier forks and components for riders who weigh more than 200 lbs, and these can be ideal for public safety use. Some manufacturers make a public safety version of their regular suspension fork, designed and tuned to stand up to the rigors of hard riding and to support heavier riders and loads. In general, suspension forks for public safety bikes should be of high quality, with easy adjustment mechanisms, reasonable weight, and low maintenance needs; they should provide stability and relieve rider fatigue.

■ Full Suspension

Fully suspended mountain bikes use a rear shock and/or coil spring to complement the front suspension fork, affording the rider a smoother ride than a hardtail bike. Most full suspension bikes have about 3 to 4 inches of travel (compression) in both the fork and rear shock. This cushion isolates the rider from the vibrations and bumps transmitted through the wheels by rough terrain or obstacles.

There are advantages and disadvantages to using a full-suspension bike for public safety cycling. In general, fully suspended bikes tend to be more expensive than their hardtail counterparts. They can also be heavier, except in higher-priced models.

As an advantage, full-suspension bikes provide a smoother ride, which translates into less fatigue for the rider. However, pedaling the extra weight of the suspension bike might negate that gain, as suspension bikes are generally 5 or more pounds heavier than a comparable hardtail. Rear suspension is also advantageous because it keeps the rear wheel in contact with the ground over rough surfaces, providing better traction and enhancing braking.

A very active rear shock can absorb some pedaling energy, making it a little slower to accelerate and slightly less efficient than a hardtail. Therefore, many shocks provide a lockout mechanism that allows the rider to cancel the shock's activity, essentially converting the bike to a hardtail when desired.

Full-suspension bikes need more maintenance and therefore might require the services of a certified mechanic to tune or repair the suspension parts like the shock and pivot bushings, or the oil and air seals in the shock body.

There are additional issues to consider when deciding whether to use a full suspension for public safety cycling. For example, most public safety bikes require a rear rack and pack system to carry equipment and supplies as well as a kickstand. Full-suspension bikes require differently designed racks and kickstands than do hardtails. These items are addressed in Chapter 4.

Careful consideration must be given to purchasing and maintaining a full-suspension bike for public safety use. The need for full suspension, as dictated by patrol area, and increased rider comfort must be weighed against the increased weight, cost, and maintenance of the equipment.

Bike Fit

Bike fit is essential to rider comfort and injury prevention. Health-related risks of riding a bike that is too small or too large include knee injuries, back pain, and arm and wrist pain. The most important aspect of bike fit is frame size, so rider size must be considered when assigning or purchasing bikes. Ideally, each rider would be assigned his or her own bike and be fitted to it prior to purchase. However, if several riders will be sharing the same bike, it may be helpful to group personnel by size and buy the bikes accordingly, then assign shifts so that no one has to ride a bike that is either too big or too small.

Even if the riders are fit to the bikes prior to purchase, additional adjustments will be necessary. Frame size is just one aspect of bicycle fit; saddle height, tilt, and fore and aft (forward and backward) adjustments are equally important. An understanding of how to adjust the bike to achieve better bicycle fit is essential to rider comfort, efficiency, and safety.

To select the proper frame size, the rider steps over the bike, stands flat-footed with the feet shoulder-width apart, and rolls the bike forward until the nose of the saddle touches the lower back or buttocks. There should be approximately 2 inches of clearance between the top tube and the groin.

Once the proper frame size has been selected, the correct saddle height must be set based on leg length. Saddle height is a personal preference based on comfort and rider efficiency, but there is a universally recognized place to start.

Have someone steady you on the bike as you sit on the saddle with both feet on the pedals, in the 6 and 12 o'clock position. Adjust the seat post to raise or lower the saddle to achieve about an 85% extension of the leg in the six o'clock position (FIGURE 3-10). This method results in a position that best uses the muscle structure of the legs and buttocks to transmit power to the pedals. Again, using someone to steady the bike, place your heels on the pedals and pedal backwards. Your hips should not rock from side to side to keep your heels in contact with the pedals; if they do, the saddle should be lowered incrementally (no more than 5 mm at a time) until the rocking ceases.

If you have a suspension seat post, read and follow the manufacturer's directions for adjusting the seat post. Suspension seat posts should sag only a small amount as you sit on them; the majority of the travel is reserved for absorbing bumps. Adjust the seat post for your weight before you adjust your

Bike Fit

Bike fit is essential to rider comfort and injury prevention. Health-related risks of riding a bike that is too small or too large include knee injuries, back pain, and arm and wrist pain.

FIGURE 3-10 Saddle height should allow 85% leg extension in the six o'clock position.

saddle height. The saddle height should be adjusted with one pedal in the six o'clock position with your heel on the pedal. Adjust the saddle height so that your legs are just barely locked straight at the knee. When this is accomplished, slide your feet back on the pedals until the ball of your foot is centered on the pedal in the riding position.

Now step off the bike and look at the top of your saddle; it should be level from front to rear. You can make minor adjustments for your personal comfort, but generally, if you tilt the saddle forward, your weight is transferred forward onto your arms, which can cause fatigue and injury. If you tilt the saddle up too much, you will increase the pressure exerted on the groin by the front of the seat, which can cause numbness, pain, or injury.

Once the saddle is level, adjust its position (fore and aft) relative to the frame and your body. The saddle is attached to the seat post by rails and can

be adjusted forwards and backwards approximately 2 to 3 inches. When you are in the saddle with your feet on the pedals in the 3 o'clock and 9 o'clock position, the hinge-point of your front knee should be directly over the axle of the pedal. You can have your helper examine this for a rough adjustment, or use a small weight hanging from a string (plumb-bob) for a more exact check (**FIGURE 3-11**). Put the end of the string on the hinge point of your knee and let the weight dangle. Gravity will pull it straight down. The string should point an imaginary line down through the ball of the foot on the pedal and through the pedal axle. Slide the saddle back or forward until you achieve this position.

Saddle rails are usually angled downward from front to rear as viewed from the side. This causes the saddle height to increase as it is slid forward on the rails and decrease with a rearward shift. Because fore and aft adjustment is made after the saddle

FIGURE 3-11 Using a plumb bob for saddle adjustment.

height adjustment, it is possible the previously set saddle height might change as a result of the fore/aft movement and should be rechecked.

Because riders of the same height may have different torso and arm length measurements, the final bike fit adjustment is the reach from the rider to the handlebar. The only way to do this is to equip the bike with a stem that achieves the best position for rider comfort. Stems are available in various increments of rise, i.e., height above the headset, and reach, or how far it projects forward past the headtube. Adjustable stems allow for setup experimentation or frequent adjustments if more than one rider uses the same bike. However, adjustable stems tend to be very heavy and can be much more expensive

than standard stems. For a fleet of bikes, it might be worth having one adjustable stem to use as a set-up guide before purchasing regular stems for individual riders.

In general, a stem with a higher rise and a short reach is preferable for public safety cycling. This allows for a more upright riding position that takes some of the body weight off the arms and hands, thus reducing fatigue, while enhancing the rider's ability to see and scan the environment. Another positive effect is a weight bias toward the rear of the bike that helps in lofting the front wheel to clear obstacles.

Once these baseline bike fit adjustments are made, the rider should let his or her body adjust to them for awhile before making further adjustments. If adjustments are necessary, they should be made incrementally, only one at a time, as, for instance, changing both saddle height and the stem might make it more difficult to identify which element caused the rider discomfort.

The above method should result in comfortable fit. There are other, more complicated methods for those who wish to have a more precise fit. Most bike shops have fit systems, tools, and measuring equipment to achieve this result.

Conclusion

All public safety cyclists should be outfitted with properly sized and fitted mountain bikes supplied by reputable manufacturers, and equipped with mid-grade or better components that can withstand rigorous use. Decisions to purchase bikes with upgraded frame materials and components should be made based upon an assessment of department needs and budget. Once the bikes have been purchased, it is critical to keep the bikes clean and properly maintained to ensure their safety and longevity.

References

May, Monte (2006). How to Buy a Public Safety Mountain Bike. *IPMBA News*, Winter, pgs 5–6.

4

On-Bike Equipment

chapter at a glance

Introduction

Selecting a bicycle that is suitable for public safety use is just the first step towards providing the public safety cyclist with a safe, effective tool and mode of transportation. The bike must be properly equipped with the necessary accessories, which must also be suitable for public safety use.

Saddles

The saddle is perhaps the most important contact point between the rider and bicycle. While the rider wants comfort from the saddle, the quality and design of the saddle could affect the reproductive health of both male and female public safety cyclists.

In 1999, the ABC News television show *20/20* aired two broadcasts: "A Bike Ride Has Its Drawback" and "Bike Riders' Lament," following an article that appeared in *Bicycling* magazine. The story revolved around the then-editor of *Bicycling* magazine, who admitted that his bike riding had brought on a distressing condition—he was unable to have erections. Urologist Dr. Irwin Goldstein admonished men to "never ride bicycles." This advice was a bit extreme, but it raised awareness about the effects of pressure exerted on the genitalia by the bike saddle.

In May 2001, the National Institute for Occupational Safety and Health (NIOSH) released the results of Hazard Evaluation and Technical Assistance Survey 2000-0305-2848, which had been conducted for the City of Long Beach, CA, Police Department. The review, conducted during two months in 2000, found that of the bike unit's 15 officers, 14 (93%) experienced numbness in their genitalia and a decreased quality of erections. This numbness occurred after 10 minutes to 3 hours of riding and lasted from 5 minutes to 24 hours.

This condition was attributed to the compression of the vascular and nerve structure (and, in males, damage to the two muscles that allow for the cremasteric response) within the genitalia of male and female public safety cyclists due to the riders' weight, body positioning and saddle design. Although a key preventive measure is the proper sizing and fitting of the bicycle to the individual rider (see Chapter 3), further studies by NIOSH point to the need for awareness of the potential risks of pressure caused by the bike saddle. As a result of their research, NIOSH released the following recommendations related to reproductive health and the bicycle saddle:

- Ensure proper bike fit.
- Dismount during rest breaks and, when possible, while talking and observing.
- Dismount if numbness occurs, and remain off the bike until it subsides.
- Minimize pressure to the perineum.
- Experiment with different saddle types, including noseless saddles.

Because of increased awareness of the need for ergonomic saddle design, manufacturers have developed many styles of bike saddles. Some public safety cyclists prefer a tapered racing-style saddle. Others opt for those that provide a cut-out, although NIOSH cautions against the use of cut-out saddles based upon preliminary research into the effects of the distributed pressure. NIOSH studies suggest the use of noseless saddles, which eliminate the potential for compression.

Whatever saddle design the rider chooses, other features to consider are the type and placement of the padding. Gel-filled saddles can be effective in absorbing additional compression and can help protect the tuberosity of the hip complex that supports the weight of the rider. Some saddles have wider bodies and heavy-duty springs, offering extra support for larger riders.

Because every person's anatomy is unique, saddle selection is a very personal decision. It may take some experimentation with different saddle types, but riders should select a saddle that offers support, is comfortable, and does not cause numbness. Riders should also follow the NIOSH recommendations to ensure proper bike fit and take frequent breaks off the saddle.

Pedal Retention Devices

The primary purpose of a pedal retention system is to keep the cyclist's feet on the pedals when going up and over obstacles. Pedal retention also helps keep the feet engaged with the bicycle during steep descents and in crash situations such as side-impact falls. For these reasons, IPMBA has identified pedal retention as mandatory safety equipment for all public safety cyclists. Although many cyclists are initially cautious about using a pedal retention system and are afraid that they will sustain additional injuries in the event of a crash, with experience and practice they soon recognize the benefits.

A secondary benefit of pedal retention is improved pedaling efficiency. Pedal retention can assist the rider in achieving the desired "good spin" of 75 to 100 pedal revolutions per minute, the rate at which a cyclist needs to pedal to maximize efficiency and conserve energy. Pedal retention enables the rider to both pull up and push down on the pedals,

exerting nearly equal force throughout the pedal revolution. This spin can be maintained at any gear through a combination of low pedal pressure and high pedal cadence. This reduces muscle fatigue and potential muscle imbalances between the bicep femoris and quadriceps muscles in the front of the leg and the hamstring complex at the rear of the leg.

The different styles of pedal retention systems available on the market accommodate a wide range of comfort levels, abilities, and skills (FIGURE 4-1A–C). Regardless of the pedal retention system used, the public safety cyclist must practice with that system, disengaging from it in routine dismounts, under stress conditions, and during crash survival exercises. It is essential for cyclists to know and understand the benefits and limitations of the particular system that will be used on their bicycles.

Good Spin

Pedal retention can assist the rider in achieving the desired "good spin" of 75 to 100 pedal revolutions per minute, the rate at which a cyclist needs to pedal to maximize efficiency and conserve energy.

FIGURE 4-1A–C Pedal retention types: A. PowerGrips, B. toe clips, C. clipless.

PowerGrips

PowerGrips consist of a 1.5-inch wide band that diagonally traverses from the rear inner portion to the front outer portion of the pedal cage. The band provides for easy in-and-out motion of the foot, but also holds the foot tightly enough to the pedal to enhance pedaling efficiency (Figure 4-1A).

Toe Clips

Toe clips, sometimes referred to as cages, are typically used in combination with straps. The straps are woven through the toe clip and can be adjusted easily to cinch them down around the footwear. Some cyclists remove the straps and use the toe clip only, but even if the straps are used, they should be kept loose enough to facilitate entry and exit. Most public safety bicycles are initially equipped with this type of pedal retention system (Figure 4-1B).

Clipless Pedals

Clipless pedal retention systems use a releasable mechanism similar to a ski binding to lock onto cleated shoes, eliminating the need for toe clips. Many experienced riders use clipless pedals, because they provide the best means of securing the foot to the pedal and are the most efficient in terms of maximizing the pedal stroke (Figure 4-1C).

With clipless pedals, the bike shoe is attached to the pedal by the cleat under the ball of the foot. The pedal releases the shoe when the heel is twisted out to the side, pivoting the ball of the foot. Although some agencies prohibit the use of clipless pedals because of the exposed cleat on the underside of the shoe, which can slip on highly polished wood floors and tiles and stonework surfaces, the development of recessed clips for use by mountain bikers has alleviated this difficulty, making clipless pedals a practical choice for public safety cyclists. There are numerous models of cycling shoes available, some manufactured specifically for public safety use.

Clipless pedal users need to be familiar with two terms: tension and float. Tension determines how tightly the pedal grips the cleat. On many pedals, the tension can be adjusted to regulate the amount of force needed to release the foot (or clip out) from the pedal. Most cyclists start by setting the tension as low as possible so they can clip out easily, but low tension increases the chances of clipping out inadvertently. As they gain experience, most cyclists increase the tension, making it more

difficult to release the foot. This allows cyclists to ride more aggressively without worrying that their shoes will detach from the pedals.

Float dictates the amount of lateral movement afforded to the heel of the clipped-in foot. Pedals typically have from 4 to 15 degrees of float. This side-to-side movement allows for some foot rotation during the pedaling revolution, which can help prevent knee and hip pain. If the float limit is exceeded, the pedals will release the shoes. The degree of float is determined by the manufacturer and is not adjustable.

Clipless pedal retention systems do have some drawbacks. Expense is a critical factor, both for the pedals and the specially equipped shoes. There is also the issue of noise generated when the public safety cyclist clips in and out of the retention system, possibly giving up a stealth or tactical advantage. Maintenance is also a consideration, as the cleat mounting bolts and tension springs need to be kept free of dirt and debris.

Headlamps

Headlamps range widely in cost and can easily become the biggest expense beyond the cost of the bicycle itself. The first and foremost factor in purchasing a headlamp is whether the public safety cyclist is going to ride the bicycle in low light conditions. If so, the next factors to consider are the requirements of the state or municipal motor vehicle code (MVC). The third consideration is whether the public safety bicycle is legally required to be equipped with a lighting system, with or without a horn or siren, to be considered an emergency vehicle.

If the bicycle will not be operated in low light conditions, is not designated as an emergency vehicle, or does not require lighting to be so designated based on the provisions of the MVC, there is little reason to justify the expense of a headlamp system. If the bicycle will be operated at night and/or is required to have lights in order to be classified as an emergency vehicle, it must be equipped with a light system comprised of both a headlight and rear lighting. (See Chapter 11 for more information on lighting and selecting a light system.)

Audible Warning Devices

As with lighting, before deciding whether to equip a public safety bike with an audible warning device, it is advisable to check the requirements of the applicable state or municipal Motor Vehicle Code (MVC). Many MVCs that require audible warning devices define parameters as to the distance they must be heard from and/or specify decibel levels. Other MVCs have provisions specifically prohibiting the use of sirens on bicycles, even those used by public safety cyclists.

Some horns available for bicycles are inexpensive and consist of a thumb-actuated striker hitting a bell, or are squeeze-toy types that force air out through a bladder, creating the noise. These types of horns and bells generally have a limited audible range. Compressed air cylinders can be used to generate louder decibel sounds, but a water bottle cage is usually necessary to hold the canister, and the plastic tubing leading to the horn can leak or get cut, rendering the system useless.

More expensive siren models operate with an electric current from a battery source. These vary in pitch, modes, and decibel level, some up to 115 db. They may be mounted separately or integrated within a headlight system. When evaluating such a siren, ensure that the wiring is protected from chafing along the frame of the bicycle or other components, and ensure that the construction will hold up to shock or being dropped. Weather resistance is also a consideration if the public safety cyclist will be operating in inclement conditions.

Bags, Panniers, and Racks

Public safety cyclists typically carry such items as a spare inner tube, an air source, a small tool kit, a first aid kit, a ticket/ordinance book, department paperwork, additional ammunition, and handcuffs. (Chapter 23 addresses medical equipment carried by EMS cyclists.) The cyclist generally carries these items in a rear-mounted rack bag or side-mounted panniers (FIGURE 4-2A-B), although some agencies also use handlebar or front-fork-mounted bags. Some public safety cyclists prefer to carry all their necessary equipment inside a backpack-style hydration pack system or regular backpack. All public safety cyclists face the question of what to carry and how to carry it; riders make refinements based upon their evolving needs and needs of the public they serve.

■ Rack Bags and Panniers

The first step in selecting appropriate bags is to determine exactly what the rider needs to carry on a regular basis as well as whether special situations will require additional equipment. The equipment will dictate the size of the bag and/or pannier to be used. A word of caution—the bigger the bag, the more equipment will find its way into it, adding weight. Another consideration in choosing to use panniers is the width they add to the bike. If panniers are selected, the rider needs to learn the limitations when negotiating through crowds and to ensure the leg clears the bag when dismounting.

Selecting Rack Bags and Panniers

When selecting a rear rack bag or pannier, assess the material construction of the bag; most are made of rip-stop nylon or Cordura®, which is resistant to abrasions, tears, and scuffs. Evaluate the strength of the bag in terms of the weight of the items to be carried. Bag strength is rated based on the amount of denier, or weight per square inch of the fabric, typically 500d–1000d. The higher the denier, the stronger the fabric and the more weight it can bear. Determine if the bag is water repellent or waterproof and if it has a liner. The degree of weather resistance required depends on the climatic conditions in which the bag will be used. Most of the time, plastic bags will suffice for protecting equipment from the elements. Examine the number of exterior pockets and whether the pockets or the main compartment are expandable. Decide whether one large compartment or a sectioned interior is preferable. Some bags have an interior foam bladder to provide shape to the bag or pannier and/or have clear plastic dividers or pockets to enable the rider to organize and locate equipment easily. Some bags have exterior Velcro® loops to hold a small hand pump or collapsible impact weapon.

Examine the quality of the zippers. They should be heavy duty, with double stitching around the edges of the zipper so that the zippers do not become stressed and rip out over time. Large pull-tabs are more practical and easy to open quickly and while wearing long-fingered gloves.

Most rack bags and panniers have reflective striping or markings on the exterior. These markings should be in a position to be visible to motorists and other bicyclists. Some also have attachments for reflectors or rear flashing lights. Finally, the bag should be able to accommodate identification markings.

■ The Rack

After determining what rear rack bag and/or side panniers will be used, as well as the weight of the items to be carried, select a suitable rack. The con-

FIGURE 4-2A-B Police and security officers typically use only rack bags (A), while EMS cyclists usually carry panniers as well (B).

struction material of racks ranges from light gauge steel or chromoly (chromium and molybdenum combined with the steel to reduce weight but maintain strength) to aluminum alloy. Rated weight varies from 15 to 50 pounds. Check the welds of the rack and the cross members to ensure that it will support the anticipated weight. Consider also the weight of the rack, as it will contribute to the overall weight of the bicycle.

Many racks for hardtail bicycles are secured with bolts to the frame of the bike in the area of the seat post and at the base of the vertical struts where the chain stay and seat stay join. If panniers are to be used, a rack that has vertical struts in a rectangular shape instead of a tapered design will prevent the bags from draping into the spokes or rubbing against the tire.

Full-suspension bicycles and disc-brake-equipped bicycles present rack mounting issues. Depending on what equipment will be carried, there are two options. For carrying a trunk/rack bag, a beam rack can be used as long as the rack's weight limit, typically less than 25 lbs, are not ex-

ceeded. Beam racks are generally mounted to the seat post rather than to the frame and do not have vertical struts for support. Quick-release mechanisms may not support the weight of the equipment carried in the bag, but a four-bolt mounting system is available to provide additional structural integrity to the rack.

In addition to having low carrying capacity, most beam racks do not accomodate panniers. If panniers are to be carried, there are two options. For full-suspension and/or disc–brake-equipped bicycles, a rack that mounts to the axle using the wheel quick-release and clamps or bolts to the seat stay or brake boss can be used. Rigid frames with disc brakes can also accommodate a rack designed to work around the brake caliper.

The last consideration will be how the rack bag and/or pannier system is secured to the rack. The rider may want to be able to disengage the rear bag or pannier from the rack quickly and carry it to an incident scene away from the bicycle. This must be balanced against the potential of the bag or pannier becoming detached when bouncing over obstacles or rough terrain. Some rear-mounted rack bags are attached by Velcro® straps that loop under the horizontal panel of the rack while others use a slide rail system and quick-release mechanism for easy removal of the bag. Panniers often use metal hooks and bungee cord-type connections.

■ Backpacks

Backpacks and backpack-style hydration packs are another option for public safety cyclists. This carry system, although limited, has the advantage of always being with the rider, even when the rider is away from the bicycle. Backpacks are also useful for riders of full-suspension bikes, whose racks have less carrying capacity than standard racks. Depending on the amount of medical equipment to be carried and the level of care to be provided, EMS cyclists may find the backpack practical. Police and security cyclists who opt to use hydration packs or backpacks need to be aware of and prepare for potential officer safety issues due to the pack being attached to the officer, therefore providing a handhold for a suspect during an altercation. Some officers mitigate this risk by wearing the straps under their shirt or jacket. This renders the pack somewhat inaccessible, so it might only be useful for hydration or rarely needed items, such as first-aid supplies.

Bar Ends

Some public safety bicycles are equipped or retrofitted with bar ends mounted to the handlebars. Bar ends come in a variety of different lengths, designs and angles, but all serve the purpose of offering additional hand positions in an effort to reduce stress and fatigue on the hand and wrist complex. Varying hand position while riding helps prevent chronic conditions such as carpal tunnel syndrome and arthritis.

The bar ends serve other purposes as well. Riders with shorter torsos or arm reach might find them beneficial, and they provide excellent protection for the fingers when patrolling in tight quarters (e.g., in tunnels or between parked cars) or when using crash survival techniques. Caution should be used when setting the angle of the bar ends so that the rider does not break a wrist during an over-the-handlebar crash. Bar ends should be at roughly the same angle as the down tube (**FIGURE 4-3**). Any angle that does not approximate that of the down tube can be considered potentially dangerous.

Bar Ends

Caution should be used when setting the angle of the bar ends so that the public safety cyclist does not break a wrist during an over-the-handlebar crash.

Kickstands

Most public safety bicycles are equipped with kickstands, which are designed to maintain the upright posture of the bicycle when the rider is disengaged from the bicycle.

The footprint on the base of the kickstand needs to be large enough to support the weight of the bicycle while on various surfaces. What may support the bike on a paved surface may embed itself into a soft surface such as grass or dirt. The kickstand should be the proper length to hold the bike nearly upright, which allows the kickstand to sink into a soft surface slightly without letting the bike fall over to the left. If the kickstand is too long, the bike will be too upright and prone to falling over to the right.

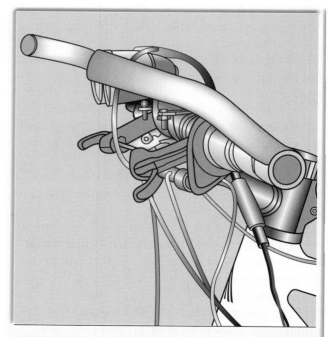

FIGURE 4-3 Bar end installed at the proper angle.

■ Bottom Bracket Kickstand

The bottom bracket kickstand, as the name implies, is attached to the frame of the bicycle near the bottom bracket. It is usually connected with just one bolt, which can be a drawback, as that bolt has a tendency to come loose, resulting in the kickstand impeding the rotation of the tire or flaring out into the pedal stroke of the rider. The bottom bracket kickstand is difficult to operate with the foot during dynamic dismounts because it aligns itself with the chain stay, preventing the toe from finding it and dropping it into place. The weight supported by a bottom bracket kickstand is not as great as that supported by a rear-mount kickstand, which may present problems when panniers are used. Weight on the rear of the bicycle can cause the bike to pivot around this type of kickstand and fall to the ground.

■ Rear-mount Kickstands

Rear-mount kickstands are a better choice for public safety cyclists. They are usually attached to the bike frame at both the chain stay and seat stay. The additional bolts and plates of this multiple connection provide a more stable stance than the bottom bracket kickstand, can support more weight, and do not come loose as readily. Rear-mount kickstands extend beyond the rear frame of the bicycle and are easier to operate during dynamic dismounts.

■ Two-legged Kickstands

Increased tubing sizes, full suspension frames, and disc brake calipers all interfere with the mounting of rear-mount kickstands unless they have been modified by the bicycle manufacturer or dealer. Center-mounted kickstands that have two legs (similar to a motorcycle center stand) may resolve this issue on rigid framed bicycles that allow regular bottom bracket kickstand mounting. The legs on twin-leg kickstands should be cut long enough to allow them to penetrate and stabilize on soft ground but short enough to allow a wide spread for stability. Although bottom bracket kickstands are not generally recommended, the twin-leg kickstands can be a practical solution for balancing rear-weighted loads if the bike cannot accommodate a rear-mount kickstand.

Water Bottle Cages

Most bicycles are equipped with at least one water bottle cage, although public safety bicycles should be outfitted with two water bottle cages. This will enable the rider to carry a water bottle to maintain a safe hydration level as well as a battery system for a headlamp or an air source for a pressurized air-actuated horn.

Water bottle cages can be constructed of steel, aluminum, alloy, or lightweight carbon fiber. The price ranges according to material. Heavy-duty water bottle cages are recommended for extremely rough terrain; lighter cages may not retain full bottles or batteries. As a preventive measure, the bolts holding the water bottle cages onto the frame should be checked periodically to ensure they do not become loose and allow the cages to fall off of the bicycle.

Cyclo-Computers

There are many features in addition to cost to consider when deciding to use a cyclo-computer. Many computers collect a great deal of information, such as miles per hour; average miles per hour; miles covered in a trip (statistics of interest to the community), weekly, or monthly (which can be useful for scheduled maintenance); time; temperature, and so forth. The more information the computer provides, the more expensive it is, but there are many good computers available at reasonable prices. Early cyclo-computer heads were mounted to the handlebars and connected to the sensor via wires, but the wires were easily damaged or detached. Wireless technology is a more practical choice. Factors to consider in deciding whether to use cyclo-computers include whether the data will be used and whether the computer head will interfere with other handlebar-mounted equipment such as headlamps, PTT radio buttons, or horns/sirens.

Conclusion

The bicycle is an emergency vehicle. As such, the same care and attention must be spent in equipping it as would be spent equipping a patrol car or ambulance. Selecting the right components and accessories can be the difference between an active, effective bicycle unit and one that rides infrequently and has little impact upon the community.

References

Schrader, Steven and Breitenstein, Michael (2000). *Health Hazard Evaluation Report: City of Long Beach Police Department, Long Beach CA, HETA 2000-0305-2848.* National Institute of Occupational Safety and Health (NIOSH), Cincinnati OH.

5

Clothing and Personal Protective Equipment

chapter at a glance

Introduction

Since the revival of policing by bike, IPMBA has partnered with uniform manufacturers to develop products that meet the unique needs of bike-mounted public safety personnel. These specialized products are designed to enhance the safety and effectiveness of public safety cyclists. Some innovations have been so successful that they have been adopted for use in regular uniforms. For instance, non-bike officers often wear bike patrol jackets, including many who responded to the World Trade Center on September 11, 2001.

The right clothing and equipment will help the public safety cyclist perform better and therefore have a greater positive impact on the community. If equipment and clothing are not up to industry standards, the productivity of the bike unit may suffer.

Clothing and Shoes

Bike jackets, shirts, and pants are designed differently than their standard uniform counterparts. The best choice is high-quality uniforms designed with input from bike personnel to make them functional, fashionable, and comfortable. Choosing a bike uni-

form based on cost alone will be more expensive in the long term.

■ Fabric

Patrolling by bike is a physical, and often harsh, outdoor activity. Uniforms must be constructed to block the wind and protect against the rain and cold, yet provide ventilation to a perspiring body. In extreme heat and cold, proper bike uniforms can prevent heat- or cold-related illness or injury.

Cyclists can generate an extra 10 to 15 degrees of body heat while riding. In hot weather, an improperly hydrated or ventilated cyclist can easily fall victim to heat exhaustion or heat stroke. An individual wearing body armor may be especially susceptible, a factor that must be taken into account when establishing a uniform standard; for instance, being permitted to wear shorts instead of long pants in hot weather is imperative. In cold weather, the heat generated by cycling is a mixed blessing. It can allow the cyclist to stay warmer while wearing less insulated clothing. However, perspiration dampens clothing and causes the body to lose heat faster and feel chilled sooner. Some items, such as cotton turtlenecks, may seem warm, but once sweaty will work against the rider. Specialized bike patrol uniforms are made of high-tech fabrics intended to both transport perspiration away from the body and protect the wearer from the environment. They are often made of specially engineered fabrics such as Coolmax™, Supplex™, and stretch knits. These fabrics will not hold moisture from perspiration, and if the fabric next to the skin is dry, the rider will stay warmer in the winter and cooler in the summer.

■ Shirts

Specialized bike patrol shirts come in polo-like pullovers and traditional button-up styles, with either long or short sleeves. Polo-style shirts have proven to be popular among bike personnel, who like the comfort and the more approachable look (FIGURE 5-1A). Polos made by uniform companies usually use Coolmax™ or other wicking fabrics similar to those used for cycling jerseys. If a more traditional look is desired, cycling-specific uniform shirts with a Class A design are available. Made of lightweight Coolmax™ or other fast wick-and-dry fabrics, these shirts have epaulets, pockets with flaps, traditional collars, and sewn-in creases (FIGURE 5-1B). They are available in both high visibility and traditional uniform colors, and in solid or duo-tone. Uniform cycling shirts of both types are typically cut longer in the back to prevent them from coming untucked while riding. They are also roomy in the shoulders and have longer sleeves.

FIGURE 5-1, A–B Bike uniforms are available in a variety of styles and colors.

■ Cycling Shorts and Pants

Sitting on seams is uncomfortable; therefore, bike pants and shorts minimize seams and place them in areas that do not have direct contact with the saddle. Bike pants hug the leg at the bottom to prevent entanglement in the chain, and the knees are often articulated for freedom of movement. Bike uniform pants and shorts should be made of a material that dries quickly after getting wet from rain or sweat. Most pants and shorts are made from materials such as Supplex™ and other stretch knits. Some pant fabrics are lined with a breathable film like Gortex™ or Ultrex™, which makes them waterproof and wind-resistant. Several companies use imported stretch knits of varying weights that are water resistant and windproof without laminates. Some bike pants are available with zip-off legs to double as shorts.

Some cycling-specific shorts and pants are equipped with a built-in chamois pad. The uninitiated believe that the chamois is there to provide padding between rider and saddle. While it can alleviate some soreness, its real purpose is to absorb moisture and reduce chafing and saddle sores.

A cyclist should not wear cotton underwear between the chamois pad and his or her skin. Cotton will retain the moisture the chamois is supposed to absorb and will increase the possibility of chafing and saddle sores. It is advisable to use special cycling underwear of Coolmax™, silk, or similar material that will wick any moisture through to the chamois.

Many uniform pants and shorts do not contain chamois pads, but are cut to accommodate cycling shorts underneath them. Many cyclists wear thickly padded shorts at first, but as they grow accustomed to being in the saddle, they often opt for thinner but still absorbent chamois.

■ Jackets

The standard riding position requires that bike patrol jackets be cut and sized so they are roomy across the shoulders, with slightly longer sleeves and back. They should be ordered large enough to accommodate multiple layers of clothing under them.

Jackets can be purchased with or without insulated liners. Nearly all jackets are lined with wickable, breathable material to help them stay dry inside. Jackets are typically available in materials like treated Supplex™, or a Supplex™-like material laminated with a breathable, waterproof film like Gortex™. The former is less expensive; the latter is more versatile and effective. Some jackets feature removable sleeves to accommodate a range of weather conditions.

■ Appearance

While bike uniforms have to be comfortable and breathable, they must also be readily identifiable as uniforms. Many public safety cyclists wear colors not worn by their non-bike counterparts, such as yellow, white, or red shirts that make them more visible. Bike patrol jackets are the most dramatically different from standard uniforms, with color combinations such as yellow or royal blue over navy blue. These brighter, contrasting colors enable motorists to see bike personnel more easily. Nontraditional shirts and jackets should have shoulder emblems and reflective stencils both front and back, to clearly identify the wearer as a part of the police, security, or EMS unit. Shoulder patches can also be worn on both sleeves of uniform shirts and jackets to facilitate recognition.

■ Shoes

Several uniform shoe manufacturers make cycling shoes designed for bike duty. Cycling shoes have narrower soles than athletic shoes, so they slide easily into toe clips. Most are compatible with clipless pedal systems. Bike patrol-specific shoes have stiff soles to keep the foot from bending during hours of pedaling, yet are flexible enough to be comfortable during periods spent off the bike, for instance, while providing medical care or pursuing a suspect. Cycling shoes should be a mandatory uniform item for public safety cyclists, especially those who operate full-time. Proper footwear can prevent such conditions as plantar fasciitis, an inflammation of the tough, fibrous band of tissue (fascia) in the sole of the foot connecting the heel bone to the base of the toes.

Personal Protective Equipment

IPMBA mandates four pieces of safety equipment and strongly recommends two others, all of which must be used by students during IPMBA training courses and should be used while on duty. Each rider should have a high-quality mountain bike, in good mechanical condition, that fits him or her

properly (see Chapter 3). In addition, all riders must be equipped with: (1) a properly fitted bicycle helmet, approved (in the United States) by Snell, ASTM, or CPSC; (2) shatter-resistant protective eyewear, for day and night; and (3) a pedal retention system (see Chapter 4). Recommended equipment includes padded cycling gloves and a ballistic vest. For the purpose of this chapter, personal protective equipment (PPE) is defined as those items worn on the body of the cyclist.

IPMBA-Mandated Safety Equipment

1. A high-quality mountain bike, in good mechanical condition, that fits the rider properly.
2. A properly fitted bicycle helmet, approved (in the United States) by Snell, ASTM, or CPSC.
3. Shatter-resistant protective eyewear, for day and night.
4. Pedal retention system—toe clips/straps, Power Grips™, or clipless pedals with appropriate shoes.

■ Helmets

According to the National Highway Traffic Safety Administration (NHTSA) and the League of American Bicyclists, 80% of all fatal bicycle crashes are the result of injuries to the cranial area. Therefore, the protection of the head is of utmost importance. While normal patrol speeds might only be 8 to 12 mph, an endo—a crash that sends the rider over the handlebars—coupled with the weight of the rider can result in significant blunt force trauma to the head, resulting in severe injuries or death. Dr. Garry Peterson, an avid cyclist and Medical Examiner of Hennepin County (Minneapolis), MN, explained that a person who falls to the ground from a standing position and strikes his head without catching himself can suffer more than enough force for a fatal head injury. The G-force in most bicycle falls is several times more severe than that.

IPMBA requires an approved bicycle helmet be worn during all training sessions and at all times while cycling. The helmet should be level, cover the forehead, and be worn with the side straps and front/chin strap tight, as shown in FIGURE 5-2, A–B .

What should public safety cyclists look for in a quality bicycle helmet? Not the cost—a helmet should be regarded as an investment in the rider's

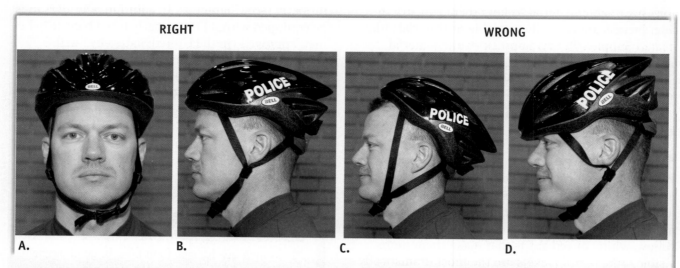

RIGHT   **WRONG**

A.   B.   C.   D.

FIGURE 5-2 A–D The helmet should be level and should cover the forehead (A); the side straps and front/chin strap should be tight (B); it should not be tilted back (C) or forward (D).

safety, not an expense. In the United States, the helmet should meet the most current impact resistance standards, which, at publication date, are: American Society of Testing Materials (ASTM F-1447 of 1999), SNELL Foundation B-95, or the Consumer Product Safety Commission (CPSC) standards. All helmets manufactured for the United States market after 1999 must by law meet the CPSC standard. Other countries have established their own standards. Details about specific products are usually available from the Bicycle Helmet Safety Institute (BHSI), which tests helmets and maintains current information on helmet safety, product recalls, and crash research.

Aside from crash resistance, comfort is the most important factor in selecting a helmet. Coolness, ventilation, fit, and sweat control are the most critical comfort needs. Airflow over the head determines coolness, and larger front vents provide better airflow. A snug fit with no pressure points ensures comfort and correct position.

Helmet Material
Most helmets are made from polystyrene or polyurethane foam (EPS) covered by a thin PVC shell. The shell helps the helmet skid easily on rough pavement to avoid jerking the neck. The shell also holds the EPS together after the first impact. Some excellent helmets are made by molding EPS in the shell rather than adding the shell later, and some use an in-mold micro-shell coupled with carbon fiber ribs.

Helmet Fit
Some helmets come in sizes, while others use plastic helmet-fit systems, known as ring fit, designed to enable a helmet to fit a wider range of head sizes. Some riders find that these one-size helmets require pulling the ring so tight for stability that the helmet causes irritation, while loosening it gives a sloppy fit. Some cyclists like the one-size option because they are quick-fitting, can accommodate unusual head shapes and sizes, and allow for wearing a sweatband or cap underneath the helmet.

Air Vents
Another consideration when choosing a helmet is the number of air vents provided. Vents help dissipate the body heat generated by the bicyclist. With ballistic protection, the equipment worn and carried, weather extremes, exertion level, and other factors, core body temperatures can increase significantly. The Bicycle Helmet Safety Institute recommends against selecting a helmet with numerous vents, as more vents reduce the protection the helmet offers. The number and spacing of vents might also contribute to sunburn if precautions are not taken to protect the scalp.

Visor
A visor may help channel air through the inside of the helmet and reduce heat build-up. It can also help keep raindrops off of the eyewear. Helmet visors must be shatter-resistant and should break off easily

in the event of impact. Although helmet visors can provide shade from the sun, they also block upward vision. When the head is tilted forward in a typical riding position, the visor can make the rider more vulnerable to an attack from above and put the rider at risk of hitting his or her head on low-hanging branches, signs, wires, or overhead beams. Such impacts, even through the helmet, can injure the rider's neck. Finally, the visor can have negative tactical considerations; for instance, it may protrude while a police cyclist is peering around a corner, revealing his or her position.

Color

The color of the helmet is primarily a matter of departmental preference. Most police departments select dark helmets because they are less likely to be seen at night, when a police officer might need to conceal his or her location. Contrary to popular belief, the color of the helmet has little effect on heat absorption.

Other Features

Most helmets have quick-release buckles on the front/chin strap and adjustment mechanisms for the side straps so that the helmet can be fitted properly for the individual rider's head size or to accommodate balaclava style hoods or other head wraps. Helmets should accept markings, such as decals, for identification purposes. A connection mount for a headlamp system might also be a consideration. Manufacturers continue to create innovative cycling helmets; for example, some integrate lights and/or reflective materials into the helmet itself.

Care

Almost all parts of any helmet can and should be washed according to the manufacturer's recommendations. Helmet pads and straps become repeatedly soaked from sweat and skin oils. Regular rinsing with clean water or mild soap and water will keep the helmet clean and odor-free and increase its longevity.

BHSI Helmet Recommendations

BHSI recommends a helmet that:
1. Meets the CPSC bicycle helmet standard.
2. Fits well.
3. Has a rounded, smooth exterior with no snag points.
4. Has no more vents than needed, because more vents equal less protection.

Replacement

The cyclist should replace his or her helmet after a crash. Although the damage may not be visible, the impact crushes some of the foam. Helmets work so well that the rider may need to examine them for marks or dents to know whether his or her head hit the ground or another object. A good test to check for helmet damage is to hold the helmet on both sides, then push and pull while looking at the polystyrene or polyurethane foam for cracks. Then grip the helmet at the front and rear, and perform the same test. If any cracks are found, replace the helmet. Most manufacturers recommend replacement after five years, but the BHSI notes that depending on usage, and assuming reasonable care, most helmets will last much longer.

■ Eyewear

There are many factors to consider when evaluating eyewear, but the most important is that the glasses meet current standards for high-velocity impact resistance and optical clarity, ANSI Z-87.1 or standard or military specifications STD-662 at the publication of this edition. Some insects can fly at average speeds of 20 to 30 mph, with a dragonfly reaching speeds of 50 mph. Coupled with the speed of a cyclist riding 8 to 12 mph, this can create a significant closing speed upon contact, resulting in serious injury to the unprotected eye.

In 2003, while on a road ride in Charleston, WV, a group of IPMBA instructor candidates witnessed an example of the importance of eye protection. A passing car struck the edge of a small stone, sending it into a nearby fence and causing a half-inch deep indentation in the wood. The officers thought for an instant that a bullet had struck the fence and realized the damage that would have occurred if the stone had struck someone's eye. This illustrates the importance of wearing protective eyewear at all times while cycling, not just while the sun is shining.

UVA, UVB, UVC Rays

Riders should consider eyewear that filters UVA, UVB, UVC rays, and IR and blue light when purchasing glasses. Bike personnel are exposed to a significant amount of sunlight and glare, and the eye needs protection from damage from short- and long-term exposure. Many glasses have extended or wraparound designs to protect as much of the eye as possible from these harmful rays and light sources.

Interchangeable Lenses

Interchangeable lenses are beneficial to public safety cyclists who work in diverse lighting and weather conditions. A frame with interchangeable lenses reduces the overall cost and is more convenient than having numerous pairs of glasses. Lenses should be easy to change quickly without damaging the frames. Many manufacturers provide carrying cases to protect the spare lenses when not in use. Some manufacturers offer sport sunglasses with interchangeable lenses that can have a set of prescription lenses mounted behind the tinted front lens. Although these glasses may be slightly heavier, they offer prescription eyeglass wearers the option of relatively inexpensive wraparound sport sunglasses with interchangeable lenses, at a greatly reduced cost over several pairs of prescription sunglasses. As with all prescription glasses, sudden changes in lighting can be problematic. Prescription eyeglass wearers may want to keep their regular glasses readily available for building searches or other inside work.

Other Factors

Non-slip nosepieces and fixed or hinged ear stems are other features to be considered. Some public safety cyclists prefer a frame that has hinged ear stems, so that when they are removed, they can be easily folded and one arm stuck in a shirt pocket for temporary storage. Many cyclists use devices that allow the glasses to hang around the neck when they are not being worn, but any officer who chooses this option should ensure that the cord will break away easily if grabbed.

■ Gloves

Riders should wear gloves at all times. Cycling gloves reduce road shock and vibration transmitted through the frame and help prevent fatigue, hand numbness, and conditions such as carpal tunnel syndrome and arthritis. Gloves can also provide protection from abrasions in the event of a crash.

Gloves worn by public safety cyclists should be designed specifically for cycling, as they contain padding that protects the carpal, median, and ulna nerves that branch off though the palm of the hand. This padding typically consists of foam, silicon gel, or a similar substance, and can range in thickness from 2 mm to 6 mm.

Depending on preference and riding conditions, public safety cyclists may use half-fingered or full-fingered gloves. Material used in the construction of the gloves can consist of Lycra, terry cloth, neoprene, or other fabrics in combination. The material might be woven with a fabric like Windstopper™ or Thinsulate™ for protection from the cold, Kevlar™ for cut resistance, or SpectaShield™ for bloodborne pathogens.

To avoid frequent replacement, select a glove with double, closely spaced stitching around stress points such as the thumb crotch, base of the fingers, and the hook and loop closure. This will resist unraveling more than a glove with single, widely spaced stitching. However, bike gloves are more likely to be discarded due to accumulated road grime, dried sweat, and skin oils. To achieve longevity, bike gloves should be cleaned regularly according to the manufacturer's specifications.

The padding and the thickness of the glove will have an operational impact on manual dexterity. Police and security officers may find that gloves affect their ability to access handcuffs; grip an impact weapon or chemical spray canister; or operate a handgun's magazine release, de-cocking lever, slide, or cylinder release mechanism. EMS cyclists may find that long-fingered gloves are impractical for handling some medical equipment and drug packaging. Those who do not intend to remove their cycling gloves prior to providing patient care should select short-fingered gloves and pack larger-sized latex gloves to wear over them.

An experienced public safety cyclist may use different gloves for different situations. Regardless of the glove, it is essential that he or she become familiar with the feel that the glove provides, not only while engaged with the handlebars of the bike but while operating various pieces of equipment as well. This familiarization should be practiced in both non-stress and stress/fatigue-related relevant training exercises with the goal of becoming proficient while using the gloves.

■ Ballistic Protection

In addition to its obvious purpose, ballistic protection can provide some crash protection for the public safety cyclist, especially to the thoracic area and skeletal structure of the ribs and spine. Public safety cyclists should refer to their departmental standard operating procedures and directives governing the use of ballistic protection. Many departments have "must wear" ballistic protection policies in place—including for their public safety cyclists. Some cyclists may be tempted not to wear it, especially during hot weather, but it should not be optional.

When deciding on ballistic protection for the public safety cyclist, consider the various fabrics that are available from the numerous manufacturers, the overall weight of the garment, and its flexibility to accommodate the extra movement of the rider. An extended back flap is a nice additional feature to protect the low back area while in the cycling position. This can be sized when the officer's measurements are taken for the ballistic vest. The body armor selected should offer the appropriate level of protection (threat level) as dictated by agency policy.

Some body armor producers provide antimicrobial covers and breathable fabric carriers to dissipate moisture. This is important for public safety cyclists because of the sweat generated by exertion. The ballistic vest can be coupled with breathable fabric undergarments. Female riders might want to avoid wearing a bra with hook closures under ballistic protection, as excessive movement can cause chafing. Sports bras that are seamless and have rolled edges and off-center stitching are good choices.

Bike officers in the United Kingdom pioneered the use of the vest carrier system, which has been adopted by some agencies in the United States. Similar in appearance to tactical vests, these are designed and cut to be comfortable while cycling (**FIGURE 5-3**). The United Kingdom version virtually eliminates the need for a duty belt, because all of the equipment is carried in secure pockets on the vest. In addition, the vest holds the officer's ballistic panels, eliminating the need to wear body armor under the clothing and greatly improving ventilation. Cycling generates more heat and perspiration than most types of police activity. Even if an officer is wearing a lightweight, breathable uniform shirt, wearing body armor between the breathable layer and the skin minimizes the breathability of the material. These external vests allow the wickable material to actually breathe better due to increased air circulation around the arms, waist, and chest.

Conclusion

As public safety cycling has become more prevalent, equipment and uniform manufacturers have responded by developing products engineered to meet the unique needs of the public safety cyclist. A public safety cyclist who is outfitted with high-quality, cycling-specific uniform and shoes is more likely to perform at a high level, because he or she will be

FIGURE 5-3 Similar in appearance to tactical vests, these vests are designed and cut to be comfortable while cycling.

comfortable. Likewise, a public safety cyclist equipped with a high-quality mountain bike, a helmet, shatter-resistant eyewear, pedal retention, cycling gloves, and ballistic protection is more likely to operate safely.

References

Beck, Kirby (2002). Bike Uniforms: We've Come a Long Way, Baby. *Law & Order Magazine,* April, pages 76–82.

Beck, Kirby (2003). Dressing for Success. *Law & Order Magazine,* May, pages 76–82.

Beck, Kirby (2005). Trends in Bike Patrol, *Law & Order Magazine,* April, pages 77–84.

Bicycle Helmet Safety Institute, www.bhsi.org.

King, Ken (2003). Helmet Safety: Separating Fact from Fiction. *IPMBA News,* Winter, pages 15–16.

Trujillo, Mitch, and Reed, Donald (2003). Bike Patrol Health & Safety: Equipment Implications for You and Your Employer. *IPMBA News,* Summer, pages 5–7.

6

Training and Policy

Introduction

The role of public safety personnel is to assist, protect, and defend the community and its members. Public safety personnel require protection, too. In order to best protect itself, its personnel, and the community, every bike unit should have written operating guidelines. These guidelines should address personnel selection, including medical and fitness screenings; uniforms and equipment; maintenance; initial and ongoing training requirements; operating conditions and restrictions, such as traffic laws and weather; and ways the bikes can and cannot be used. Having such policies in place can help reduce the risk of both injury and lawsuits. Just as administrators should not put officers behind the wheels of patrol cars and medics in the drivers' seats of ambulances without driver training and policies, they should not send personnel out on bikes without bike-specific training and guidelines governing the safe and legal operation of bikes within the context of the jurisdiction and the department.

Types of Policy

There are many different approaches to policy writing, and bike unit guidelines must be written in adherence to the department's standard format and process. Poli-

cies may be referred to as, for example, rules and regulations, general orders, special orders, policy manuals, standard operating procedures (SOPs), standard operating guidelines (SOGs), uniform regulations, standing orders, or commander's instructions.

Bike unit policies should use a format, writing style, and philosophy that are similar to existing policies. It is helpful to become familiar with the policies of similar units, such as fire prevention, motorcycles, or K-9, prior to drafting the bike unit policies. Input from both line personnel, especially experienced, certified police and EMS cyclists, and supervisors should be solicited; they are in the best position to point out the strengths and weaknesses of their own guidelines. Bike personnel are encouraged to author their unit policies in order to prevent someone unfamiliar with the operational needs of a bike unit from establishing the guidelines.

Safe and Legal

Administrators should not send personnel out on bikes without bike-specific training and guidelines governing the safe and legal operation of bikes within the context of the jurisdiction and the department.

Bike Unit Policy Content

A general statement of purpose should set the context for the bike unit. The bike unit should be established as a specialized operation with a definitive organizational chart, even if it simply means designating an officer in charge (OIC) who is capable of making administrative decisions for the unit. In addition, the bike unit policy must address the following topics, many of which are discussed in more detail throughout this book.

- Primary and Special Bike Uses
  - Patrol
  - Community policing
  - Traffic enforcement
  - Drug operations
  - Public order
  - Targeted enforcement
  - Special events
  - Basic and advanced life support
  - First responder
  - Critical incident emergency response
  - Search and rescue
- Hours/Seasons of Operation
  - Special shifts, 24-hour shifts, day and night shifts

- Labor agreements, contracts, and memoranda of understanding
- Year-round or seasonal considerations
- Restrictions due to temperature, rain, snow, sleet, etc.
- Minimum annual riding requirements
  - **Personnel Selection**
    - Physical fitness standards
    - Medical screening
    - Ongoing fitness requirements
  - **Uniforms**
  - **Equipment**
    - Bicycles and accessories
    - Personal protective equipment
  - **Maintenance**
    - Preventive
    - Periodic
    - Emergency repairs
  - **Training**
    - Initial
    - Firearms
    - In-service training (type, duration, and frequency)
    - Conferences
    - Requalification
  - **Supervisory Responsibilities**
  - **Motor Vehicle Code and Traffic Laws**
  - **Prisoner/Patient Transport Procedures**
  - **Tactical Considerations (police and security)**
    - Traffic stops, vehicle pursuits, and felony stops
    - Undercover and stealth operations
    - Emergency deployment
    - Use of force
    - Park and ride
  - **Bicycle Crashes**
    - Injury
    - Property damage

▪ Training

One of the most important topics to address in bike unit policy is training. The bicycle is more than just a mode of transportation. Most people know how to operate a bike on a basic level, but not everyone knows how to ride one effectively on duty. To ride a bike on duty requires an understanding of how a bike works and a mastery of the skills that enable the cyclist to focus not on the act of riding, but on the job. In order to achieve this level of mastery and to be able to use

the bike as a tool for patrol or EMS delivery, specialized training (FIGURE 6-1) is necessary and should be written into the operating guidelines.

Both initial and in-service training should be designed to meet the "three Rs": training should be realistic, relevant, and recent. As *Canton v. Harris (489 U.S. 378, 109 S. CT. 1197 1989)* illustrates, proper training can provide protection from criminal and civil litigation. At minimum, training should consist of the IPMBA Police, EMS, or Security Cyclist Course. In-service training should consist of at least eight hours of bike-specific training annually, either refresher or topic-specific. Armed personnel should attend bike-specific firearms training annually and be required to qualify yearly with their firearm while wearing full bike uniform. If possible, the firearms trainer should be a certified basic police cyclist or instructor, and the training course must be supported by a written lesson plan. Training records should be maintained at the department and by the bike team members.

▪ Vehicle Code and Traffic Law

As discussed in Chapter 8, bicycles are recognized as vehicles in most jurisdictions. Therefore, public safety cyclists must operate their bicycles in accordance with the local vehicle code and traffic law. Bike unit policies must adhere to the laws of the jurisdiction or jurisdictions in which the bikes are used. Teams who are writing bike policy should address the following questions:

- What is the legal status of bicycles in your state?
- Are there any regulations or ordinances restricting use of bicycles in your jurisdiction?
- Are there restrictions concerning cyclists' use of earphones (this may affect the selection of communications devices)?
- How far to the right are you required to ride? What circumstances allow you to ride otherwise? Can you ride double? When and where?
- Are bikes permitted on sidewalks? Are cyclists required to ride in bike lanes or on sidepaths if they are present?
- Must bikes be equipped with audible warning devices?
- What kinds of lights and/or reflectors are required?
- What hand signals are legally acceptable?
- What local bike licensing or registration requirements exist?

FIGURE 6-1 Operating a bike as an emergency vehicle requires appropriate training.

- Can bikes be considered emergency vehicles? If yes, are there special equipment requirements? If yes, under what circumstances can bikes violate traffic law (e.g., riding on sidewalks, opposite to traffic, in the center of a lane)?
- Are there mandatory training requirements for public safety bike personnel?
- Does the command staff understand the legal limitations and liabilities that affect bike patrol operations? If they do not, who is in the best position to educate them?

Knowing the state and local laws pertaining to bicycles will not only help you operate safely and effectively, it will help reduce your liability. Public safety cyclists are held to a higher standard of accountability for the way they ride. They should follow the rules of the road at all times, only acting counter to them during necessary performance of duties, and then only in accordance with established policy and the law (**FIGURE 6-2**). To ride in any other manner invites a negative response. Addi-

tionally, it could lead to a suspension or termination, unnecessary restrictions on a unit or, in severe cases, termination of the bicycle unit.

■ Bicycle Crashes

Bicycle crashes are inevitable. They sometimes cause injury and/or property damage. The agency that has a policy in place with proper legal support will fare best when a crash occurs. Departments should establish policies regarding crashes prior to the first crash. Departments must implement guidelines for reporting and responding to bike crashes involving bodily harm, damage to the bike, or damage to a third party's property to provide protection to the individual and their agency.

An agency's response to a bicycle crash will typically mirror its response to a crash involving an ambulance, police vehicle, or fire apparatus. If the bike is not defined as a vehicle or emergency vehicle, it may be treated similarly to a pedestrian or equestrian. In accidents involving personal injury or death, public safety cyclists without adequate

FIGURE 6-2 Bike personnel must adhere to traffic law.

policy and legal protection could be criminally charged. The penalties could be as simple as a traffic fine or as significant as a felony conviction, which for a public safety official can be accompanied by loss of employment.

Administrative, Criminal, and Civil Liability

Training and policy can help guard against administrative, criminal, and civil liability. Public safety personnel have an obligation to set a good example for the other members of the community. In the operation of emergency response vehicles, legislation often allows for exceptions. The strongest concerns should lie in those agencies that knowingly and willfully violate these regulations without legal foundation. This type of action will ultimately lead to negative ramifications, either criminal or civil.

The risk of negative litigation arises when a situation falls outside the normal scope of a legal guideline or agency policy, or both. Those who act without knowledge of legal guidelines and do not have an agency-specific policy governing bicycle issues, and those who give little or no consideration to policy within the law and their potential effect on bike unit operations maintain the highest risk. To operate with little or no consideration of these policy issues invites administrative or disciplinary actions, criminal fines, and civil liability for public safety agencies and individual employees.

The issues surrounding criminal liability are most dramatic when the offender, i.e., the public safety cyclist, lacks knowledge of his or her duties and responsibilities. To best serve the individual, agency, and government, appropriate policies must be in place, supported by legal foundation, and updated regularly.

Conclusion

Clear policies and procedures are essential to the successful operation of a bike unit. Without such policies, the unit may be underutilized, lack professionalism, and fail to realize its potential. Model and actual policies for police and EMS bike units are available through the IPMBA office, for the purpose of assisting members in drafting and implementing appropriate policies that successfully integrate the bike unit into agency operations.

References

IACP National Law Enforcement Policy Center (2004). *Bicycle Patrol Model Policy and Concepts and Issues Paper.* International Association of Chiefs of Police (IACP), Alexandria VA.

7

Fundamental Cycling Skills

Introduction

Public safety cycling presents unique challenges and thus requires unique skills. Some cyclists ride primarily on the street, where they must take into account rules governing traffic flow. Others prefer to ride on trails, which calls on different skills. Some ride in urban areas, but not necessarily in traffic. Public safety cycling demands proficiency in all of these environments in all kinds of weather. In addition, public safety cyclists frequently ride in areas where bicycles typically do not belong, such as on sidewalks and in crowds.

In order to prepare for riding in these conditions, there are skills that even the novice rider should consider essential. The IPMBA Police, EMS and Security Cyclist certification courses teach all of these skills, but the skills addressed in the courses should be considered the minimum standards. It is vital that every public safety cyclist continue to develop new skills while maintaining proficiency in basic skills.

In order to develop these basic skills, the rider must understand a few things about how the bicycle responds to input from the rider. The rider can affect the bicycle's movement in only a few ways: pedal pressure, steering, braking, and weight transfer. Each has infinite implications. It might seem

that with only four types of input, skills development would be a relatively simple process. Experience has shown otherwise.

Simply stated, the entire bicycle is designed to respond to rider input. This is important to understand during the process of developing skills. Every crash is the result of improper input under a given set of circumstances. The right balance of various simultaneous inputs, delivered through the proper receptors on the bike, is the basis of skills development. This chapter will refer to these four inputs frequently as it addresses specific maneuvers.

Inputs and the Bicycle's Receptors

For each of the four types of rider input, the bicycle has at least one receptor, or feature, that accepts rider input. These receptors are usually specific parts of the bicycle. This chapter will discuss each input, its receptor, and the mechanical variables that affect how the bike responds.

Pedal Pressure

Pedal pressure is defined as the amount of force the rider applies to the pedals. Pedal pressure affects the crankarms, chainring, rear hub, spokes, rims, and finally, the rear tire. Most riders grossly underestimate the importance of proper pedal pressure, particularly as it apples to riding at slow speeds.

Gear selection regulates the amount of pedal pressure required. Generally, lower gears are suited for slow-speed riding, but selecting a lower gear may also decrease the pedal pressure required to make the bike move. In many, but not all, circumstances, lower pedal pressure can provide a greater degree of control. This will be addressed later in this chapter.

Steering

It seems obvious that steering a bicycle is a function of the handlebars, but it really involves a lot of other parts as well. The stem, headset, forks, hub, spokes, rim, and tire are all mechanical factors. From a rider input standpoint, a combination of weight transfer and handlebar position also affects steering. Most crashes are at least partially the result of mistakes in steering input.

Braking

Mechanically speaking, brakes are responsible for stopping a bicycle, but they do much more. Brakes can also regulate pedal pressure, facilitate proper body positioning and weight transfer, and change the physics that keep the bike under control.

Braking involves more than simply bringing the bike to a stop.

■ Weight Transfer

The vast majority of the input a rider imparts to a bicycle involves weight transfer, but most of the time it is very subtle. Mechanically, weight transfer input is imparted to the bike at every point that the rider's body contacts the bike and, in some cases, even where it does not. Nearly everything on the bike is designed to accept weight transfer input, which makes the mechanics of weight transfer complex. The angles at which the tubes that make up the bike's frame are welded together, the height of the saddle and handlebars, the length and angle of the stem, the length of the crankarms, and the distance from the bottom bracket to the rear axle all play a part in processing weight transfer input. Every part that moves, and some that do not, has an effect on how the bike responds to weight transfer, yet it tends to be the single most neglected part of teaching bike riding skills. Any rider who masters the art of weight transfer is destined to be a very skillful rider.

Basic Skills

Several skills and maneuvers are essential tools for any public safety cyclist, and this chapter will refer to them as "basic skills." This does not mean that those skills are unimportant or that experience will automatically ensure mastery of them. The proper development of these skills serves as the necessary foundation for more advanced skills; a weak foundation will impede progression into more complex skills. Many riders who have difficulty with more advanced skills find it necessary to correct the bad habits that resulted from lack of attention to the basic skills. Therefore, concentrate on building a strong foundation; the growth and development of your skills depend on it.

Correcting Bad Habits

Many riders who have difficulty with more advanced skills find it necessary to correct bad habits they developed when they began to ride.

■ Falling

Falling off a bike does not require a lot of skill. People do it all the time, and most have never trained or practiced for it. Falling off a bike while maintaining an awareness of your actions and maintaining control of your body is a skill. If you intend to improve your riding and develop new skills, it is a good idea to consider a few basic principles involved in the mechanics of falling. It is possible to learn how to minimize the risk of injury caused by various types of falls. Some IPMBA instructors teach these techniques in a controlled environment, with spotters, coaches, and a variety of safety equipment in place (FIGURE 7-1).

First, it is important to realize when a fall is unavoidable. In almost every fall, there is a brief moment when an experienced and skillful rider has enough information to know that it is time to prepare for a fall.

Truly skilled riders are not afraid of what it feels like to lose control of the bike. They expect to lose control on occasion, and they always have a backup plan for how they will react when that moment arrives, so it is really not a complete loss of control. While they may eventually end up on the ground, their process for getting there looks quite different from the process of someone who "just fell." Having a plan and having the skill to execute the plan make a real difference. In general, falls are the consequences of other mistakes, but falling is a part of learning to ride. Obviously, nobody wants to fall, but learning to do it properly and under control can remove a lot of the fear that prevents riders from improving.

Lateral Falls

A lateral fall occurs when the rider simply falls sideways. Sometimes the bike is barely moving and just stalls, such as when the bike contacts an object unexpectedly, leaving no time for the rider to remove a foot from the pedal retention device. This kind of fall is almost always the result of failure to anticipate the situation that caused the fall.

The skilled and unskilled rider will react very differently in this situation. It is helpful to analyze the actions that caused the situation and the potential results. The unskilled rider will usually fight to free the trapped foot from the pedal, all the way to the ground. Just before contact with the ground, the rider will reach out with one or both arms to catch himself.

FIGURE 7-1 Falling techniques may be taught in a class, using spotters annd safety equipment.

The less skilled rider tends to try to stay as far away from the ground as possible for as long as possible. The rider may stay in the saddle or at least try to stay upright. This high center of gravity may buy some time, but once the tactic fails, it ensures that the rider will gain as much speed as possible before striking the ground, thus increasing the force with which he will land. At the last minute, the rider will reach for the ground, extending his arms. Because the rider does not have a plan of action, one arm may catch the entire body weight and all of the momentum created by his high center of gravity. Even if the rider extends both arms, they are likely to be out of position. All of these factors create a situation that is likely to cause injury. What should the rider have done?

Imagine that you are carrying a sack of groceries when you realize that the bag has torn. Most people will instinctively squat toward the ground.

Without thinking about it, they are trying to lessen the distance that the groceries will have to fall, reducing the speed of the impact and subsequent breakage. This is an automatic response, but it usually does not engage when the same person is about to fall off a bike. Still, the first principle is the same: Lessen the falling distance and reduce the speed of the fall.

From the rider's point of view, this is done by crouching as much as possible, maybe even to the point that the crotch is touching the top tube of the frame, while the feet remain engaged in the pedal retention system (FIGURE 7-2). Now, the impact with the ground will be only a fraction of its original force. This alone may be enough to produce a drastically different outcome.

Rather than reaching for the ground, the rider should keep both hands on the bars and pull the bike over so that the first thing to contact the

FIGURE 7-2 Crouching lessens the falling distance and reduces the speed of the fall.

ground is the end of the handlebar. The pedal may strike the ground next, but the goal is to put as much of the bike on the ground as possible before the rider gets there. This accomplishes two things. First, it allows the bike to hit the ground at one of its strongest points. Bike stems are incredibly strong, and this is to where most of the impact on the bicycle will be transferred. Second, it prevents the rider's weight from contributing to the amount of force that the bike will have to absorb. The rider should look away from the ground and attempt to avoid hitting it for as long as possible.

Once the bike is on the ground and the rider is positioned to land a fraction of a second later, the impact of the fall will be about the same as if someone pushed the rider over while he was in a squatting position. This is generally not enough impact to cause serious injury.

A lateral fall can be thought of as a process of two falls, not one. The first fall gets the bike on the ground. The second gets the rider on the ground. In both cases, the key is control.

Even during a lateral fall at higher speeds, the same principles and techniques apply. Of course, this will usually involve the loss of lateral traction to one or both wheels, so things will happen much faster. Obviously, the potential for injury will increase with speed, but mastering this technique and putting it into practice will help mitigate the damage.

Backward Flips

A backward flip happens when the front wheel rises up far enough to overcome the rider's ability to bring it back down by weight transfer input. If the rider can free his feet from the pedal retention devices, both feet normally land on the ground; if the rider cannot free his feet, the rider will land very hard on his back.

If the rider cannot free his feet, he must resist the urge to reach out and must instead keep both hands on the handlebars. This is very scary and completely unnatural, but it can help the rider avoid serious injuries. Keeping a grip on the bars does two things. First, it reduces the likelihood of upper extremity injuries by preventing awkward attempts to break the fall with the arms. Second, it prevents the twisting of the rider's body in relation to the long axis of the bike. If the rider's feet remain fastened to the pedals and the bike twists in relation to the rider's body, the potential for injury to the ankles and legs rises dramatically. This potential continues to increase through the hips, back, and neck.

If the rider is able to free his feet, both feet will naturally end up on the ground. At slow speeds, it is usually easy to control the bike and hold on long enough for a relatively uneventful placing of the front wheel back onto the ground. At higher speeds, the rider will probably release the bike and allow it to fall, usually very violently. Still, this is a better option than accompanying the bike on its wild ride.

There is one other option for getting the front wheel back on the ground, but it requires a great deal of control and skill. The rider can tap and quickly release the rear brake lever, which can cause the front wheel to contact the ground. If the brake is not immediately released, the bike will come to an abrupt halt, which could cause injury or damage.

Endo Falls

The term endo is short for "end over." Endo falls occur when either the rear wheel rises and passes the front wheel, roughly along the same axis as the frame of the bike, or when the rear wheel rises far enough to pitch the rider off the saddle and over the handlebars.

The endo can be the most devastating crash a rider can sustain without contact with an immovable object. The rider often somersaults through the air before contacting the ground, which often results in a broken clavicle (collarbone), arm, or even neck. Once an endo starts, it is almost impossible to recover control of the bike (FIGURE 7-3). Some very

FIGURE 7-3 Once an endo starts, it is almost impossible to recover control of the bike.

skilled riders can control rear wheel lift and actually use it as a technique for laterally repositioning the rear wheel in certain situations. There is also a maneuver known as a stoppie, which amounts to a rear wheel wheelie. This technique is truly an advanced skill and is not recommended for public safety work.

True endo crashes almost always happen at higher speeds. Learning the proper way to execute an endo fall is almost impossible to explain in a book, but the most valuable rule for surviving an endo fall is "don't fight physics." Once this type of fall reaches a certain point, there is nothing you can do to recover. The trick is to realize when it is happening and make a few adjustments to your body mechanics very quickly. The point of no return is reached when the rider is already airborne and the only part of the body still touching the bike is the hands on the bars.

At this point, the rear wheel has already risen far enough off the ground that the rider is headed over the bars and onto the ground. The body has usually completed half of a somersault in the air, and there is nothing that can reverse that—hence the "don't fight physics" advice. The rider has only one thing working in his favor—momentum—and should use it to his maximum benefit.

Tuck the chin against the chest and allow your body to complete the mid-air flip. Try to relax. Do not reach for anything. Most of the time, being upside down in the air is so disorienting that extending the arms in any direction will result in unnecessary injury. Keep the arms close to the body and the legs in front with the knees slightly bent in roughly the same position as when doing a sit-up. If all goes well, you will contact the ground in this seated position. The hands will move naturally to either side of the buttocks, which can help to break the fall. The bend in the knees will allow for the soles of the feet to contact the ground. The momentum may allow you to regain your balance while standing. Of course, all of this is assuming the ideal outcome.

When the rider does not complete the flip in the air, the body is still in the ideal position to avoid injury, even if the rider lands on the back or shoulders. This position will allow for the body to continue rolling until the rider lands in a seated position.

Endo crashes are always dramatic and scary. If you find that you use this technique frequently, it is time to evaluate what you are doing wrong that gets you into this position in the first place.

■ Gear Selection

Regardless of riding conditions, gear selection is arguably the most critical decision a rider makes. Selecting the wrong gear can adversely affect balance and control; produce fatigue; cause chronic injury to the knees, ankles, and feet; and cause premature wear on bike components. Gear selection is often a matter of personal comfort, not rigid, absolute rules. Riders of equal ability may choose different gears in the same situation. Gear selection depends on a variety of factors, including current riding conditions, level of skill and experience, and what your body tells you about the gears you choose. Watching more experienced cyclists may give you some ideas for experimentation, and there are general rules to follow, but selecting the right gear will ultimately be your choice.

An understanding of how shifting systems work will make it easier to understand how to use gears properly. On multi-speed bikes, each gear combination simulates the effect of larger or smaller wheels. Large (high) gears mimic large-sized wheels, allowing the cyclist to ride faster and longer while pedaling moderately. Smaller (lower) gears simulate the effect of smaller wheels, enabling the rider to pedal up hills, into headwinds and over different surfaces with less effort.

Most public safety cyclists prefer the middle chainring for the speeds and conditions of normal patrol. This includes riding at relatively slow speeds and in most urban settings. Choosing gears in the middle range also eliminates the need to make drastic changes if conditions dictate sudden shifts to lower or higher gears. Changing gears should always be done under light pedal pressure; making drastic changes under heavy pedal pressure can result in broken or thrown chains. Choosing medium-range gearing for patrol can reduce the time needed to allow for the chain to move, which provides an advantage, particularly when the situation calls for sudden increases in speed. Cross-chaining, or allowing the chain to ride on either the largest front chainring and largest rear cog, or smallest front chainring and smallest rear cog, should be avoided (FIGURE 7-4). This will eventually destroy the chain and damage the chainrings.

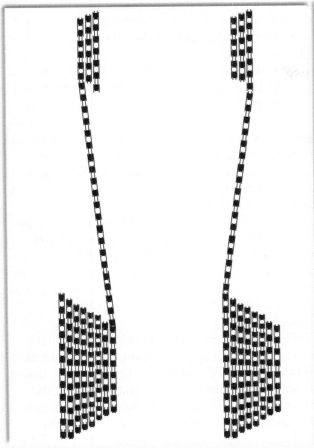

FIGURE 7-4 Avoid cross-chaining, or allowing the chain to ride on either the largest front chainring and largest rear cog, or smallest front chainring and smallest rear cog.

Selecting Gears

Gear selection may be the most critical decision a cyclist makes. Selecting the wrong gear can adversely affect balance and control; produce fatigue; cause chronic injury to the knees, ankles, and feet; and cause premature wear on bike components.

railleur arm. This can be particularly beneficial in situations where repeated hard bumps, such as on a stair descent, might cause the chain to bounce off.

While gear selection is often discussed in terms of maintaining a particular cadence, the real issue is maintaining a comfortable pedal pressure for the speed of the bike. The implications are obvious for sustained road speeds, but the issue is no less critical for slow-speed riding. The combination of proper gear selection and brake application can have an enormous effect on the ability to control the bike. Choosing gears that allow for the steady, even application of power to the rear wheel can help the rider make small corrections to the bike's position, negating the need for big corrections that might have been required only fractions of a second later. No matter what your speed, always try to keep the pressure required to move the bike at a comfortable level, considering your own fitness, skills, and capabilities.

■ Braking Techniques

Many crashes involve the improper application of brakes or the improper balance of braking with other inputs. Braking is unique because it is the only input the rider can impart to a bicycle that can be shared equally and simultaneously with both wheels independent of weight transfer. For this reason, mastery of braking may be considered the most important skill. Nevertheless, in many situations, the rider should consider that there are really two separate aspects to controlling the bicycle: controlling the front wheel and controlling the rear wheel.

Lockdown

As the name implies, lockdown is simply the application of both the front and rear brakes

It usually takes less than one second to change gears properly. With a little forethought, it is usually easy to anticipate and plan shifts. The most common mistakes in changing gears occur when the rider is on a steep climb. Some riders wait until the current gear becomes too difficult to continue the climb and then try to shift to a lower gear. By then, the next lowest gear is probably not going to be adequate either, and the damage to the bike may have occurred already. If you know that you will have to change gears in a particular situation, do it early.

The need for higher gears is obvious in situations in which speed is required, but there are other circumstances that might require higher gears. Using the large (front) chainring will leave less slack in the chain, causing the rear derailleur to put the most pressure on the spring in the de-

simultaneously, with sufficient force to keep either wheel from rolling. This technique is not normally used to stop the bike, but to keep it from rolling after it stops and during quick dismounts. Its greatest value is during a failed attempt at another maneuver. For example, if a rider attempts to climb a set of stairs and the bike stalls, both brakes are applied at the same time to hold the bike in place. The rider places one or both feet on the ground and holds the brakes until everything is back under full control. As simple as that sounds, it is rare to find riders who actually practice it.

The advantages to using the lockdown technique are numerous. First, it prevents the bike from rolling out from under the rider, which could damage the bike or injure others. Second, it holds the bike in place and provides a stable object for the rider to use in regaining balance and control. Whether the rider decides to completely dismount or to straddle the bike, it is always better if the bike is immobile.

While developing other basic or more advanced skills, the rider should practice the lockdown until it becomes an automatic response, keeping in mind that it should not be used at high or even moderate speeds. Lockdown is only used when the bike is already stopped or at low enough speeds that the rider can safely straddle the bike and place both feet on the ground.

Maximum Braking

Maximum braking is a technique that is used to bring a bicycle to a stop or to drastically reduce its speed when it is rolling too fast for the rider to dismount safely. Mastery of this skill is critical to learning more advanced skills, not because more advanced skills involve riding at high speeds, but because the position required to execute the maneuver is applicable to many other situations.

Maximum braking requires two primary inputs from the rider: weight transfer and braking, or more accurately, braking to prevent uncontrolled weight transfer. The concept of applying brakes with the greatest practicable force is not hard to understand, but the indiscriminant application of brakes can have serious consequences.

There are two main factors to consider when executing maximum braking maneuvers. First, about 80% of the braking power on a bicycle comes from the front brake. While it makes sense to want to use that brake to its full potential, over-application of

the front brake can cause weight transfer that is sufficient to not only lift the rear wheel off the ground, but also to toss the rider off the bike. This can result in an endo crash.

To counteract this weight transfer, the rider must (1) keep all moveable weight as far back and as low as possible and (2) balance braking input to the front and rear wheels so that weight transfer is kept within acceptable limits. It is critical that braking not occur until the rider can maintain correct weight transfer and body positioning. Braking too soon will prevent getting into the proper position to maintain control under maximum braking.

To control the weight transfer, place the pedals in the 3 o'clock and 9 o'clock position (parallel with the ground) and rise off the saddle. Next, straighten the arms and legs, keeping them slightly flexed to absorb shock, and push as far back and as low as possible over the rear of the bike (FIGURE 7-5).

The braking input should be applied to both brakes, but primarily to the front, although some modulation will be required to keep the bike under control. This is not to suggest that pumping the brakes is a good idea. The sudden application/release/application of brakes will cause the front shocks to load and unload rapidly while simultaneously bouncing the weight distribution back and forth along the long axis of the bike. This upset in balance may cause the over-application of the front brake during a moment when the contact patch of the front tire (the amount of surface area that the tire has in contact with the ground) is at its smallest because weight has transferred to the rear. This will cause the front tire to skid, which results in a loss of lateral traction. At this point, it is almost certain that the wheel will slip out from under the bike, causing a crash.

The rear tire will sometimes skid under maximum braking, which means that the rear tire is not providing all of the stopping power that it could. Weight transfer moving to the front of the bike

Braking

It is critical that braking not occur until the rider can maintain correct weight transfer and body positioning.

FIGURE 7-5 Maximum braking requires controlled weight transfer.

causes this rear tire skid. If you do not stop the skid, enough of your weight could be transferred forward to cause an endo. When you hear your rear tire start to skid, slightly reduce front brake pressure until you notice the rear tire starting to turn again. This will reduce the forward weight transfer and help enable you to stop as quickly as possible.

Regardless of where you are riding, ride with two fingers on the brake levers at all times. Having to find the brakes when you need them may only take a fraction of a second, but that could be the difference between maintaining and losing control. Having your fingers on the brakes is a lot like already having your sidearm loaded and a round in the chamber when you begin your shift as a police officer. You would not want to take the time to load

if you needed your gun right away. The same principle should apply to your brakes.

■ Curb Ascents

Curbs are the obstacles that public safety cyclists will encounter most frequently in urban settings. Like the maximum braking technique, learning the curb ascent is critical to learning more advanced skills. Even if the rider never encounters curbs in an assigned work area, this skill represents another important building block in the foundation of skill development.

Although the process of riding over curbs is commonly referred to as curb hopping, there are usually no hops involved. When performed properly, the maneuver is almost completely silent, and the bike never leaves the ground. For this reason, curb hops are more accurately referred to as curb ascents.

As with braking, the bike becomes two separate entities when clearing curbs. The front wheel and the rear wheel each clear the obstacle separately, and there are distinctly different maneuvers to get each over the curb.

90-Degree Curb Ascents

Ideally, curb ascents should be executed while approaching the curb at a 90-degree angle and at no faster than walking speed. As the front wheel approaches the curb, the rider must lighten or loft the front wheel sufficiently to clear the curb. There are two ways to do this.

The first, which is not recommended, involves jerking the handlebars just before the tire contacts the curb. If the bike is rolling at sufficient speed, the wheel comes down on the top of the curb. While this usually works just fine, there is little room for error. Timing is critical. If the rider jerks the wheel up too soon, it will come down before it clears the curb and cause the front of the tire to strike the curb. This can result in damage to the

FIGURE 7-6 Curb ascents should be executed while approaching the curb at a 90-degree angle and at no faster than walking speed.

bike or injury to the rider, who is unexpectedly bounced toward the front of the bike.

The preferred method, known as the lofting method, involves leaning back on the bike with the arms straight and applying sufficient pedal pressure to cause the front wheel to lift off the ground (FIGURE 7-6). This method permits the rider to loft the wheel off the ground for a much longer period of time and with greater control. Even if the wheel comes down too soon, it is already unweighted and will usually roll over the curb with little effort. Whenever possible, this method is best choice. Riding under control with larger margins for error is always a better choice than relying on perfect timing for success.

Immediately after lofting the wheel onto the curb, the rider should stand on the pedals, transfer weight forward, and keep the pedals in the power position, which is usually at 2 o'clock and 8 o'clock. Most riders will have a power, or "chocolate," foot as Hans Rey, the famous trick rider, calls it. Place the foot that feels strongest or most comfortable in the 2 o'clock position. When the rear tire contacts the curb, pedal the bike over the curb. Gear selection is important, so practice this technique until you learn which gears are appropriate for different curb heights. Generally, a lower middle-range gear is a good place to start. Taller curbs usually require lower gears, but choosing a gear that is too low can result in the power pedal progressing to the bottom of the crank rotation before the maneuver is complete or the rear tire losing traction because of the disproportionate application of torque. Again, experience and practice are the best ways to learn about gear selection.

When done properly, this maneuver is absolutely silent and does not jar or bounce the bike. If the rear wheel slips when applying pedal pressure, it is possible to use the handlebars to push the bike so that the rear wheel climbs over the curb.

Again, this is a slow speed maneuver. Attempting to execute this maneuver at higher speeds will result in the rear wheel bouncing into the air while the rider's weight is already forward, almost certainly causing an endo crash. There are other methods for clearing curbs and other obstacles at speed, but these are not considered basic skills. Learning to clear curbs in this manner will help build a foundation for clearing many other, much larger obstacles. Every rider should consider this to be an essential skill and practice it often.

Angled Curb Ascents

At times, it may be necessary to clear a curb at less than a 90-degree angle—usually because an object prevents the rider from a straight approach to the curb. For this maneuver, approach the curb as close to parallel as possible. When the front tire is an inch or two away from the curb, stop the bike and place a foot on the curb. Lift the front wheel and place it on top of the curb. Position the pedals in the power position with the power foot ready (FIGURE 7-7). Roll the bike toward the curb until the rear tire is against it, then simultaneously push forward on the handlebars and apply pressure to the pedal. The rear tire should climb onto the curb easily and the crank rotation should put you back on the saddle, ready to reinsert the free foot into the pedal retention and resume riding. As with the 90-degree curb ascent, gear selection may be important, particularly with a heavily loaded bike. Experience will teach you which gears work best.

■ Descents

Steep Descents

For a variety of reasons, steep descents can be tricky. In essence, steep descents change the geometry of the bike's frame by moving the contact patch of the front tire forward of its normal position, effectively increasing the rake of the front fork. The bike will behave as if the front axle has moved an inch or two in front of its mounts, which means that all steering input will be exaggerated. Consequently, small turns of the handlebars will be met with increased resistance. If the rider is not prepared for this response, the bars can turn unexpectedly, even to the point of being jerked out of the rider's hands. To overcome this, it is important to maintain a firm grip on the bars and keep the front wheel straight.

Another consequence of steep descents is that the rider's weight is transferred forward. The steeper the descent, the more weight will transfer. This has two effects. First, it compounds the problem of exaggerated steering resistance. Second, it causes the rear wheel to lighten considerably, maybe even lifting off the ground. All of these inputs differ drastically from those of normal riding,

FIGURE 7-7 With a foot planted on the sidewalk and the front wheel on the curb, place the pedals in the power position.

and drastic inputs from the rider are necessary to counteract them.

If you noticed that many of these same effects are produced during maximum braking maneuvers, you are already on the way to identifying corrective measures. The answer to the weight transfer problem is exactly the same as under maximum braking. Review the section on maximum braking and follow those guidelines for steep descents. However, proper body positioning is only part of the solution.

Depending on such factors as rider skill and angle of the steps, it may be critical that the front wheel remain straight or in line with the length of the frame. Steep descents increase both rider input and the bike's resistance to steering input, which means that the rider may have to apply considerable force to hold the handlebars straight. As long as the front wheel remains on axis with the frame, this usually is not difficult. However, even the

slightest deviation will result in increased lateral leverage on the wheel. That said, as long as the rider is able to sense and provide the force required to control the bike, turning the wheel should have no negative effect.

The elbows should not be locked while maintaining the maximum braking posture, and importantly, neither should the knees. Stiffening the legs, particularly on rough terrain such as stairs or rocky hills, may cause the rider to bounce into the air, taking the rear wheel off the ground and completely upsetting the balance of the bike. The arms and legs should work as shock absorbers.

The last concern is with braking input. Even with the rider in proper position and taking all necessary measures to maintain control of the bike, there are limits. Improper use of the brakes can have the unfortunate effect of showing you when you have passed those limits, particularly when the front brake is applied with too much force. With the rear wheel already lighter than usual, the front brake can quickly bring the rider past a point of no return.

There are varying degrees of steepness. In some cases, both brakes can be applied sparingly with good results, although the rear brake is almost always ineffective. Sometimes, very steep descents are best managed with little or no use of brakes, particularly on rough terrain. Although it can be a bit unnerving, it may be best to let the bike roll through the descent until the brakes can be applied safely. For this reason, it is always wise to plan ahead. Look for relatively level spots on the descent where heavy braking can be used to reduce speed, and always plan for where you will end up at the bottom. If you do not believe that there is sufficient room to slow or stop the bike at the bottom of the descent, do not attempt it. Experienced riders usually find that it is safer and easier to ride down a steep descent than to walk down with the bike, but the consequences of failure are not worth the risk. You may fall while walking the bike down a steep descent, but that is better than a 20 mph crash resulting from attempting to ride under conditions that require more skill than you possess.

Some descents may not be steep enough to require radical adjustments to weight distribution but may still present challenges for the rider. Long descents while riding on the street can be as tricky as short, steep ones, particularly when conditions require hard braking or sudden turns. The gyroscopic effect of rapidly spinning wheels causes them to resist changes in direction, but once that effect is overcome, steering inputs become exaggerated. (If you need to prove this to yourself, remove the front wheel from your bike and have someone spin it while you hold each side of the axle. Now, try to turn the spinning wheel parallel to the ground.) This is why turning and braking on fast descents always feels treacherous. When you combine that with the bike's reaction to adjustments in weight distribution and transfer, the effect is amplified. For all of these reasons, high-speed, downhill inputs should always be delivered gradually. The bike must be given time to stabilize after the initial application of steering or braking inputs. After the bike begins to feel under control again, the force of the input can be increased. It is probably safe to say that the only exception to this rule is when executing the maximum braking technique, because maximum braking does not attempt to change the direction of the bike. Therefore, the gyroscope effect is not at work against multiple inputs. Braking while traveling in a straight line is far safer than attempting to turn while braking.

Stair Descents

Descending stairs is exactly the same as any other steep descent, with one additional consideration. Because the contact patches of both tires may be considerably less than on a consistent, even surface, braking may be completely ineffective. In some cases, the treads of the stairs may be positioned so that the tires only contact the edges of the stairs during the descent, meaning that, even under the best circumstances, only a small percentage of the normal contact patch is ever touching anything. The rest of the time, the tire is completely in the air. Obviously, brakes will not work.

In addition, the exaggerated steering input and subsequent resistance described in the Steep Descents section will be multiplied by the additional force of the bike's momentum. They will also come in pulses because there will be no resistance while the tire is in the air, but resistance will be even stronger when the tire comes in contact with the edge of the step. It may be even more necessary to ride out the stairs until you reach the bottom. Again, be sure that you have adequate room to stop the bike at the bottom before you begin the descent.

Descending stairs can be a lot of fun, and is usually not nearly as difficult as it appears, but stairs can be very unforgiving. While you are learning, always practice with at least a couple of spotters (FIGURE 7-8).

■ Parking Blocks

Riding over parking blocks is a terrific way to practice combinations of varied inputs, which is the gateway to more advanced skill development. Although it may not look very difficult, the skill required to ride over a parking block quietly and under control uses the techniques required to execute the curb ascent, then a quick steep descent, then the curb ascent again, and finally, another steep descent. Learning to make such adjustments rapidly can prepare you for learning much more advanced skills.

Of course, it is possible to ride over a parking block by simply riding a wheelie over it with the front tire and allowing the rear tire to bounce over. If you are satisfied with that method, you will

FIGURE 7-8 Descending stairs can be fun, but stairs are unforgiving. Always practice with a couple of spotters.

probably find that learning new skills will be very difficult. As mentioned at the beginning of this chapter, basic skills form the foundation for learning advanced skills. Without a proper foundation, you will have a hard time breaking old habits in order to learn more advanced riding skills. This is an excellent opportunity to practice some discipline and perfect your skills as a beginner.

To ride over a parking block the proper way, approach it as if it were a curb with a sidewalk on the top edge. Loft the front wheel and let it touch the top of the block. As the front wheel rolls down the other side of the block, gently apply the brakes and quickly transition to the steep descent posture. As the bike levels off again, move your weight forward, slow the bike, and wait for the rear wheel to contact the block. Then, complete the second step in the curb ascent maneuver by pedaling the wheel onto the top. As the rear wheel rolls over, move your weight back again, assuming the steep descent position, and applying the brakes sufficiently to allow the rear wheel to crawl, not drop, off the back side of the block. Practice this until you can do it

without hearing the chain bounce. Obviously, one can ride over a parking block without all of these adjustments, but this an important step in building a strong skills foundation. Working towards perfecting this maneuver can lead to remarkable control and confidence, prepare you for learning other skills, and make your everyday riding safer.

■ Quick Turn/Rock Dodge

Both the Quick Turn and Rock Dodge are avoidance techniques intended for those situations when objects have appeared in your path so quickly that you have no time to prepare for avoiding them by maximum braking or scanning to the rear and swerving. When performing either of these maneuvers, it is important not to use the brakes. Applying the brakes during either of these maneuvers results in conflicting inputs to the bike, which often results in loss of control. In this case, the most common result of conflicting input is the loss of lateral grip on the front tire. When lateral traction is lost, the front tire will slide sideways in relation to the direction the tire is pointed. All steering input becomes irrelevant, and the front brake will be ineffective. The front wheel will probably fall over no matter what the rider does at this point, and the rest of the bike will follow. Even experienced and very skilled riders seldom recover from a laterally sliding front tire.

The Quick Turn and Rock Dodge maneuvers both involve rapid steering input and weight transfer. A Quick Turn is used primarily as a collision avoidance technique. After the Quick Turn is completed, the bike will be traveling in a different direction. The Rock Dodge is usually intended for avoiding a surface hazard and then continuing in the same direction.

Steering input on a bicycle is almost always accompanied by weight transfer to begin the turn. Normally, this is done almost subconsciously and feels quite natural. A right turn is normally accomplished by the rider leaning to the right and then turning the handlebar/front wheel to meet the angle of the lean. At this point, the rider's weight is transferred slightly to the right and the front wheel is turned to the right to catch the bike as it falls. Usually, this happens smoothly and effortlessly.

The problem is that when it has to happen very quickly, it is very difficult to keep all of those inputs in the proper order and delivered to the proper degree. If the slight left turn input is delivered too quickly, the rider's weight may also transfer to the left, causing the bike to veer left too far. Transferring the weight to the right before the bike begins to fall to the right results in a right side fall. The Rock Dodge and Quick Turn are used to minimize the possibility of a fall in either direction.

Rock Dodge

While riding, a cyclist continually scans the pavement several bike lengths ahead for hazards. If a hazard appears, the cyclist normally scans to the rear to ensure it is safe and then swerves to the left (the traffic side) of the obstacle. If this is not possible, the cyclist should perform a Rock Dodge. In a Rock Dodge, the cyclist makes a quick back-and-forth movement of the front tire, either to the left or right of the hazard, to avoid striking it with the front wheel, which could cause the bike to lose control (**FIGURE 7-9**). The rear wheel may hit the object, but this is unlikely to cause loss of control. The Rock Dodge enables the rider to miss the object and continue to ride in the same "line."

Start the Rock Dodge by quickly turning the handlebar quickly to the opposite direction of the side to which you wish to pass the obstacle. Immediately lean in the direction you want to travel around the obstacle and turn the front wheel in the same direction at the same time. Adjust your weight

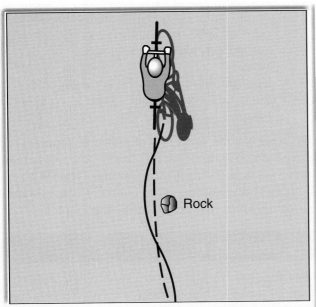

FIGURE 7-9 In a Rock Dodge, the cyclist makes a quick back-and-forth movement of the front tire, either to the left or right of the hazard, to avoid striking it with the front wheel.

to keep the turn under control, then, after clearing the obstacle, straighten the bike and continue traveling in the original direction. The turning motion is very subtle; extreme motion could result in a crash.

An alternative to the Rock Dodge would seem to be standing up on the pedals and simply riding over the obstacle, but there are a few potential problems with this technique. First, getting into position may require time that you do not have, whereas when properly executed, the Rock Dodge is an almost reflexive, instant action. Second, the object could be one that you must avoid at all costs, for instance, a child or small animal.

Quick Turn

The most common circumstance that would require a Quick Turn maneuver occurs when a vehicle makes a left turn in front of you after failing to yield right-of-way. When the maneuver is complete, you will be riding in the same direction as the vehicle.

The Quick Turn starts similarly to the Rock Dodge. Start by turning the handlebar quickly in the direction opposite the one in which you wish to turn. Immediately lean in the direction you want to turn, simultaneously turning the front wheel in the same direction. As the bike begins its turn, adjust your weight to keep the turn under control, and continue turning until you have completed the maneuver (**FIGURE 7-10**).

It is common for this situation to lead to a very close call, but the consequences of not acting immediately could be a collision with a moving vehicle whose driver either does not see you or does not care. It can be a violent and frightening maneuver to make, but failure to take this action is far worse.

■ Climbing Hills

For public safety cyclists, the most important reason to learn the skill of climbing hills is for more efficient energy expenditure. You must be able to function physically when you reach your destination, especially in emergency situations. Although hills challenge aerobic capacity and strength, a reasonably fit public safety cyclist should be able to master hill-climbing techniques with a little practice.

There are varying opinions in cycling as to the best way to climb: seated or standing; shifting before or after you meet resistance of the hill; staying in a gear until your cadence slows and then downshifting, or trying to maintain the same cadence and shifting gears accordingly. The type of terrain is

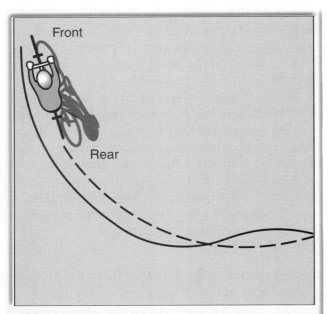

FIGURE 7-10 In a Quick Turn, adjust your weight to keep the turn under control, and continue turning until you have completed the maneuver.

also a factor. The best method for any cyclist is largely dictated by physical capabilities and experience in a given set of circumstances.

According to cycling experts, seated climbing is more efficient than standing, especially on longer climbs. Standing requires more muscles, raises your heart rate, and uses more energy and oxygen.

Stay relaxed to conserve energy and use a light touch on the handlebars. To pull maximum air into your lungs, keep your back straight and your chest open. Position your hands on the handlebars and relax your arms so that your elbows are wider than your hips. If you are short, slide back on the saddle to generate more force through the top of the pedal stroke and to encourage your heel to drop through the bottom of the stroke. If you are tall, slide forward, positioning your hips so they come close to lining up with the bottom bracket to generate maximum muscle force.

Carry as much momentum as possible into the hill. As you meet resistance from the slope of the hill, continue pedaling until your cadence slows, and then downshift. Stay in that gear as long you can maintain your cadence, and again downshift. Remember that it is important to lighten the pressure on the pedals to allow for the shift to occur.

On very steep climbs, this may require shifting earlier instead of waiting until your cadence drops. Concentrate on pedaling in circles instead of mashing down on the pedals with each stroke. This will allow more muscles, like the gluteals and hamstrings, to share the work with the quadriceps.

There are times when it is appropriate to stand: when you need a break (standing lets you stretch your muscles and open your lungs) and when you are about to crest a hill. When you are ready to stand, shift into the next higher gear and stand when one foot reaches the top of the pedal stroke to minimize momentum loss. Avoid leaning forward as you stand, and keep your weight centered over the bottom bracket. You should feel like you are running on the pedals, allowing the bike to rock gently, but not excessively, from side to side.

Bicycling magazine offers advice for climbing hills with a smooth seated stroke, which allows you to apply more force more evenly and efficiently. While following these steps, concentrate on pushing each pedal forward, then pulling it back.

1. When your crankarm is at the 11 o'clock position, push it as though you are walking down a set of long, shallow steps. Think forward and down.
2. Keep the same amount of pressure until the crankarm reaches the 5 o'clock position.
3. As the pedal passes through the 5 o'clock position, pull back and up on the pedal as if you are scraping mud off the sole of your shoe.
4. Keep pulling up with the same amount of force until you are back to the 11 o'clock position.

Like other cycling skills, hill climbing becomes easier with practice. Riding a hilly route just one or two times a week will significantly improve your hill-climbing ability and therefore your ability to respond to an emergency that occurs at the top of a hill.

Conclusion

All of the skills in this chapter should be considered essential for every public safety cyclist. These represent the most basic tools required to ensure your safety and effectiveness, regardless of where you ride. Even as you add more advanced skills to your riding capabilities, it will always be necessary to maintain proficiency at the basic level. As you practice more advanced skills, you will not only get better at the basics, but you will gain an understanding of how important it was to build the foundation that supports your progression into becoming a better rider.

As you move into the Continuing Skills Development chapter, keep the basic skills in mind. No matter how advanced a rider may become, the basic skills are the ones that are used most.

References

Cote, Alan. How to Conquer Long Climbs. *Bicycling* magazine. www.bicycling.com.
Yeager, Selene. Fly up Hills. *Bicycling* magazine. www.bicycling.com.

8

Vehicular Cycling

chapter at a glance

Introduction

To understand the principles of vehicular cycling fully, it is essential to know the laws surrounding bicycle use. Most states in the United States define bicycles as vehicles; thus, as vehicle operators, cyclists have the legal right to use the roadway. Even in the few states that do not define bicycles as vehicles, the laws generally give a person riding a bicycle upon a public roadway all the rights, duties, and responsibilities as any other vehicle operator. Therefore, whether or not bicycles are defined as vehicles, cyclists in every state have the right to use the roadway. Not only is it the cyclist's right; it is usually the safest place to operate.

The Rules of the Road

The basic rules of the road as listed in each state's motor vehicle code (MVC) affect all roadway users, motorized or not. The rules include posted signs, traffic signals, and right-of-way rules. Some laws by their very nature do not and cannot affect cyclists, such as those pertaining to motor vehicle equipment. Likewise, other laws exist that are directed only at cyclists.

Every state requires cyclists to ride with the flow of traffic, and in most states, the statutory language requires cyclists to ride as far to the right of the roadway as is practicable. Others require cyclists to ride as close as practicable to the right-hand curb or edge of the roadway. Practicable is defined as "possible to practice or perform." Therefore, to ride a bicycle as far to the right as practicable means to ride as far to the right as can be accomplished safely.

Cyclists are vehicle operators; as such, they need to ride in the streets and be recognized by motorists as legitimate users of the transportation system. To achieve this, cyclists must ride in a way that demonstrates that bikes belong on the roads. In short, cyclists must drive their bikes as if they are driving their cars. This concept is known as vehicular cycling. It is especially important for public safety cyclists to follow the rules of the road, because they are in uniform, highly visible, and expected to set a good example for the general public.

■ How Far Right Is Far Enough?

The law does not require cyclists to ride as far right as possible. If it did, cyclists would have to either ride in the gutter or balance precariously along the edge of the pavement. By using the word *practicable*, the law permits the cyclist to decide the safest place, within reason, to ride. The law generally can be interpreted to mean that cyclists shall ride as far right as is safe in the appropriate lane. Generally, the usable width of the road begins where a cyclist can ride without increased danger of falls, jolts, or blowouts. A road may have a gravel shoulder, its edge may be covered with sand or trash, or the pavement may be broken. Closer to the center of the road, the pavement is better and is more likely to be swept clean of sand and debris. The right side of the road begins here (FIGURE 8-1).

The decision of where to ride is based upon a number of factors, including:

■ Experience: Where a wide shoulder exists, many experienced cyclists ride just to the right of the solid white line if the road conditions are favorable. Even though they are closer to passing traffic, doing so places them where they are most likely to be seen by drivers waiting at intersections and least likely to encounter debris. Inexperienced cyclists may feel more comfortable riding a farther distance from the passing traffic; however, the cyclist is actually safer while riding closer to traffic because there is a reduced need to swerve to avoid hazards on the shoulder. Riding along the fog line, in a predictable manner, is safer than swerving onto the roadway to avoid holes, grates, parked vehicles, and other obstacles.

- Equipment (road bike or mountain bike): Surface hazards that may be a danger to a cyclist riding a bike with skinny, high-pressure tires and no suspension may pose no danger at all to a person riding a bike with wider tires or a suspension to absorb shocks or bumps. The rider, knowing his or her own equipment and his or her limitations with the equipment, determines the safest legal place to ride.
- Perception of the dangers: Surface hazards and moving hazards vary in their degree of danger, both inherently and as perceived by the cyclist. The same cyclist may perceive similar hazards differently in different situations.

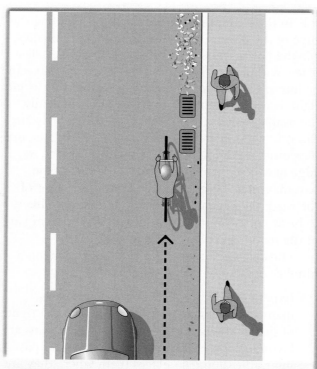

FIGURE 8-1 Ride as far to the right as practicable and safe.

- The condition and width of the roadway, including the shoulder.
- The presence of bike lanes and whether their use is mandatory.
- The need for 3 to 4 feet of wobble space.
- The likelihood of a pedal striking the curb.
- Movements made within the lane (e.g., preparing for a vehicular-style left turn).

The Wobble Lane

The decision of exactly where a cyclist should ride is largely dictated by the need for a 3-foot to 4-foot wobble lane. Bicycles are single-track vehicles that require balance to remain upright. Cyclists balance by subtly moving the front wheel back and forth, movements similar to those needed to balance a baseball bat upright in the palm of the hand. The resulting wobble, which is more noticeable at slow speeds than at higher speeds, causes cyclists to need a 3-foot-wide wobble lane for safe travel. That is, the practical width of rider plus bicycle, including the wobble space to balance, is at least 3 to 4 feet wide; therefore, an equally wide safe travel lane is necessary.

For instance, if a cyclist is riding on a road with a curb and gutter, the joint where the asphalt and concrete gutter apron meet would be to the cyclist's right. The gutter apron is generally not a safe place to ride and should not be considered part of the wobble lane. Instead, the right edge of the wobble lane would be aligned with the edge of the asphalt. Likewise, if a cyclist is riding on paved shoulder that tends to collect debris, the wobble lane would begin to the left of the debris. If cars are parked along the road, the wobble lane begins about 3 feet away from the cars; riding more closely can put the cyclist at risk of being hit by a car door as it opens or by cars pulling out from side streets and driveways.

■ Exceptions to Riding on the Far Right

Cyclists do not have to ride only on the far-right side of the road. Most MVCs allow them to leave the right side when making a turn; when passing a slower-moving vehicle or bicycle; to avoid a hazard; and when the width of the street makes it unsafe, especially in situations where riding too close to the roadway edge would encourage a driver to pass despite having insufficient room. In these situations, the cyclist should "take the lane," that is, ride in the center of the traffic lane.

Each person operating a bicycle or a motor scooter at a speed less than the normal speed of traffic on a roadway shall ride as near to the right side of the roadway as practicable and safe, except when:

- Making or attempting to make a left turn.
- Operating on a one-way street.
- Passing a stopped or slower moving vehicle.
- Avoiding pedestrians or road hazards.
- Approaching a location where a right turn is authorized.
- Operating in a lane that is too narrow for a bicycle or motor scooter and a vehicle to travel safely side by side within the lane.

Wrong-Way Riding

Riding against traffic is not only illegal; it is extremely dangerous. An unexpected roadway position, coupled with a bike's speed, removes the cyclist from the scanning pattern of the majority of motorists (FIGURE 8-2). Based on habit and experience, motorists focus on oncoming traffic—the traffic that is legally approaching in the opposite lane. Wrong-way cyclists are about three times more likely to be involved in a crash and are involved in nearly one third of all bicycle-motor vehicle crashes. Wrong-way riders also pose a threat to cyclists who are riding legally. When appearing from behind parked cars or other cyclists, a wrong-way rider can cause a head-on crash with another cyclist at closing speeds of up to 40 mph. This can be fatal for either cyclist. Fear of vehicles approaching from behind does not justify riding against traffic.

"New cyclists fear that they will be hit from behind by fast motorists, almost to the exclusion of any other fear of motor traffic. This fear is created by parents, teachers, police officers, motor-vehicle driver education, and other social forces. However, this fear is entirely unwarranted, because about 90 percent of car-bike collisions are caused by conditions or actions in front of the cyclist, where they can be seen and therefore avoided by proper avoidance actions. Of the 10 percent of accidents that are caused by conditions behind the cyclist, six percent are caused by the cyclist swerving in front of the car and only four percent by the overtaking motorist. Of this 4 percent, half are caused by

motorists who do not see the cyclist (generally in the dark) and often by motorists who have been drinking; some by motorists who misjudge the width of their vehicles, and very few by motorists who are out of control."

—John Forester, *Effective Cycling*, MIT Press, 1992.

Riding on the wrong side also prevents cyclists from seeing the regulatory signs and traffic control devices that are posted and positioned for traffic traveling on the right. Riding in a predictable, lawful manner increases personal safety by maximizing the opportunity for other drivers to see and respond to bicycles as vehicles.

The Speed Positioning Principle

When cycling on a roadway, it is important to adhere to the speed positioning principle. This principle dictates that the slowest moving vehicles operate in the far right lane and the fastest vehi-

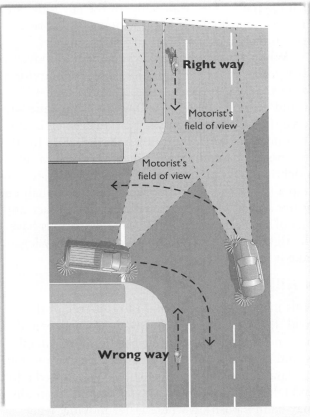

FIGURE 8-2 Riding the wrong way removes the cyclist from motorists' fields of view.

cles operate in the far left lane. At times, the cyclist is the slowest vehicle on the road and must ride on the right side, on the shoulder, or in a bike lane. At other times, for instance, when descending a hill or riding in congested traffic, a cyclist will be as fast as the other traffic, if not faster. In that case, the cyclist should move to the left and take the entire lane.

The cyclist should also take the lane on narrow roadways that do not allow a cyclist and a motor vehicle to pass safely side-by-side within the same lane. A narrow lane is usually one that is less than 12 feet wide. A typical passenger car or pickup is 6 feet wide, and trucks can be 8 or more feet wide. The cyclist's profile, including the wobble lane, is roughly 3 feet wide. Some states require motorists to allow at least 3 feet when passing a cyclist; therefore, a 12-foot-wide lane would be required for a passenger vehicle to pass a cyclist legally within the same lane. A truck would require an even wider lane. The typical interstate highway lane is 12 feet wide, and some lower-speed streets may have lanes that exceed 12 feet, especially on the curbside lane. However, most streets upon which a cyclist rides have travel lanes narrower than 12 feet.

While an inexperienced cyclist would move as far right as possible in attempt to make room for a faster-moving vehicle to pass, a skilled cyclist would move to the left—taking the entire lane—to force the motorist to pass legally, that is, by using the oncoming lane. By trying to make room for the motorist to pass, the cyclist may be forced to ride in a debris-filled gutter or on a gravel edge. They may trap a tire in the joint that separates the asphalt and gutter apron, hit the curb with a pedal, or face any one of several fall-provoking events. Cyclists have the right to the lane if they need it, and may legally take it if necessary.

Hills

Hills may cause an exception to this rule of the road. If the traffic lanes are relatively narrow and have no shoulder, the speed-positioning principle would normally put the cyclist in a position to take the lane. If, however, a cyclist has just crested a hill and takes the lane on the downhill side, he or she may be in a position where faster-moving, rear-approaching traffic may not expect a cyclist. Even though cyclists can travel faster than usual while descending a hill, they should stay farther to the right and wait until they are considerably beyond the hillcrest before moving out into the traffic. This gives overtaking motorists time to see them and respond accordingly.

Passing

Whether passing a motor vehicle or another cyclist, it is always safest to pass on the left. Drivers expect to be passed on the left, so they look back to the left before they pull out into traffic or change lanes. In addition, a cyclist who passes a slower vehicle on the right could become trapped if the vehicle suddenly turns right or pulls to the shoulder.

One Third of the Lane Rule

Another basic rule of vehicular cycling is the one third of the lane rule. When approaching an intersection, cyclists should occupy the appropriate one third portion of the right-most lane that goes to their destination. For example, a cyclist who is approaching an intersection with the intention of turning right should be in the right one-third of the lane. A cyclist stopping at a controlled intersection and planning to go straight should stop in the middle one third of the lane (but slightly to the left or right because the center of the lane tends to become slick from oil drippings). This position allows room for drivers turning right on red to pass easily. A cyclist who is making a left turn at the intersection should stay in the left side of the lane, close to the centerline. This will signal the cyclist's intent to motorists and will allow straight-through motorists to pass safely on the right.

Left Turns

Cyclists and motorists are safer and more predictable when they make turns from the lane nearest their destination. Traffic law requires vehicles to change course from the correct lane. Left-turning vehicles should move into the left lane (or the left turn lane, if one is available) before changing course. Bicycles are no exception, and they may legally leave the right side of the road or shoulder to make a left turn (**FIGURE 8-3**). Cyclists preparing for a left turn should scan to the rear (known as a "rear scan" or "shoulder check") before moving to the left. When there is a gap in traffic, they signal and move toward the centerline. Once near the centerline, they signal their intention to turn and wait for a gap in oncoming traffic. Overtaking cars can pass on the cyclist's right. In this position, the cyclist is visible, predictable, and communicating to other traffic, and is both acting and being treated as the driver of a vehicle.

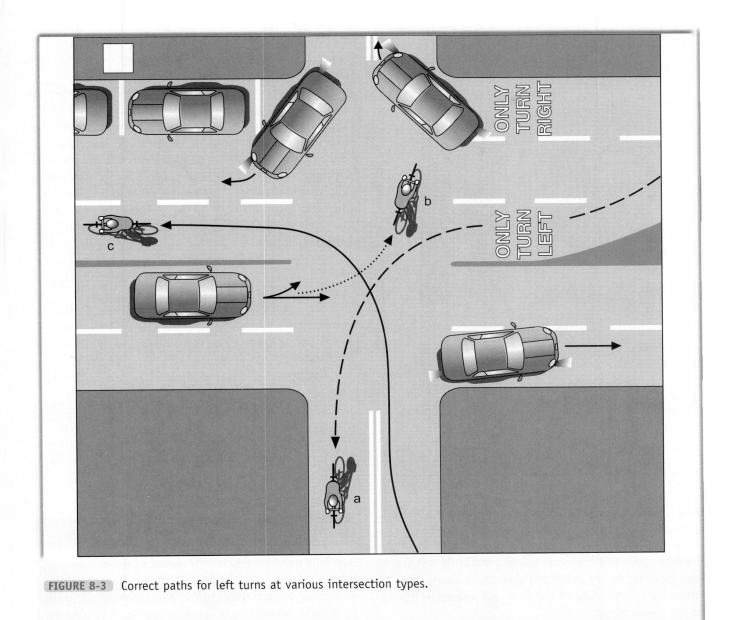

FIGURE 8-3 Correct paths for left turns at various intersection types.

■ Channelized Intersections

If the intersection is channelized with turning lanes, the cyclist legally must use them (**FIGURE 8-4**). Many inexperienced cyclists feel uncomfortable leaving the right side edge, regardless of what type of lane it is. If there is a right-turn-only lane (RTOL), they will often still ride on the right side and go straight at the intersection. This frequent violation by cyclists creates unpredictable, and potentially unsafe, situations at intersections. The proper way to proceed straight when one or more RTOLs are present is to ride in the right one third of the right-most straight-through lane. Right-

turning cyclists should use the right-most RTOL, if more than one is present.

When making a left turn from a left-turn-only lane (LTOL), the cyclist must cross the straight-through lanes and enter the right one third of the LTOL. After completing the turn, the cyclist will already be positioned in the right one third of the roadway. If there are two or more LTOLs, the cyclist must ride in the right-most lane. If the LTOL is wide enough to safely accommodate a cyclist and a motorist side-by-side, the cyclist should use the right one third of the LTOL.

Some intersections have multiple destination lanes. Cyclists approaching these lanes need to

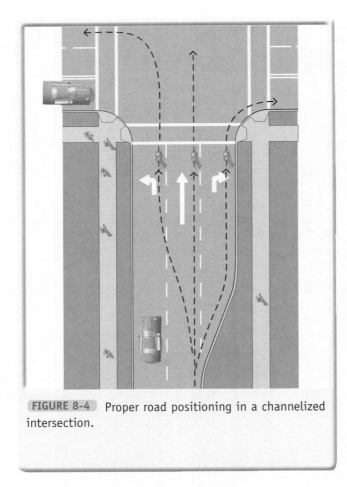

FIGURE 8-4 Proper road positioning in a channelized intersection.

remember the basic vehicular cycling rule requiring them to ride in the right-most lane that goes to their destination, while following the one third of the lane rule. If a cyclist is using a multiple destination lane, he or she must position the bike in the appropriate one third of the lane, according to his or her destination.

■ Passing at Intersections

Cyclists may find themselves in heavy traffic that backs up from controlled intersections. If there is room along the right side of the lane to pass safely, the cyclist may do so but must be cautious of right-turning vehicles. If there is insufficient room to pass on the right, the safest method for the cyclist is to get in line with traffic and take the lane through the intersection, thus avoiding conflict with right-turning vehicles. It is not difficult for a cyclist to keep up with traffic when starting out at an intersection, but once through the intersection, the cyclist should move to the right unless traveling at the same speed as the cars or if the road is not sufficiently wide.

■ Traffic Circles

A traffic circle, also known as a rotary or round-about, is a left-curving street with several side streets going off to the right, like spokes. In other words, traffic goes around the circle to the left and leaves it by turning right onto a spoke. In traffic circles with more than one lane, the right lane is a right-turn lane used by entering and exiting traffic. Cyclists who enter the traffic circle with the intention of turning right at the first exit should stay in the right lane. Those who are proceeding past the first exit should change lanes to the inside while entering the circle and ride around the circle at the outer edge of the inside lane. They may signal to the left while in the inside lane to communicate to drivers that it is safe to pass on the right as they exit the circle. To exit, the cyclist moves into the outside lane while approaching the desired exit point, using the normal procedure and hand signals (FIGURE 8-5).

Because of the traffic circle's left curve, cars go straight to turn right. For this reason, it is especially dangerous to cross an exit of a traffic circle in the right lane. Bicyclists who always keep to the right will perceive traffic circles as very dangerous, but it is surprisingly easy to ride around in the inside lane. Drivers typically drive more slowly on the inside, because they are following the curve.

■ Merging and Changing Lanes

Cyclists must be constantly aware of the traffic around them. In addition to keeping their eyes searching ahead, they should also monitor the traffic behind them with rear scans (sometimes known as shoulder checks), that is, glancing backwards over the shoulder. When performing a rear scan, the natural tendency is to turn in that direction. In order to avoid collisions, the cyclist must learn to maintain a straight line of travel while looking over the shoulder. Although most rear scans are over the left shoulder, cyclists should practice scanning to both the left and right while maintaining control of the bike.

Most bicycle/motor vehicle crashes involve events happening in front of the bicyclist, but a cyclist who pulls into a travel lane without checking to see if it is clear greatly increases the chance of being struck from the rear. Statistically, this is one of the most deadly crash types; hence, it is imperative that cyclists understand how to merge and change lanes safely.

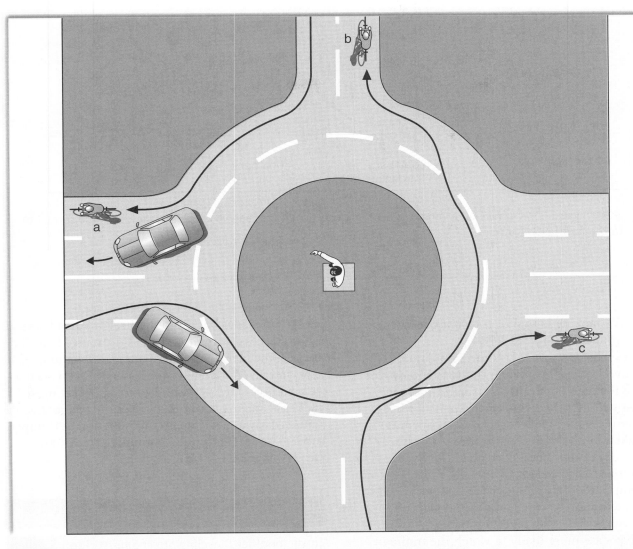

FIGURE 8-5 In a traffic circle or rotary intersection, (a) keep to the right if you will take the first exit, (b) and (c), ride in the inside lane if you are going past the first exit.

▪ Lane Changes

The lane change requires two rear scans and two moves to the left (**FIGURE 8-6**). The first step in changing lanes is to check over the left shoulder for traffic. If traffic is far enough back and not overtaking rapidly, signal with an extended left arm. If traffic is near but moving slowly, an extended arm may be a way to request permission to move in front of the vehicle. After determining it is safe to enter the stream of traffic, pull into the left portion of the lane in which you are currently traveling. Perform another rear scan and signal before moving into the right-hand side of the next lane.

When changing lanes from left to right, the method is the same, except it is necessary to check for traffic over the right shoulder. If the travel lane or shoulder comes to an end or merges with another lane, the technique required is the same: scan to the rear and make the move.

▪ On and Off Ramps

Roads with entrance and exit ramps onto other roads, or merges and diverges, can present challenging traffic conditions. Drivers on both the through streets and merge/diverge lanes must make frequent scanning movements for traffic in multiple direc-

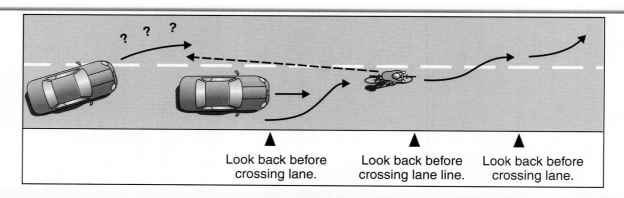

Look back before crossing lane.

Look back before crossing lane line.

Look back before crossing lane.

FIGURE 8-6 Cross a lane in two steps: one to move from one side of the lane you are in to the other, the second to cross into the next lane.

tions while making lateral or traversing movements into or around traffic (FIGURE 8-7).

The cyclist is most at risk for a rare but often deadly overtaking crash when traffic is entering or crossing the lane the cyclist is using. A merging motorist will usually be looking over his or her shoulder or to the side to check for an opening. Actions taken by the cyclist are best based on the speed of the traffic as much as any other factor.

On lower speed roadways, where traffic is moving 30 mph to 40 mph, the driver does not need to accelerate as hard to catch and merge with traffic. The slower speeds may tend to bunch up traffic, and drivers are more likely to watch the traffic in front of them. Here a cyclist riding on the through street should try to stay in the right-most lane that goes to his or her destination. As with a right-turn-only lane, the cyclist may have a lane or more between himself and the edge of the roadway, which may put the cyclist in a conflict with merging drivers. If the approaching driver recognizes the cyclist and slows or yields, motorists following that vehicle will most likely also slow. However, the cyclist should always be prepared to stop or evade.

On high-speed highways where traffic is moving in excess of 50 mph, the driver is often accelerating to highway speed and looking behind and laterally for a gap in traffic. The threats in front of the car are rare, so the driver is less concerned about what is in front of the vehicle. This situation is far more dangerous for the cyclist. It may be prudent for the cyclist to move to the far-right shoulder of the merge lane to avoid high-speed overtaking crashes. If the

merge lane fades back into the straight-ahead lane, it is only necessary to move across the merge lane once. If the merge lane turns into a deceleration lane and diverge lane, it is necessary to traverse it a second time. To diverge and exit, the cyclist must make the move to the right side of the merge/diverge lane as early as possible. In this situation, it is imperative to be assertive and communicative with the drivers of vehicles.

The Moving Blind Spot

In the booklet *Bicycling Street Smarts,* John S. Allen describes a situation he calls the moving blind spot. The blind spot may occur when the cyclist is making a left turn in front of multi-lane traffic. If the vehicle in the left-most approaching lane (the one closest to the cyclist) is large, it may block the cyclist's view of cars approaching in the right-most lane. The large vehicle may be stopped to make a left turn, or allowing the cyclist to proceed. This is potentially dangerous as an oncoming vehicle may be in another lane, out of view (FIGURE 8-8). The cyclist should ride as if there is another car approaching rather than riding blindly across the intersection.

A second type of moving blind spot can occur if the cyclist is crossing a through street and a larger vehicle is approaching to make a right turn. While the right-turning vehicle may not present a risk, it may hide a moving vehicle that is continuing through the intersection. It is unlikely that

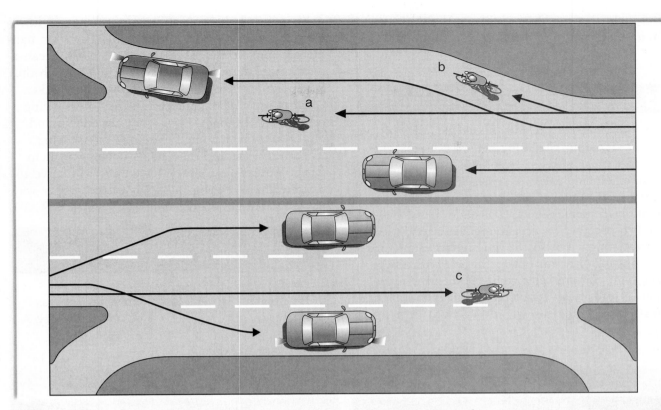

FIGURE 8-7 If passing an on- or off-ramp (a), ride in a straight line. Use the right side of the ramp to enter or exit (b). If the distance between the on and off ramps is short (c), hold your line to avoid merging left and then right again.

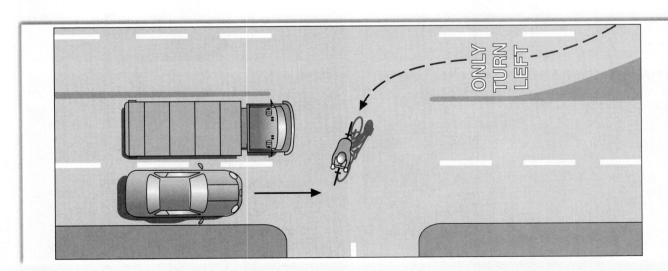

FIGURE 8-8 Avoid the moving blindspot by always crossing multiple lanes as if an unseen car is approaching.

the straight-through driver will see the cyclist; therefore riding through the intersection could prove deadly.

Hand Signals

Every rider must learn and follow the rules of the road for signaling. Signaling is a way of communicating with motorists and other cyclists, thereby greatly enhancing safety. Cyclists use their arms and hands to signal turns, lane changes, and deceleration. In some states, cyclists are legally required to use the left arm to signal turns. Putting the arm straight out to the left signals a left turn, while putting the arm out to the left with the elbow bent upwards at a right (90-degree) angle signals a right turn. As of the publication date, 23 states had accepted the alternative right turn sig-

nal of putting the arm straight out to the right. However, removing your right hand from the handlebars puts you at risk of an endo crash because if you need to stop suddenly, you might grab the left brake lever, which controls the front brake. Cyclists must also signal when they are slowing or stopping by pointing the left arm down and out at a 45-degree angle with the palm facing backwards. Using proper hand signals will help ensure your safety, and your actions will serve to educate the motoring public as to the proper way to ride a bicycle on the roadway (FIGURE 8-9A–D).

Riding Defensively and Assertively

Competent cyclists ride both defensively and assertively. These two styles are not contradictory. A

FIGURE 8-9 A. Left turn signal B. Right turn signal C. Alternate right turn signal D. Slowing/stopping.

defensive cyclist is always alert and anticipates the mistakes of other drivers. A defensive cyclist is prepared to evade or stop for threatening obstacles or vehicles. An assertive cyclist understands he or she is part of traffic and operates within the rules. An assertive cyclist will take the entire traffic lane if necessary, signal and request right of way from motorists, and generally operate as he or she would in a car. Cyclists who are defensive and assertive epitomize the basic tenet of vehicular cycling as articulated by John Forester in *Effective Cycling:* "Cyclists fare best when they act and are treated as drivers of vehicles."

Public safety cyclists in uniform enjoy a respect from motorists most cyclists do not experience. That allows the public safety cyclist to be especially assertive when necessary to respond to an urgent call. But even uniformed cyclists must never forget that not every motorist sees cyclists, and it isnecessary to remain defensively vigilant. As is the case when driving, it is always best to make eye contact with a driver to assure that you have been seen and recognized before riding in front of any vehicle.

Partner and Group Riding

Public safety cyclists often ride with a partner or, on occasion, a group of riders. Whether riding on- or off-duty, they should be able to ride both single file and side by side with ease, and transition smoothly between the two. When riding with other cyclists, communication is important because it can prevent collisions among riders.

Although there are several transitioning methods for group riding, IPMBA recommends that the lead rider in a single-file line of cyclists be regarded as the number 1 rider. When transitioning to double file (FIGURE 8-10A), the number 1 rider communicates his or her intention to move, scans, and then moves to the left. The number 2 rider continues to ride straight forward, moving up next to the number 1 rider. All other riders follow suit. To transition back to single file (FIGURE 8-10B), the number 1 rider communicates his or her intention to move, scans, and then accelerates slightly while moving to the right, in front of the number 2 rider. The number 2 rider allows the number 1 rider to merge into the line while maintaining speed.

There are a few rules to group riding, whether in single or double file, or on- or off-duty. First, maintain space between cyclists. About one bike length is appropriate under normal circumstances, although more space should be allowed while ascending or descending hills. Closely following another rider increases the risk of a crash if your wheels touch or if the rider in front of you makes a sudden, unexpected move or stop.

Second, ride steadily and predictably. All riders should maintain a steady pace and ride in a straight line without swerving from side to side.

Third, call out road hazards. Riders in the front of the group should warn those behind of hazards ahead, such as rocks, potholes, sand, gravel, glass, or oncoming traffic, and should make every effort to steer smoothly around the obstacles. Riders at the back should alert those in front to traffic approaching from the rear.

Fourth, ride single file, unless traffic, road conditions, and local statutes permit riding two abreast. If you need to pass another rider, look back to ensure it is clear, move to the left, and communicate your intention to pass.

Although they are rarely as serious as car-bike crashes, crashes involving two or more cyclists are more common. Whether riding with a partner or in a group, communication is essential for preventing such crashes. In addition, adhering to a standardized method of transitioning can help reduce the chance for miscommunication and ensure greater predictability.

Bicycle and Pedestrian Facilities

Like roads, bicycle and pedestrian facilities typically are governed by state or local laws. Cyclists should be aware of the rules regulating such facilities and use them accordingly.

At times, local jurisdictions will attempt to use the presence of bike facilities, such as bike lanes, routes, and paths, to ban cyclists from certain roadways. However, whenever state laws recognize bicycles as vehicles or grant cyclists the same duties and responsibilities as motorists, regulating the riding of bikes on the roadway rests with the state. In almost all states in the United States, the use of bike lanes and shoulders is optional, not required. In 2006, only seven states (AL, CA, HI, MD, NY, OR, PA) required the use of a bike lane if one was present, and only four states (AK, CO, MD, NY) required the use of shoulders. State law normally grants authority to

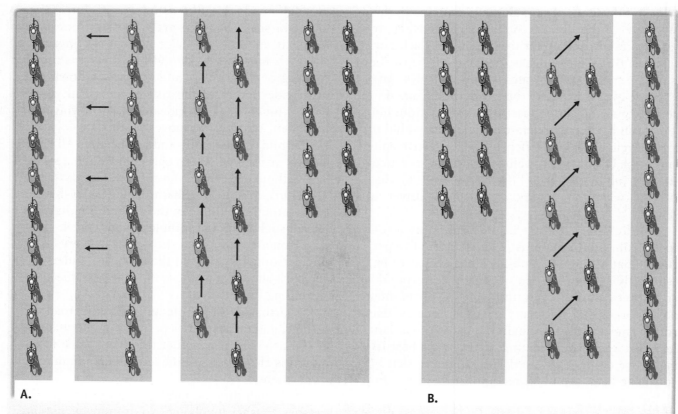

FIGURE 8-10A-B Transitioning diagram. A. Transitioning from single to double file. B. Transitioning from double to single file.

local jurisdictions to regulate cycling on pedestrian facilities only.

■ Bike Lanes, Paths, and Routes

Many people use the terms *bike lane, bike route,* and *bike path* synonymously. However, there are significant differences among them.

Bike Lanes

Generally, a bike lane refers to a section of the roadway designated by painted lines and other markings. It is a portion of the road that is restricted from most motor vehicle use, not a sidewalk or sidepath. The purpose of a bike lane is to provide an area in which cyclists can operate on-road, safely and in a vehicular manner. Unfortunately, bike lanes seem to suggest to other road users that cyclists should ride exclusively in them; however, as mentioned above, this is rarely the case. While many bicyclists would prefer to ride on properly designed and well-maintained bike lanes, there are times when cyclists need to have the discretion to avoid riding in bike lanes, as in situations when

they are not the safest part of the road for cyclists. It is not uncommon for bike lanes to collect debris, have poor pavement, or be used for parking, legal or otherwise.

Bike Routes

A bike route is a signed or mapped route that aims to facilitate bike travel. It may take the cyclist on regular roads, onto sidewalks and bike paths, or into bike lanes. Bike routes typically follow low-traffic roads with the goal of providing a safe, pleasant ride. Unfortunately, except in areas where the bicycle is well-integrated into the transportation system, many bike routes are designed for meandering rides with no particular destination. Use of bike routes is never required by law, but some motorists think a cyclist using the road is "off the bike route," when in fact the cyclist is merely taking a more direct route to his or her destination.

Bike Paths

Bike paths are typically multi-use trails (**FIGURE 8-11**). There are many different types of bike paths, includ-

FIGURE 8-11 Multi-use trails attract a wide variety of trail users.

ing sidepaths, which are separated from but parallel to the road, and paved recreational trails, such as rail trails. These are often characterized by the presence of joggers, in-line skaters, dog-walkers, and equestrians. Though they are away from the road, the presence of so many types of users traveling at very different speeds with no traffic regulations often makes such paths more dangerous than roads. In addition, sidepaths typically have speed limits, and cyclists usually do not have right-of-way, making them impractical for many cyclists. As is the case with bike lanes, very few states mandate the use of bike paths by cyclists, although many motorists believe otherwise.

■ Sidewalks, Crosswalks, and Pedestrian Zones

Because they are pedestrian facilities, laws that prohibit or restrict the riding of bikes on sidewalks, in crosswalks, and in pedestrian-only zones are imposed by local regulation, such as city and county ordinances. Some local jurisdictions allow cyclists to ride their bikes on residential sidewalks but not in business districts. Some do not allow cyclists on sidewalks at all. In some locations a cyclist riding upon a sidewalk or within its legal extension, the crosswalk, is legally considered a pedestrian. As such, rules like direction of travel, equipment requirements, and even stop signs, which do not apply to pedestrians, do not apply to cyclists either. In areas such as this, the cyclist must yield to actual pedestrians as a matter of safety. Because rules vary dramatically from place to place, it is important that you check the laws in the areas in which you will be riding.

The legality of operating a bike on pedestrian facilities has a unique impact on uniformed cyclists, who are bound to uphold the law and set a good example. Some jurisdictions have made exceptions for public safety cyclists operating on patrol, in emergency situations, or both. The exception may apply to police cyclists only, not EMS or security.

Conclusion

As John Forester stated, the basic tenet of vehicular cycling is that cyclists fare best when they act and are treated as drivers of vehicles. In order to operate safely and effectively, cyclists must recognize that bicycles are vehicles and that they have the same rights and responsibilities as the drivers of motor vehicles. They must understand the concept of road positioning and learn the techniques that will give them the skills and confidence to operate safely in traffic. Most importantly, they must be intimately familiar with the state laws and local regulations governing the operation of a bicycle as a mode of transportation and as an emergency vehicle.

References

Allen, John (2001). *Bicycling Street Smarts*. 2nd Edition. Rubel BikeMaps/Rodale Inc., Cambridge, MA.

Forester, John (1993). *Effective Cycling*. 6th Edition. MIT Press, Cambridge, MA.

Hazards and Crashes

Introduction

Public safety cyclists must apply their skills in a wide range of practical situations and are often confronted with dangerous riding conditions caused by a variety of hazards. Cyclists can greatly enhance their safety by learning techniques to recognize and avoid such hazards, thus minimizing the risk of falls and crashes. The skills chapters discuss in more detail many of the cycling techniques that can be employed to avoid hazards and minimize the risk of injury from crashes.

Common Crashes

In order to prevent falls, collisions, and related injuries or death, it is important for cyclists to recognize the common crash types. Although motor vehicles are the most common and dangerous hazard that cyclists encounter, according to *FHWA-RD-99-07, Injuries to Pedestrians and Bicyclists*, motor vehicles account for only 33% of all bike crashes resulting in injury or death. Bicyclists are more likely

to crash with a fixed object, another bike, a pedestrian, or a dog; they could also fall or go off the road.

Common Bike Crash Types

Bike Overturn (fall)
Bike Off-road
Bike/Fixed object
Bike/Bike
Bike/Pedestrian
Bike/Dog
Bike/Motor vehicle

Common Cycling Hazards

Hazards can generally be divided into three categories: surface, visual, and moving. Minimizing the risk of injury and/or property damage is contingent upon a cyclist's ability to anticipate, recognize, and avoid such hazards. Ignoring hazards often results in damage to the bike and/or the rider.

■ Surface Hazards

A surface hazard is an obstacle on the riding surface that can cause the cyclist to lose control or fall. Found on roadways, sidewalks, trails, and off-road areas, surface hazards include water, ice, potholes, railroad tracks, sewer grates, broken glass, sand and gravel, expansion joints, pavement cracks, and miscellaneous objects such as dead animals, car parts, and tree branches. In some situations, the cyclist can employ specific techniques to negotiate surface hazards, but in general, avoidance is the best approach.

Sand, gravel, wet leaves, metal plates, manhole covers, and painted areas on the roadway can cause a bicycle to lose traction and fall, especially when turning, braking, or accelerating. Roads often become slippery at intersections, especially the centers of each lane, where oil and other fluids collect. Look for slippery areas as you approach intersections, and ride straight and upright through them. If you are turning, you may be able to initiate the turn prior to or after the slippery area. If you need to slow down, brake before the turn. The small area of the tire in contact with the ground is not large enough to provide the traction necessary to both slow the bike and allow it to turn, especially if a surface hazard is present.

Sewer grates present a hazard to cyclists if the openings in the grates run parallel to the direction the bike is heading, especially if the openings are wider than the tire. If your wheel gets trapped, you will be vaulted over your handlebars in an endo crash. A similar type of crash, known as a diversion crash, can occur when an object causes the front wheel to divert in an unexpected direction. Such crashes often result when the front wheel becomes trapped in a parallel crack, or the side of the tire strikes an object, such as a curb or railroad track. As with all surface hazard-related crashes, they are more easily prevented through avoidance than any other way. Stay away from parallel cracks in riding surfaces. Coast over cracks, railroads tracks, and ridges as close to a 90-degree angle as possible, with your pedals in a horizontal position (FIGURE 9-1). When riding over bumps or on rough surfaces, rise off the saddle and use your legs and arms to absorb the shock.

Cyclists may experience a diversion fall if trying to escape a deep crack that has trapped a wheel or when trying to get onto a paved surface that is at a higher grade than the one on which they are riding. If you ride off the paved surface with the side of a tire against the edge of the roadway and cannot stop, it is best to lighten the front wheel and reposition it away from the edge. If you try to climb slowly up onto the pavement or out of the crack, your likelihood of diverting increases. Try to move a foot or two away from the pavement edge before attempting an ascending move. Then turn at a sharper angle (about 45 degrees) back onto the pavement. These moves must be done with the same kind of attention used when ascending curbs or other obstacles as described in Chapter 7. It is often safest to simply stop as quickly and safely as possible to avoid a fall from one of these potential diverters.

Many surface hazards, like debris, rocks, or small potholes, can be avoided by steering around them or employing the Rock Dodge technique. The Rock Dodge will prevent you from swerving out in

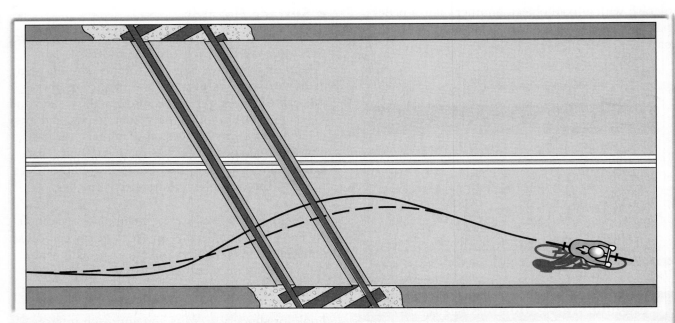

FIGURE 9-1 Ride across railroad tracks at as close to a 90-degree angle as possible.

front of any overtaking traffic, a common cause of potentially fatal crashes. This technique is described in Chapter 7.

A seldom-recognized hazard is the curb itself. If you ride too close to the curb, a pedal may come down on top of it, launching the bike upward and to one side, causing you to fall in front of oncoming traffic. The best way to avoid the curb is to avoid riding in the gutter; the "ride as far right as practicable" rule does not necessitate riding in the gutter.

Weather can also cause surface hazards. Moisture may make the riding surface more slippery than usual, especially metal surfaces and painted lines, and can increase the hazard of oil and other fluids. Avoid puddles, pools, and potholes filled with water. What lies beneath the surface could be far worse than it appears.

Cold-weather riders may encounter ice and snow. The thin layer of ice covering roads, known as "black ice," can be one of the greatest winter risks because it is so difficult to see. Turning on black ice can be especially challenging because the bike can easily slide. It is helpful to keep the bike as upright as possible, which often involves offsetting the upper body to the side, toward the direction of the turn.

Braking on black ice is also hazardous because it causes the ice to melt slightly, creating a layer of water, which makes it even more slippery. The brakes must be applied carefully and with a strong bias towards the rear brake. Transferring the weight backwards over the rear wheel will also help maintain traction.

Black ice should be avoided whenever possible. The mix of grit, sand, and other debris that collects at the side of the road can provide much greater traction than black ice, as does untracked snow.

Untracked snow also provides a better riding surface than car tracks. It is easier to push through the snow than it is to maintain balance on an area with numerous, diversion-causing ruts. Riding on trafficked snow is similar to riding in the sand; heavy pedal pressure and constant steering are needed. It can be very hazardous, especially when other traffic is present. Riding in undisturbed snow is preferable, although it is important to watch for peaks and valleys in the snow, which can signal debris or potholes.

Common Surface Hazards

Holes, cracks, road edge deterioration or drop-off
Curb and gutter joints or grade differences
Curb tops
Loose sand, debris, or glass
Skewed railroad or trolley tracks
Expansion joints
Drainage grates
Standing water
Ice and snow

■ Visual Hazards

Visual hazards prevent cyclists and motorists from seeing one another. They also affect the cyclist's ability to see the riding surface and detect other types of hazards. Environmental visual hazards include darkness, fog, rain, and glare. Visual screens are objects that block the view, including parked cars, hedges, buildings, groups of pedestrians, and hills.

Environmental Visual Hazards

Cycling in low-light conditions can be extremely dangerous. A large percentage of fatal bicycle crashes occur during darkness. Cyclists must strive to be as conspicuous as possible when riding after dark, especially in traffic. There are times that police cyclists may want to be inconspicuous for tactical reasons, but cycling in traffic is not one of them. Motorists must see bicyclists in order to avoid crashing into them. See Chapter 11 for a detailed discussion of nighttime conspicuity, and Chapter 18 for night patrol.

Rain, fog, blurry windshields, and glare from oncoming headlights reduce drivers' ability to see. If riding in these conditions is necessary, the cyclist should seek out bike lanes, sidewalks (if legal), off-road options, and lightly traveled roads with lower speeds. Cyclists riding in fog or rain in the daylight may choose to use their headlights to enhance their visibility to drivers in front of or approaching them. Traffic vests or high-visibility uniform parts will also help make a public safety cyclist more visible.

Glare is especially dangerous to cyclists when the sun is low on the horizon. Motorists easily can be blinded by the sun and may only be able to see a portion of a driving lane. The driver may see just enough to feel assured that no other motorist is approaching; a cyclist may get lost in the glare. This problem can be compounded by dirty, hazy, or bug-smeared windshields, which intensify the effects of glare, whether from the sun or oncoming headlights.

Glare frequently contributes to car/bike crashes that result when a motorist makes a left turn in front of a straight-through cyclist or when an overtaking motorist passes and then turns right in front of a cyclist. Being aware of the position of the sun and your direction of travel in relation to it can help you avoid these mishaps. If the sun is on the horizon behind you, it is possible that an oncoming motorist may not see you. Pay attention to oncoming drivers who appear to be slowing. Because not all motorists use their turn signals, watching for turning front tires may alert you if the car is making a left turn.

Motorists driving into the sun may also have a hard time seeing cyclists traveling in the same direction. Be aware of this and stay a bit further to the right, if road conditions permit. Use extra caution at intersections and places where motorists are likely to turn or merge. If a car overtakes you and slows, watch its front tires, which will alert you if the motorist will be making a right turn. If the car turns, either use the maximum braking technique to stop, or execute a Quick Turn to the right (as described in Chapter 7) to stay on the inside of the motorist.

Glare also increases the probability of motorists pulling away from stop signs, or out of driveways or alleys, into the path of the cyclist.

Visual Screens

Visual screens are objects that obstruct the view, including shrubbery, parked vehicles, buildings, pedestrians, hills, and similar objects. As with other visual hazards, recognition of the hazard is the most important part of avoiding it. Once a visual screen is noted, you can make adjustments in your riding or searching technique to prepare for possible consequences, such as a car pulling out in front of you or a pedestrian entering the roadway.

Hills present a unique hazard. While riding up long or steep hills, a cyclist may become fatigued and distracted. After cresting the hill, most cyclists take the traffic lane, which is appropriate if the cyclist is traveling at the same approximate speed as other traffic. However, a cyclist who is moving more slowly than the traffic cresting the hill should stay farther to the right side of the lane until he or she is far enough away from the hillcrest to give overtaking motorists time to see him or her and react appropriately.

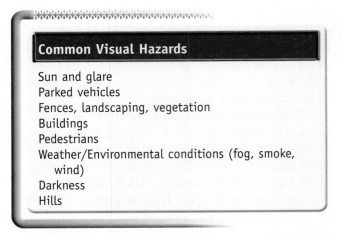

Common Visual Hazards

Sun and glare
Parked vehicles
Fences, landscaping, vegetation
Buildings
Pedestrians
Weather/Environmental conditions (fog, smoke, wind)
Darkness
Hills

■ Moving Hazards

A moving hazard, as the name implies, is anything that moves and that may collide with cyclists or cause them to fall. Common moving hazards include cars, other bicycles, pedestrians, skaters, and animals.

Motor Vehicles

Whether parked or in motion, motor vehicles are considered moving hazards. Parked vehicles are moving hazards because of the risk of a car door suddenly opening or a car pulling out from a parking space. When approaching or passing parked cars, the cyclist must look for passengers or other indicators that the car is occupied, such as brake lights, flashers, visible exhaust, or an open door. Defensive cyclists treat all parked cars as occupied; they scan to the rear and move out into the traffic lane at least one door's width away from the vehicle (FIGURE 9-2). This helps the cyclist avoid a crash or an unpredictable swerve around the door if it is opened suddenly.

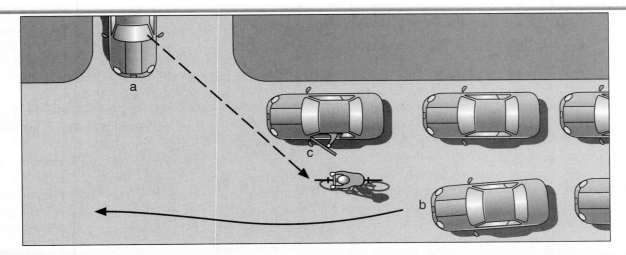

FIGURE 9-2 Ride a safe distance from parked cars in order to be seen by motorists entering the road (a), avoid being closely overtaken by passing cars (b), and avoid being hit by a car door (c).

Causes of Common Bicycle-Motorist Crashes

Motorist Unexpected Turn
    Motorist left turn—oncoming
    Motorist right turn—parallel paths
    Motorist left turn—wrong-way cyclist or riding
       to the left of the motorist
Motorist Stop and Go
    Motorist disobeys traffic control device at an
       intersection
    Motorist fails to yield right-of-way when exiting
       an alley or driveway
Motorist Overtaking (striking from behind)
    Bicycle not seen—improper lights/reflectors
    Motorist out of control—for instance, DUI
    Motorist taking counteractive measures
    Motorist misjudged space—improper passing
    Cyclist's path blocked—evading an object and
       entering motorist's path

Source: Cross-Fisher Study, 1977.

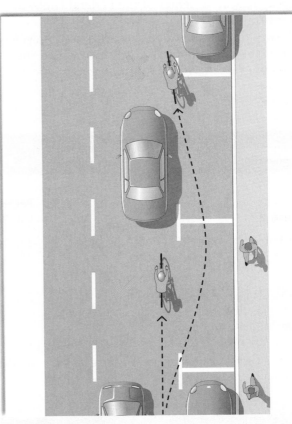

FIGURE 9-3 Skilled cyclists maintain their line of travel.

If a line of cars is parked along the street with wide gaps between the cars, inexperienced cyclists may weave around the cars. Skilled cyclists ride predictably, maintaining their line of travel until they have passed all of the cars and it is safe to move back to the right (**FIGURE 9-3**). This prevents cyclists from being hidden from view and from having to swerve in and out of traffic.

The 1977 Cross-Fisher study resulted in the NHTSA classification of bicycle-motor vehicle crashes. The three most common adult bike-car crash types are the motorist unexpected turn, the motorist stop-and-go, and the motorist overtaking, the last of which is the most frequently fatal.

Studies conducted by the Highway Safety Research Center (HSRC) and published in 1999 used police accident reports to identify the various types of car-bike crashes and those that resulted in very serious or fatal injuries to the cyclist. Several types of accidents had identifiable characteristics (referred to as "over-represented variables") that set them apart from the norm. These variables include such factors as the age of the cyclist and the driver as well as the road conditions. Highlights from these studies appear in TABLE 9-1 . More detailed crash reports are available from the Turner-Fairbank Highway Research Center of the Federal Highway Administration.

Most conflicts between motorists and bicycles occur at intersections and driveways, where the motorist is turning or pulling out into traffic.

Once you have spotted a vehicle that is turning or that may pull out in front of you, prepare to take evasive action. Although you should be prepared to stop quickly if necessary, you should also assert your right to the road by continuing to pedal and holding your line. The term "hold your line" simply means continue to pedal forward in a straight line, without moving to the right or left (FIGURE 9-4). By continuing to pedal, you will communicate your intention to proceed through the intersection. The same message can be communicated to oncoming drivers who wish to turn left in front of you. If you stop pedaling, the motorist may think you are turning right or yielding to them so that they can turn.

Vehicles turning in front of a cyclist create a very common bicycle/motor vehicle crash scenario. Cyclists can do several things to reduce the chances of this type of crash: First, enhance conspicuity, especially at night. Nearly half of the fatal car-bike crashes occur at night or in low light conditions. Second, ride with traffic unless tactical reasons dictate otherwise. Third, watch for oncoming cars that appear to be slowing, whether or not they are signaling for a turn. As with cars overtaking and slow-

TABLE 9-1 Bicycle/Motor Vehicle Crashes			
Cause	Percent of All Car/Bike Crashes	Percent of Very Serious or Fatal Car/Bike Crashes	Over-Represented Variables
Car turns left into path of oncoming cyclist.	12.2%	11.7%	Bicyclists from 20-44 years old. Drivers older than 65 years.
Car runs into cyclist while traveling in the same direction (half involve the cyclist going straight; half involve a cyclist turning left from the right hand edge of the road).	8.6%	14.6%	Drivers from 16-19 years old. Darkness Two-lane roads
Car hits cyclist at right angle in intersection with no signal or stop sign.	21.7%	10.5%	Bicyclists from 15-19 years old. Wrong-way cyclists.
Car hits cyclist at right angle in intersection after bicyclist runs stop sign or stoplight.	16.8%	18.9%	Bicyclists from 0-14 years old.
Car hits cyclist at right angle in mid-block after cyclist rides out from driveway.	11.8%	14.2%	Bicyclists from 0-14 years old.

Source: www.velonews.com, accessed May 4, 2007.

FIGURE 9-4 Holding your line enables drivers to predict your intentions accurately.

ing, watch the front tires to see if they begin to turn. Fourth, if it is safe to do so, visually or audibly signal to the driver to make sure you are seen. Should the motorist turn anyway, you may need to apply maximum braking or make a Quick Turn with the motorist. If the oncoming car turns left in front of the bike, you should perform a Quick Turn in the same direction. If an overtaking vehicle turns right in front of the bike, you should perform a Quick Turn to the right to stay on the inside of the vehicle.

A cyclist must also remain alert for situations that might cause a motorist to take evasive or counteractive actions that may in turn cause the motorist to enter the cyclist's lane. Anticipate what you might do if you were driving a car and decide what action to take. For instance, if it is obvious that a motorist is approaching debris in

the road and might swerve to avoid it, slow down or move into a position that will enable the vehicle to take this action without putting you in danger.

Other Moving Hazards

In addition to motor vehicles, cyclists must also avoid confrontations with pedestrians, dogs, cyclists, and other moving hazards. Riding appropriately for the existing conditions, remaining aware of one's surroundings, and being prepared to take evasive action are essential for avoiding such hazards.

Pedestrians can be hazardous to cyclists in many settings. Cyclists operating on the road risk crashing into pedestrians who enter the street both at and between crosswalks and from between parked cars. In residential neighborhoods, children are likely to dart out in front of an oncoming bicyclist. While operating on multi-use trails, cyclists are usually legally required to yield to pedestrians. They should be especially aware of children, who tend to act unpredictably, and should operate at a speed appropriate for the trail conditions. They should also provide an audible warning (voice or bell) when approaching pedestrians from the rear. Skaters, especially in-line, pose a unique hazard in that they tend to use more space than a pedestrian or jogger. Public safety cyclists who operate on sidewalks, routinely or on an emergency basis only, should be particularly cautious of pedestrians, who have right-of-way and may be entering and exiting the walkway from the street as well as from businesses and homes.

Dogs and other animals are a frequent hazard, especially in neighborhoods and on trails. Unleashed dogs are likely to give chase and may even attempt to bite the rider's leg. Techniques for dealing with dogs include shouting, exiting their territory as quickly as possible, and squirting them in the face with a water bottle. Leashed dogs can also be a problem, especially if the leash is long. If the dog owner is not in control of the animal, the rider can easily become entangled in the leash and crash.

Other cyclists are also considered moving hazards. If they are operating in a vehicular manner, their actions should be predictable, but not all cyclists adhere to traffic laws and regulations. Be alert for cyclists passing on the right, ignoring traffic control signs and signals, and failing to signal. Wrong-way riders are an even greater hazard because they approach from an unexpected direction. Police cyclists should use education and enforcement to encourage safe cycling behavior when they encounter other cyclists who are operating recklessly or in violation of the rules of the road.

Even cyclists with whom you are riding can present a danger. If the principles of group and partner riding presented in Chapter 8 are not followed, one cyclist can easily cause others to crash. Transitions from double to single file and vice versa must be communicated clearly and executed cleanly. Riding partners should always communicate their intended actions to one another both to avoid crashes and to ensure that they are not separated unintentionally. This communication is often nonverbal among partners who have ridden together long enough to have developed routines.

When multiple cyclists are riding single file, the most common and serious type of crash occurs when cyclists allow their wheels to overlap. If the front rider makes a sudden lateral move to avoid an object, for example, and bumps the overlapped front wheel of the rear rider, the result can be a type of diversion crash in which the balance of the rear cyclist is suddenly and unexpectedly diverted. Therefore, drafting with other cyclists is inadvisable unless all the cyclists are skilled in drafting. If riders agree to draft, communication is essential to avoid the types of chain reaction crashes that can easily occur when cyclists are riding close to one another.

Common Moving Hazards

Motor vehicles
    Car doors being opened
    Parked cars pulling out
    Extended mirrors and other items on vehicles
Other cyclists
    Wrong-way riders
    Riders in a group
    Your partner
Pedestrians
    Skaters
    Joggers
    Persons with strollers or carts
    Wheelchair users
Animals
Wind, wind blasts

Conclusion

Cyclists are at risk from a number of hazards found in the cycling environment. These risks are generally divided into three categories: surface, visual, and moving. Recognizing the various types of hazards and the situations in which they are likely to be encountered is an important part of minimizing the risk of crashes and crash-related injuries. For many risks, avoidance is the best approach, but an understanding of when and how to take evasive action is also essential.

References

IceBike: Home of the Winter Cyclist, www.icebikers.org. Accessed January 22, 2007.

Mionske, Bob (2003). Legally Speaking: Crashing by the Numbers. *Velo News*, www.velonews.com/news/fea/4193.0.html.

Stutts, Jane C & Hunter, William W. (1999). *Injuries to Pedestrians and Bicyclists: An Analysis Based on Hospital Emergency Department Data.* FHWA-RD-99-078.

Tan, Carol (1996). *Crash-Type Manual for Bicyclists.* University of North Carolina Highway Safety Research Center. Pub # FHWA-RD 96-104.

Turner-Fairbank Highway Research Center, Federal Highway Administration, www.tfhrc.gov/safety/pedbike.

Continuing Skill Development

Introduction

As discussed in Chapter 7, the development of more advanced skills does not mean that the fundamental skills are no longer needed. Regardless of how advanced one becomes as a rider, there is always an underlying force at work: mastery of the basics. Until a rider truly understands how rider input affects the way a bike behaves, progression will be difficult. Being satisfied with the attitude of "it wasn't pretty, but I did it" will allow for the omission of critical building blocks that should be included in your foundation of skills, a lot like skipping grade levels in school. If you have jumped ahead in this book by skipping over Chapter 7, do yourself a favor—go back and read that material now. The reason will become clear.

Many skills that most riders consider to be intermediate are simply basic skills carried to extremes or executed in rapid succession. For example, imagine a bike class. An eight-foot long, 10-inch-wide line is drawn on the pavement. Everyone in the class is asked to ride on top of that line from one end to the other without allowing either tire to roll off of it. Within about 10 minutes, everyone can do it with ease. It is a basic skill.

Then, a railroad tie of the same dimensions is set out. Now the line that was on the pavement is 10 inches above the ground (**FIGURE 10-1**). People have much more trouble, and it takes a lot longer before everyone is comfortable with riding the same line. If the railroad tie is then set on pallets and raised 3 or 4 feet in the air, most people will decline to even attempt to ride it. Why? It requires the same amount of skill to ride a straight line on the ground as it does to ride one that is 4 feet high!

There are two primary areas of difference. The first is the consequences that will accompany failure. A 4-foot fall is going to hurt a lot more than simply riding off of the line on the ground. The other consideration deals with the rider's perception of the amount of skill required to ride the same line when it is elevated above ground level.

This is why the basics are so important. A good rider must have absolute confidence that he or she has mastered the basic skills before moving to more advanced skills. That confidence is the foundation that will enable the rider to attempt new things. Basic skills are the basis of even the most difficult and complex maneuvers.

For example, consider riding over a 1-foot-tall wall from one parking lot into another. Instead of

FIGURE 10-1 Riders apply the same principles to riding on a railroad tie as to riding a straight line on the ground.

seeing a foot-tall obstacle, look at it as a 1-foot curb ascent. The skill required to ride this obstacle is exactly the same as the skill required to ride over a 4-inch curb. They both require the same rider inputs; the difference is that the actions must be imparted to the bike much more aggressively. The wheel will have to lift higher off the ground, which requires more room and greater weight transfer; weight transfer is rider input. The rear tire will still roll into the wall, just as it does with the smaller curb. The rider will have to transfer his or her weight forward more aggressively to begin the climb; more rider input. The rider will have to apply a lot more pedal pressure than with the small curb, and push the handlebars forward with greater force; again, rider input. In each case, even though the rider input may be greater in magnitude, the exact same principles apply when riding over the big curb and the smaller one. Applying the basics will get the rider over the wall, but if the rider has not mastered the basics, he or she is likely to fail.

Before attempting to ride any obstacle or learn a new maneuver, it is a good idea to walk the bike through the maneuver. Place one hand on the handlebars and the other on the saddle. Feel the forces that the bike will encounter as it rolls through the process of the maneuver. Make note of the position of the bike at each phase and imagine what you will feel as the rider. At what points are there drastic angles that could pitch you forward or back? Where does the bike meet resistance that will need to be overcome? Where might the bike pick up speed that you will need to control? What inputs must you be prepared to deliver that will counteract these things, and how important is the timing? Will your chainring or pedals strike an object that could cause damage or result in a crash? If things begin to go wrong, where are the bailout points? Where can you successfully stop the bike before committing to riding the obstacle? All of this is part of the mental preparation necessary for the first attempt at riding the obstacle. By completing this process, you may avoid injury or damage to the bike, because it is akin to a test run with nothing at risk. You may even decide that the forces that the bike will encounter in this situation are too extreme for you to overcome.

Master the Basic Skills

A good rider must have absolute confidence that he or she has mastered the basic skills before moving on to more advanced skills.

Some of the skills in this chapter are truly more advanced than those covered in the fundamental cycling skills chapter. They require different applications of concepts and rider input, and it may take a lot longer to learn them, but the benefits can be tremendous.

As you practice these skills, remember: frustration usually results in bad decisions. Do not try going faster or making extreme moves. The trick is always proper technique. Always ride under control, even on a failed attempt. Mastering new skills takes time and practice. The psychological effect of repeated failures may cause you to believe that you will never master the maneuver, but taking a break will help alleviate the frustration that can be a barrier to success.

Trackstanding

The trackstand is one of the most valuable skills that a rider can learn. Trackstanding involves holding the bike in a stationary position without placing either foot on the ground (FIGURE 10-2). Most riders who can trackstand are very accomplished riders, but that does not mean that only very accomplished riders can learn to do it. It is more accurate to say that good trackstanders can become exceptional riders.

Trackstanding is a huge confidence-builder. The reason for this is easy to understand. Executing a trackstand demonstrates that the rider has a remarkable comprehension of bike physics, rider input, and control. Really good trackstanders seldom get hurt.

One of the most common misconceptions about trackstanding is that it is really just riding so slowly that the bike comes to a complete stop. While using that approach may get you in position to sit motionless for a few seconds, a true trackstand can last indefinitely. If you can't hold a trackstand for more than 30 seconds, then you do not yet understand how it works.

FIGURE 10-2 Trackstanding at traffic light will enable a quick start when the light turns green.

The name *trackstand* refers to a technique used by velodrome racers at the start of a race. Velodromes are closed-circuit oval tracks with steep banking. In the past, velodromes were typically made of wood that resembled the flooring on a basketball court. Normally there were only two riders on the track at a time. In order to gain an advantage over his or her competitor, one rider would try to take a position behind and slightly offset from the rider in the front, with the front wheel turned up the banking. Both riders would sit almost motionless until one or the other wiggled slightly or appeared to lose concentration. The split-second bobble presented an opportunity for the more controlled rider to burst ahead and build a slight lead over the other one.

Learning its history can provide some guidance on how to approach learning the trackstand. Find a slight incline and slowly ride along so that the up-

hill side is to one of your sides. (For the purpose of this discussion, assume that your right side is uphill.) Turn your front wheel up the hill and put your power foot at 2 o'clock. Some find it easier to do this while standing on the pedals, but most prefer to stay on the saddle. Try it and practice it both ways. Gently apply both brakes and feather your pedal pressure so that you can make very fine adjustments. Normally, it is best to do this in a low gear, but remember that the lower the gear, the more quickly the bike will respond to pedal pressure input. This may cause the bike to react more quickly than you can accommodate in order to maintain a proper balance of inputs. This can be controlled with braking input, with the goal of smooth application of pressure on the pedal and drivetrain.

As this happens, there are times that the bike may want to fall to the right. Applying pressure to the pedal will cause the bike to lean back toward the left, allowing the rider to regain control. The trick is to keep the bike in a position so that it only tends to fall toward the right.

If you find that you frequently have to turn the wheel to the downhill side to avoid putting your foot down, you have not yet grasped the technique. The bike's center of gravity has shifted too far to the left, either because your weight transferred that direction, or, more likely, because you applied pedal pressure too quickly.

Learning this skill causes most riders to get very tense. Enable yourself to relax. Trackstanding is mostly about an indefinable, but essential, element of "feel." As stated earlier, this is a demonstration of control and a comprehension of bike physics. If you are too tense to feel what the bike is doing and how it responds to your input, learning this skill can be very frustrating.

Once you have mastered this skill, the incline will no longer be necessary. By understanding and applying principles of bike physics, you can impart the same forces on the bike that the incline would. Mastering this skill to this degree will not happen overnight; it is very difficult to learn, but it can be done.

In learning the trackstand, there is one magic moment that will let you know that you are on the right track. When you can allow the bike to roll backwards slightly, then smoothly catch it and move forward slightly, you are beginning to get a feel for what is involved in mastering it.

Learning to control a trackstand will improve virtually every aspect of rider skills. When a rider understands and demonstrates this level of control, a whole new world of developmental opportunities will open.

Learning the Trackstand

When you can allow the bike to roll backwards slightly, then smoothly catch it and move forward slightly, you are beginning to get a feel for what is involved in mastering it.

Stair Climbs

Especially for those working in urban areas, climbing stairs is a valuable skill. Even if you work or ride in areas where stairs are not common, learning the technique can make riding rough, steep inclines much easier.

Some riders mistakenly believe that riding up stairs is a maneuver that requires a lot of speed. Nothing could be farther from the truth. Proper technique will negate the need for the momentum that some deem necessary. Substituting speed for technique seldom results in success, but it will certainly raise the consequences of failure, potentially resulting in damage to the bike, injury to the rider, and a poor public image.

Before attempting to climb any set of stairs, walk the bike through them. Look at the angle and determine whether you will be able to position yourself on the bike to make the climb. On any climb, the rider has to maintain a position that prevents the bike from flipping over backwards. If the weight is too far forward, the rear tire will not have enough traction to keep the bike moving. The steeper the climb, the less room there is for error. If the stairs are too steep, avoid them. If the stairs are constructed in such a way that both tires strike the edge of the steps at the same time, they will be nearly impossible to ride, especially if there are more than six or seven of them.

Once you have determined that climbing a particular set of stairs is within your capabilities, the procedure is something like a prolonged curb ascent. Choose a gear that would be a little lower than the one you would select for a similar incline without the steps. Approach the stairs at a speed that you would find acceptable if you knew that you were going to run directly into the first step. Loft the front wheel, just as you would if this were a curb ascent.

Two things are important here. The angle of the bike should be the same as the angle of the stairs when the front wheel comes down (FIGURE 10-3). If it is much more than that, the front wheel will slam down on the steps when the rear wheel contacts the edge of the bottom step. This will bring the bike to a sudden stop, probably ruining any chance of making the climb. Proper angle will also ensure that as much of the movement of the bike as possible is used to maintain forward motion. Energy that is transferred into the steps by improper angle is energy that could have been used to help with the climb. In addition, proper angle helps provide for a smoother transition at the beginning of the climb, which is critical to maintaining balance. It is equally important to make sure that the entire wheelbase of the bike is put to use. This will provide maximum reach and take the bike as far up the stairs as it can go before it meets with any resistance.

Once the bike is positioned so that the front wheel is on the steps and the rear wheel is against the bottom step, you are ready to pedal up the stairs. Now, the biggest challenge is figuring out how to balance the bike so that it does not flip over backwards, while maintaining enough weight on the rear tire to provide the necessary traction. You will be very close if you keep your body at a 90-degree angle with the ground; not the steps, but the ground.

On some very steep climbs, following this rule will put too much weight on the front wheel. The only way to overcome this is with a very unnatural bit of rider input. It is possible to lighten the front wheel by quickly jerking straight up on the handlebars. If this technique is required, you will be pulling the bars straight toward your abdomen, right about hip level. If it is necessary to do this on any one step, it will probably be required for each of them. It is difficult, but not impossible to learn. The trick is that the wheel must only be unweighted for a split second. If it comes up too far, the bike will either flip or stall.

It is also important to remember that each set of stairs is unique. Many complicated factors define what is required to climb different sets of stairs. Sometimes, these factors will be too extreme to overcome. Tread measurements vary. Angles vary. Even the materials used to build the stairs can have

FIGURE 10-3 The angle of the bike should be roughly the same as the angle of the stairs.

an effect, but once you learn the proper technique, it will be much easier to figure out what adjustments will be required. You must then determine whether you have developed the skills needed for those particular conditions.

Climbing stairs takes patience to learn. Most everyone experiences a lot of failures while practicing this skill. The lockdown technique, as described in Chapter 7, should be used as necessary.

Multiple Obstacles

Even the simplest of obstacles can be challenging when the rider encounters several obstacles in rapid succession. If you have mastered the basics, some circumstances will require that you act quickly to apply them. In a sense, this is a more advanced skill in itself.

For example, assume you are riding through a steep ditch at a 90-degree angle. The ditch is smooth and only about 3 feet deep. There are no other obstacles, but it is very steep.

As you enter the ditch, prepare for a steep descent. You will need to be in the maximum braking position with your weight transferred as far back and as low as possible. As the front wheel rolls through the bottom of the ditch, you encounter a problem. The rear of the bike is still going downhill, but the front has begun its climb up the other side. Now where should you position your weight? You are executing a steep descent and a steep climb at the same time (**FIGURE 10-4A-C**).

The goal is to transition from the descending position to the climbing position with perfect timing. You have to move your weight forward as the bike transitions to the new angle. You have to

FIGURE 10-4A-C Overcoming multiple obstacles requires a keen sense of timing and an understanding of weight transfer.

change the position of your pedals from the 3 and 9 position to the power position to begin the climb. You may also have to release the brakes at just the right moment to avoid an endo that would result from the application of the brakes as the front tire meets with the added resistance of the far side of the ditch. This all requires a keen sense of how the bike is reacting to these outside forces and what rider input will be required to counteract these forces. None of these techniques is hard, but the timing is critical. You could loft the front wheel during the descent to get the bike in position for the climb, but again, if your timing is off you are almost sure to crash.

What is required is the perfect execution of several basic skills. What appears to be a single object (a ditch) are really two obstacles that will be encountered in very rapid succession, and each will have to be treated as a separate obstacle. In addition, you will have to control the front and rear wheels separately and treat each one as its own entity.

The point is that it is not very difficult to ride down a steep incline. It is not very hard to ride over a small obstacle. And it is not very hard to climb a small, steep hill. It can be very tricky to do all of those things in 2 or 3 seconds when each maneuver requires drastically different kinds of rider input. Learning to make these kinds of transitions rapidly is the key to developing your skills. Riding through a ditch is just one simple example. You will encounter others every day.

Off-Road Riding

One of the best ways to develop and practice the rapid application of various skills is off-road riding. Trail riding can present challenges that riding on the street will almost never duplicate. The obstacle courses created by nature can help you develop skills that will make you a better rider, no matter where you ride. Take the skills that you learn on the street and apply them to trails, and the other way around. When you encounter new obstacles, there is very little chance that they will require new techniques. Always think about an obstacle that you have not ridden in terms of one that you have.

Conclusion

In the chapters covering fundamental and more advanced skills, you have been provided with information that should put you on the path to improvement as a rider. You have read about building a foundation, then relying on it to support more advanced skills development. You have been provided some basic tools to get you started. Now it is up to you.

Learning new skills can be a lot of fun or very frustrating. Regardless of what skills you have right now, the most important factor in learning new skills is attitude. Ride with people who are more advanced than you. Watch and analyze their techniques, then assess what you are doing right or wrong. Ask questions. Continually reinforce your foundational skills, and always remember that you must progress at your own pace. Do not skip steps, and do not mistake success for mastery of any particular skill.

Finally, bicycle skill development is about progression. There is simply no substitute for spending time on the bike. The more you ride and challenge yourself, the faster you will improve.

11

Cycling at Night

chapter at a glance

Introduction

Cycling at night presents a variety of challenges. Daytime hazards become even more treacherous at night, and public safety cyclists must take precautions to ensure their safety. These steps include implementing measures to both see and be seen. For EMS providers, being seen is almost always an advantage. Police officers are faced with the difficult choice between being seen while riding in traffic and maintaining stealth when observing illegal activity or approaching suspects. Security officers, depending upon their responsibilities, will fall somewhere on the spectrum between visibility and stealth.

Hazards of Night Cycling

Night patrol can expose a public safety cyclist to a different world and a unique set of hazards. Some of those hazards are as follows:

- Cyclists may not be seen in traffic, especially during foul weather.
- Shadows and darkness hide surface hazards.
- Shadows and darkness affect depth perception and could make obstacles more dangerous.
- Darkness makes it more difficult for cyclists to be located.

- Darkness amplifies sounds, especially for the "bad guys."

In order to both see and be seen, and to avoid these hazards, cyclists use a combination of active and passive lighting.

Active Lighting

The term active lighting generally refers to any light source that involves a bulb and a battery or generator. For public safety cyclists, a battery is the practical choice. Active lighting serves two purposes. The first is to illuminate the area around the bike while riding or working around it. The second is to make the bike visible to motorists or others who may need to avoid it.

In either case, proper lighting is a very high priority for public safety cyclists (FIGURE 11-1). Active lighting for police officers not only provides an illuminated work area, it may also provide a tactical advantage. Bright and/or flashing headlights are a very effective means of disorienting a suspect, particularly when the light is directed from a variety of angles. EMS cyclists generally require a well-lit work area but realize no advantage in blinding a patient with more light than is necessary. Headlights with easily adjustable angles may be a good choice for these applications, but the same

FIGURE 11-1 Public safety bikes should be equipped with high-quality front and rear lights that meet their needs and local regulations.

thing can be accomplished by twisting the mount on the handlebars to direct the beam. Some bike medics prefer to use helmet-mounted lighting systems. These provide for hands-free use and the more precise direction of light than systems that are attached to the bike itself; however, some medics find the use of such systems to be awkward.

■ Lights

Any public safety cyclists who will be operating at night must, at minimum, meet the legal standards for bike lighting as defined by the applicable vehicle code. In most areas, this includes a front light and rear reflectors or taillight. However, most public safety cyclists require more powerful and versatile lighting than the lighting the law requires.

■ Illumination and Visibility

Illumination is the ability of a lighting source to brighten or make luminous a particular unit area on an intercepting surface at any given point. Visibility is a measure of the ability of radiant energy (in this case, light) to evoke visual sensation—in other words, the greatest distance at which the naked eye can identify the source of the light.

Some lighting sources are both illuminating and visible, while other lighting sources are visible, but not very illuminating. When operating a public safety bicycle in low light conditions, it is important to have a headlamp that can perform both functions, but illumination becomes more critical. It is equally important to have a highly visible taillight.

■ Lighting Standards

The brightness of a light is measured in lumens, which are a measure of the amount of light that falls on an area at a certain distance from the source. Although commonly believed to be a measure of brightness, watts refer to a measurement of electrical output from a source. As defined by the *IES Lighting Handbook,* a watt is a measure of electrical power. It defines the rate of energy consumption by an electrical device when it is in operation. As such, wattage is important because it affects battery life, and subsequently the length of time one can patrol in the dark. Different types of lights require different wattage to produce similar lumens. For example, a 12-watt headlamp with a halogen, light-emitting diode (LED), or high-intensity discharge (HID) bulb will all produce different lumens, with the HID bulb being the most illuminating. (It would take a 40-watt halogen bulb to equal the lumens produced by a 12-watt HID bulb.) The standards for both front and rear lighting are defined in this chapter.

■ Headlamps

The bicycle of any public safety cyclist operating at night should be equipped with a headlight that pro-

duces at least 42 lumens measured at a distance of 10 feet from the light and 9 lumens when measured 20 feet from the light. This can be achieved through the use of various bulb and battery types.

Bulbs

The bulbs and filaments found inside of headlamp systems can be of various components, the common ones being halogen, LED, and HID. A halogen system uses a tungsten filament and the injection of the reactive elements iodine or bromine (halides) into the inert argon gas contained within the bulb. The gas zenon is generally found in HID systems and produces an extreme white color. LEDs, which use numerous diodes, are very visible, but when they first became available they were not bright enough for illumination. As technology has developed, however, the LED has become a viable illumination option for public safety cycling use.

Batteries

The source of energy for headlamps usually comes in the form of a battery or battery pack. These batteries can be disposable or rechargeable and are available in many different technologies, all of which have benefits and drawbacks. Many low-cost and inexpensive headlamp systems that operate on disposable AA, AAA, or 9-volt alkaline batteries do not produce enough light to meet the needs of public safety cyclists. While the headlamp system itself might be inexpensive, the batteries, even the rechargeable ones, need to be replaced frequently, which can become expensive and inconvenient.

Rechargeable battery systems have become the industry standard for the public safety bicycle. The primary technologies used in these battery systems are nickel metal hydride (NiMH), nickel cadmium (NiCad), sealed lead acid (SLA), and lithium ion (LiIon).

Headlamp Features

Although the bulb and battery are the most important features when selecting a headlight, there are other factors to consider. Headlamps can have a fixed headlamp head, one that pivots and rotates to illuminate areas to the side of the bicycle's pathway, or a system with a combination of fixed and pivoting heads. Pivot points can be a source of breakage, so care needs to be used when operating such a headlamp.

Some headlamp heads contain a single beam while others have two or three separate but still fixed beams within the head. Other systems have two or three independent beams. Colored lenses such as red or blue can also be found on many of the major headlamp systems available to public safety cyclists. These lenses can be integrated with the headlamp head or can be separate lenses that flip into place over the headlamp. Headlamp systems with multiple beams in the head can also flash back and forth, which can be used to attract attention when operating in emergency response mode.

Most headlamps have the ability to operate in an energy-saving mode to conserve battery power when the full capacity of the headlamp is not necessary. These step-down modes can be a single setting or multiple settings, depending on the manufacturer and the technology used in the control head.

The control head, or on/off switch, also varies among models. Some headlamps can go from on to off in one mode, while others have to cycle through various settings to turn the system off—a disadvantage if one wants to operate in a stealth mode.

Other Considerations

There are other factors to consider in headlight selection, some of which are related to the conditions in which the bike will be ridden. If the cyclist will be riding in inclement weather, the headlamp system should be water resistant or waterproof. The connection should be sealed well enough to prevent moisture from entering and damaging the battery. The wiring system(s) from the headlamp to the battery source should also be checked to determine if it will hold up to the constant movement of the handlebars without causing chafing to the wires. It may be helpful to select a system with an integrated rear light.

The ease with which the headlamp and battery can be removed from the bicycle should be considered. This can be a concern from a security standpoint, for recharging purposes, and if the system is needed to provide a light source away from the bicycle.

■ Rear Lighting

Most jurisdictions require that bikes be equipped with rear reflectors or flashing red lights. In some, reflectors are required even if lights are also in place. Whether or not it is required by law, all public safety bicycles should be equipped with a steady or flashing rear light (FIGURE 11-2).

Rear lights come in two basic types, LED and

FIGURE 11-2 Whether or not it is required by law, all public safety bicycles should be equipped with a steady or flashing rear light.

strobe. The LED is very directional. How or where it is aimed or mounted can affect its effectiveness. LED lights often have several settings, including steady and flashing. LED taillights that use AA or AAA batteries are very energy efficient and the LEDs never burn out. Some rear lights are hard-wired to the light system battery, which can reduce the life of the battery's charge, but they are convenient to operate.

A strobe is a multidirectional device. It causes a backsplash of visible light to nearly everyone around it. Strobes tend to exhaust batteries very quickly.

A significant percentage of cycling deaths each year are the result of motor vehicles striking cyclists from behind, often because the cyclists are operating without rear lights. Only under such circumstances as described in Chapter 18 should a public safety cyclist consider riding without a red or flashing rear light during the night and at other times when the visibility is poor.

Passive Lighting

Passive lighting refers to retro-reflective devices that do not provide their own light sources. There are two basic types of retro-reflective devices. The first includes prismatic reflective materials, such as Reflexite or standard plastic reflectors. The other employs something known as "glass bead technology" such as that in Scotchlite™ material.

Retro-reflective materials can provide a high degree of visibility as long as the viewer is positioned directly along the same plane as the reflected light source (FIGURE 11-3). Retro-reflective materials, like a standard bike reflector, return light directly back to the source. The farther one gets from the path of the light source, the less reflected light one would see. If you shine a light on retro-reflective material and stand directly behind the light, it will appear at its brightest. As you move away from the light, the reflection will begin to diminish until it becomes no more reflective than any normal material like the other, non-retro-reflective areas of the uniform. For example, a cyclist wearing retro-reflective material would appear unusually bright to the driver of a car while the headlights are pointed at the cyclist. Yet, at that same moment, a pedestrian standing next to that car would see less light reflected from the cyclist. Compared to active lighting, passive devices are inexpensive and versatile. Many can be washed hundreds of times without losing effectiveness. They are available in a wide range of colors and sizes, and can be cut to fit as needed. Even small amounts of reflective material can pay great dividends when it comes to safety.

Placing retro-reflective material on the back of the uniform will help bike patrol members stay visible in traffic without becoming visible to suspects. Some police and security officers fear that their retro-reflective material will "give them up" if they walk under a streetlight. However, the badges many police officers wear create a bigger tactical problem than does reflective cloth tape. Their shiny surfaces reflect light in many directions. A cloth or embroidered badge is a better choice for night operations.

Except in unusual circumstances, such as tactical medical operations, EMS bike team members should try to wear as much retro-reflective material as possible. Being seen, day or night, is the first step to being avoided by vehicular traffic.

Detection and Recognition

A disproportionate number of cycling deaths occur at night. Most often, these involve cyclists being struck from behind by motorists who do not see them or fail to accommodate them. In addition, there are more chemically impaired drivers on the road at night, vision problems are more pronounced, and reaction times are reduced. Well-prepared cyclists can take steps to lessen the effects of darkness on safe cycling, but this requires a thoughtful, systematic approach.

Many inexperienced cyclists who ride at night believe that being seen will protect them from the threat of vehicular traffic. The use of active lighting, bright clothing, and reflectors may call attention to the fact that something is on the roadway as drivers approach, but drivers often fail to identify what the object is.

Detection—being noticed—is only half of the objective. The other half is recognition that the object ahead is a cyclist. Recognition identifies the object as one that is moving, both forward and laterally. An approaching driver must react to a cyclist in a manner that differs from how he or she would react to a mailbox, barricade, or other stationary object. Moving objects take longer to pass than stationary ones, and in the case of a bicycle, there is likely to be some side-to-side movement. The extra time and space required for a vehicle to

FIGURE 11-3 Retro-reflective material on the bike and uniform provides a high degree of visibility.

pass translates to extra time for contact with the cyclist.

Recognition can be accomplished fairly easily by emphasizing two features that distinguish cyclists from other objects, thus creating a signature. The first is the unique shape of a person. This can be done by accenting the head, torso, arms, and legs with reflective tape or visible clothing. Because the head is highest, it may be most effective to add reflective material to the helmet. Additional reflective material may be added to supplement the outline of a person.

The second feature, and the one that is most effective in identifying a cyclist, is to accent the motion of pedaling. While most states require a red reflector on the rear of the bike, the most critical reflectors are probably those on the rear of each pedal. These reflectors positively identify the object as a bicycle and are most likely to produce the required caution from the driver of an approaching vehicle.

As long as the recognition factor is not ignored, the more reflective material on the bike or the rider, the better. While it is obvious that reflective surface area is critical, several small reflectors are more effective than one large one. If using reflective tape, cut it into small pieces and distribute it to different parts of the bike. Again, to draw attention to the pedaling motion, concentrate on the moving parts, particularly the crankarms.

Identification of the Object

Detection—being noticed—is only half of the objective. The other half is recognition that the object ahead is a cyclist. Recognition identifies the object as one that is moving, both forward and laterally.

Stealth and Visibility

EMS cyclists are almost always at an advantage when they are highly visible. The same is not always true for law enforcement and some security officers. Many police agencies use bicycle officers in drug enforcement or other covert activities. These officers are at an advantage when they are not seen or heard until they choose to be. Often, they will employ a variety of techniques to maintain stealth. The use of flat black paint on frames, handlebars, rims, and cranks is common. The use of reflectors or active lighting may be kept to a minimum. Anything that may produce glare or a reflection will be eliminated if possible.

The same is true of clothing, including helmets. The shininess of a helmet can be eliminated through the use of a dark nylon helmet cover. Some departments use different uniforms for day and night patrol. Some use an all-dark uniform, which enhances the officers' ability to use shadows for concealment when necessary. However, every bike patrol member should keep in mind the safety aspect of being able to be seen when it is necessary, such as when in traffic. Other ways to maintain stealth are discussed in Chapter 18.

Conclusion

Cycling at night exposes the public safety cyclist to various hazards. These hazards can be alleviated through training, practice, and common sense. Proper active and passive lighting can reduce the risks of being struck by an automobile dramatically. Operating more slowly and with greater caution can enable the rider to detect surface hazards in time to avoid them. Taking shadows and darkness into consideration prior to attempting to clear even a familiar obstacle can reduce the risk of a crash or fall. Operating in pairs and communicating your location will enhance rider safety. Perhaps most important is knowing your beat. When working at night, it is crucial to know every inch of the patrol area, especially the normal surface and other hazards. Slow down and take time to see, hear, and sense more of what is around you.

Reference

Gatlin, Nick (2002). Reflections on Being Seen. *IPMBA News*, Summer, page 10.

12

Bicycle Maintenance and Repairs

Introduction

There are two kinds of maintenance: preventive maintenance and repairs. Both are necessary to keep a public safety bike on the road. Preventive maintenance keeps a bike in good working order and prevents small problems from developing into large ones. Proper maintenance and repair are important not only for rider safety, but also because they extend the life and serviceability of the bike fleet. All public safety cyclists should be able to repair flat tires, adjust brake and derailleur cables, and repair or replace broken or worn chains. These repairs are often needed in the field. Public safety cyclists should also clean and lube their own bikes. However, bikes must be taken to a trained mechanic—either in-house or at a bike shop—for periodic safety checks and repairs unless the cyclist is properly trained and experienced in making those repairs.

All but the most basic adjustments and repairs are beyond the scope of this book. Readers who wish to learn more about bike maintenance should consult a bike repair book or attend a training course such as the IPMBA Maintenance Officers Certification Course.

The ABC Quick Check

One of the fundamentals of preventive maintenance is called the "ABC Quick Check." This should be completed every time you ride, both at the beginning of your shift and whenever the bike has been out of your sight. The ABC Quick Check requires just a few visual and physical checks. If the bike needs repairs or adjustments beyond your ability, it should be scheduled for maintenance with a qualified mechanic. If the ABC Quick Check does not reveal any problems with the bike, you are ready to start your shift.

■ "A" Is for Air

Check the tire pressure. Tires should be inflated to the rated pressure printed on the sidewall (pounds per square inch). Stay within the range, going higher or lower depending upon the type of surface on which you ride the most. Use a gauge to verify the tire pressure (FIGURE 12-1). Check for damage to the sidewalls and tread. Damage to the sidewalls can result if the brakes are not adjusted properly. If the bands are showing, the tire needs to be replaced immediately. If this is noticed in the field or if a flat is caused by a sidewall tear, use a folded dollar bill, piece of cardboard, or a tire boot between the sidewall and tube for a temporary fix.

FIGURE 12-1 Using a tire pressure gauge is the most accurate way to ensure proper tire inflation.

■ "B" Is for Brakes

Check the brakes for wear and adjustment. This is extremely important if your agency uses pool bikes that are shared by multiple riders. To check the brakes, hold the brake lever down and roll the bike forward and back. If it is possible to pull the brake lever to the handlebar, the brakes need to be adjusted and/or serviced. The rule of thumb dictates that the distance between the handlebar and the en-

FIGURE 12-2 The distance between the handlebar and the engaged brake lever should be approximately the width of a thumb.

FIGURE 12-3 Grip the crankarms, not the pedals, and attempt to move them sideways.

gaged brake lever should be no less than the width of a thumb (**FIGURE 12-2**).

Visually inspect the brake pads for wear. Pads for rim brakes have depressions to indicate wear; when these are no longer visible, it is time to replace the pads. Pads for disc brakes should be replaced when they are thinner than 1.0 mm. Check the cables and housings, making sure the cables travel smoothly, there are no kinks, and the ends are not frayed. If the cables stick, lubricate as described in the lubrication section of this chapter, and if they are frayed, have them replaced. Check disc brakes for leakage from hydraulic lines. Hydraulic lines should be serviced by a qualified technician.

■ "C" Is for Crank

Check the crank set. This is part of the drivetrain of the bicycle, comprising the bottom bracket, the crankarms, and the chainrings. To check the crank set, take the left and right crankarms (not the pedals) in your hands and attempt to move them sideways (**FIGURE 12-3**). There should be no lateral movement. If both move, there is a problem with the bottom bracket and the bike should be taken to a mechanic. If only one moves, that crankarm is loose and must be secured prior to riding the bike.

■ "Quick" Is for Quick-Releases

Quick-release hubs need to be tight, but not too tight. If the quick release is too tight, the bearings in the wheel may be compressed, causing damage. The proper pressure has been obtained if pushing on the lever while closing the quick release leaves a

FIGURE 12-4 Quick releases on wheels should face up and backwards.

momentary impression on the palm of your hand. The closed levers should face up and backward to minimize the chance of them catching on anything while you ride (**FIGURE 12-4**). They also should always be positioned on the non-drive side. Quick-release brakes, which are opened when removing or installing wheels, need to be in the closed position. When closed, the brake pads should not rub against the rims. The security of all other quick releases, such as the seat post, should also be checked.

■ "Check" Your Derailleur

"Check" reminds you to check that your derailleur and shift levers are working properly. Take a brief, slow ride to ensure both components are functioning smoothly. This ride should also be used to ensure that all bike systems are working properly. Pick the bike up a few inches above the ground and bounce it. If a quick release on the wheel(s) is not engaged or has malfunctioned, a clunking noise will be heard. This can also be used to noise test the bike to ensure that mechanical issues or items in the rack bag will not compromise an officer's stealth advantage.

ABC Quick Check

A: Check Air pressure.
B: Check Brakes.
C: Check Cranks.
Quick: Check Quick releases.
Check: Take a short ride to Check that everything is working properly.

Rules of Maintenance

Performing the ABC Quick Check can reveal damage and wear. It is best to fix these potential problems before they become more significant. Sometimes, even with preventive maintenance, breakdowns occur. Whether you are preventing or fixing a problem, it is wise to adhere to the three basic rules of maintenance: keep your bike clean and lubricated; do not try to fix what you do not understand; and never try to fix anything without the correct tools.

Three Rules of Maintenance

RULE 1: Keep your bike clean and lubricated.
RULE 2: Do not try to fix what you do not understand.
RULE 3: Never try to fix anything without the correct tools.

Tools

To maintain a bicycle, it is necessary to invest in bike-specific tools, which are available from a variety of manufacturers. In many instances, substituting general tools for bike-specific tools can result in further damage to the bike.

Every bicycle should be equipped with a basic tool kit. These tools can be used to make adjustments and perform emergency repairs. Not all bikes require the same tools (some are make- and model-specific) so purchasing tools that fit the specific bike should be part of equipping it for duty.

Basic Bicycle Tool Kit

2-, 3-, 4-, 5-, 6-, and 8-mm Allen wrenches
Spare tube, patch kit, and pump (Schrader or Presta to match the valves)
Tire levers
Small chain rivet tool
Screwdriver

Cleaning

Keeping a bike clean is an essential part of keeping it well-maintained. A clean bike not only presents a professional image, it will perform better and last longer. Routine cleaning can help the rider locate damage or wear before a breakdown occurs. A frequently ridden bike should be washed once a week, especially in the winter, or any time it gets dirty.

Most cleaning can be done with soap, water, and a brush. Soap and water are easier on you and the environment than stronger solvents, which are generally only needed for the drivetrain, if at all. Avoid using the high-pressure sprayers at pay car washes to clean your bike. The soaps are corrosive, and the high pressure forces the soaps into bearings, pivots, and frame tubes, causing extensive damage over time.

■ Cleaning the Bicycle

Using a bike stand is highly recommended when scrubbing a bike. In the absence of a bike stand, the bike can be hung from a garage ceiling with rope, stood upside down on the saddle and handlebar, or balanced on the front of the fork with the front wheel removed.

Clean the wheels while they are on the bike. Remove the wheels to clean the frame, fork, and components.

If the bike has a chain hanger (a little nub attached to the inner side of the right seat stay, a few centimeters above the dropout), hook the chain over it. If not, pull the chain back over a dowel stick or an old rear hub secured into the dropouts. Fill a bucket with hot water and dish soap. Scrub the entire bike and wheels with a stiff nylon-bristle brush. Leave the chain, cogs, chainrings, and derailleurs for last. Rinse the bike with water, either by hosing it off with a low-pressure spray or by wiping it with a wet rag.

Avoid getting water in the bearings of the bottom bracket, headset, pedals, or hubs. Also avoid getting water into the lip seals of suspension forks, as well as any pivots or shock seals on rear-suspension systems. In addition, most metal frames and rigid forks have vent holes in the tubes to allow expanding hot gases to escape during welding. The holes are often open to the outside on the seat stays, fork legs, chainstays, and seat stay and chainstay bridges. Avoid getting water in these holes, especially if you have to use a high-pressure car wash.

■ Cleaning the Drivetrain

The drivetrain consists of an oil-covered chain running over the gears and derailleurs. It is exposed to the elements and therefore collects a great deal of dirt. Because the drivetrain translates the rider's energy into the bike's forward motion, it should move freely. Frequent cleaning and lubrication keep it rolling well and extend the life of your bike.
The drivetrain can often be cleaned sufficiently by wiping down the chain, derailleur jockey wheels, and chainrings.

- To wipe the chain, turn the cranks while holding a rag in your hand and grabbing the chain (FIGURE 12-5).
- Holding a rag, squeeze the teeth of the jockey wheel in between your index finger and thumb as you turn the crank (FIGURE 12-6).
- Slip a rag between cogs of the cassette and work it back and forth to clean each cog (FIGURE 12-7).
- Thoroughly wipe down the derailleurs and the front chainrings with the rag.

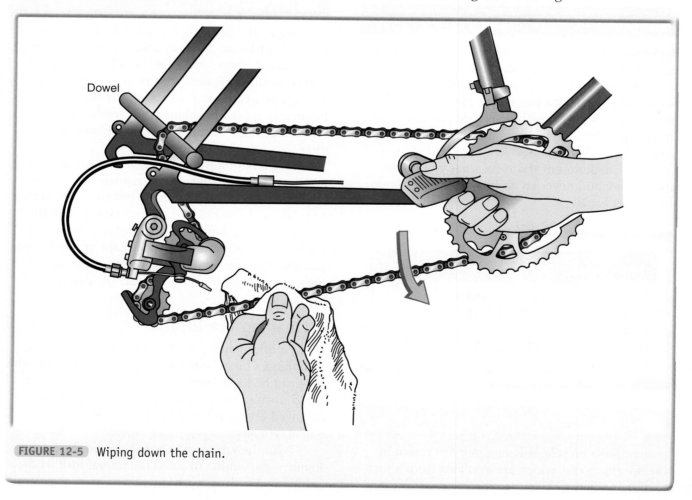

Dowel

FIGURE 12-5 Wiping down the chain.

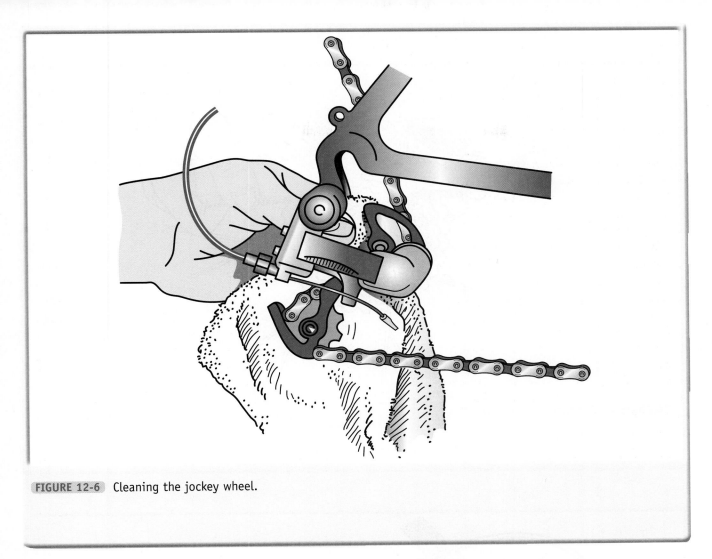

FIGURE 12-6 Cleaning the jockey wheel.

Your chain will last much longer if you perform this quick cleaning regularly and follow the cleaning by dripping chain lube on the chain and wiping it down lightly. You will be able to avoid heavy duty solvent cleanings, which are necessary when the chain is excessively dirty. You can get it just as clean as with a solvent if you wipe the chain down thoroughly after lubricating it and cleaning in between all of the outer links with cotton swabs. Although they will not fit between the inner link plates, the roller will spin with them.

Remove packed mud from the derailleurs and cogs with the soapy water and a stiff-bristled scrub brush. Use a different brush than the one used for cleaning the frame, because the bristles will become oily and smear the dirty lubricant onto the frame. Wipe the derailleurs and cogs with a cloth after brushing.

■ Solvent Cleaning of the Chain

If you frequently wipe down your chain and lubricate it sparingly by putting lube only on the chain

rollers where it is needed, you can minimize the need for solvent cleaning. However, if solvent cleaning is necessary, work in a well-ventilated area, pick an environmentally friendly solvent, and use as little of it as possible.

Because all solvents take moisture out of your skin, wear gloves, even with "green" ones. A self-contained chain cleaner with internal brushes and a solvent bath is a quick and convenient way to clean a chain (**FIGURE 12-8**), and it can be done without

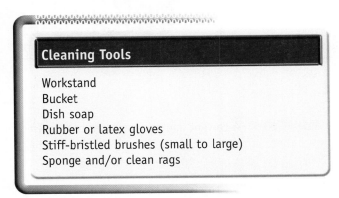

Cleaning Tools

Workstand
Bucket
Dish soap
Rubber or latex gloves
Stiff-bristled brushes (small to large)
Sponge and/or clean rags

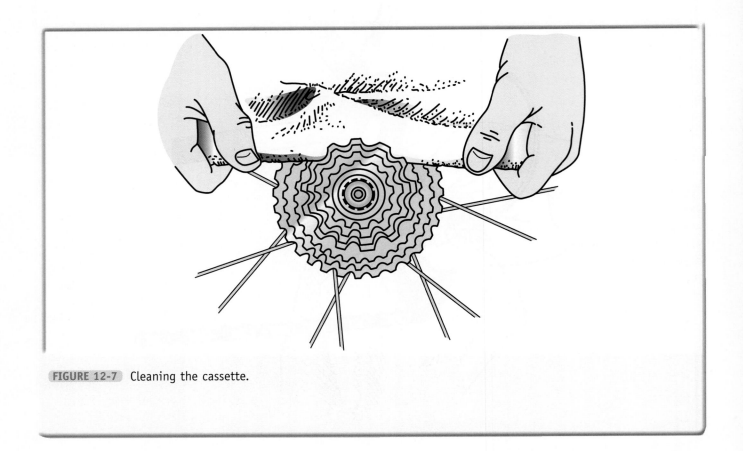

FIGURE 12-7 Cleaning the cassette.

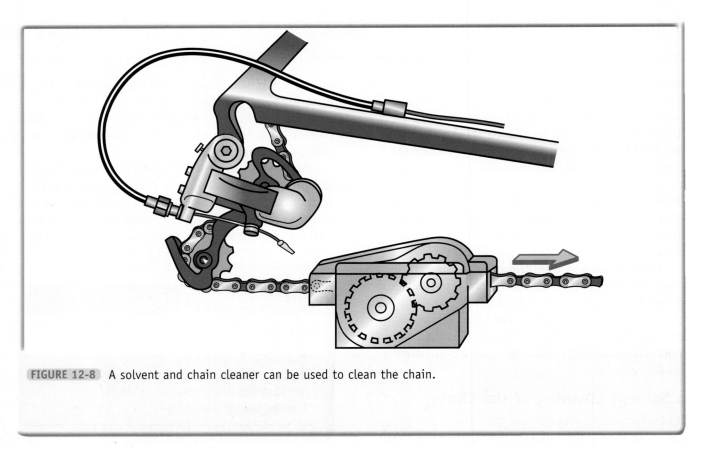

FIGURE 12-8 A solvent and chain cleaner can be used to clean the chain.

the risk of chain breakage caused by opening and closing the chain. A nylon brush or old toothbrush dipped in solvent is good for cleaning cogs, pulleys, and chainrings and can be useful for a quick clean of the chain as well.

Lubrication

Once the bicycle is cleaned, lubricants can be applied. Lubricants should not be applied to dirty bicycles as they will simply attract more dirt. Always use a high-quality, bicycle-specific lubricant. Some water-repellent sprays and lubricants contain solvents that can damage both parts and paint. Bicycle lubes can be dry, wet, or wax-based, and are designed for various weather and riding conditions. In general, wet lubes are recommended, but which type to use ultimately depends on personal experience and preference.

■ Chains

To lubricate a bicycle chain, drip a small amount of lubricant across each link (only one drop of lubricant per link), moving the chain periodically (not continuously) to gain access to all of the links. Do not be tempted to back pedal the crank slowly while dripping lubricant onto the chain. While this is better than not lubricating the chain at all, it will cause you to apply too much lubricant. The excess lubricant will attract dirt, which will result in the chain wearing out more quickly. After applying the lubricant, wipe the chain off lightly with a rag.

■ Cables and Housing

In order for your derailleurs and brakes to function properly, you must have clean, smooth-running cables (**FIGURE 12-9**). Cables and housings become more difficult to operate as they age, due to their exposure to dirt and grime. If any cable is frayed or kinked or has any broken strands, have it replaced by a qualified mechanic. If the cable is not sliding

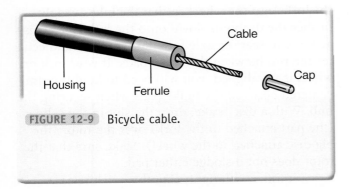

FIGURE 12-9 Bicycle cable.

well, lubricate it. Use molybdenum disulfide grease if you have it; otherwise, try a chain lubricant. Standard lithium-based greases can eventually gum up cables and restrict movement.

Derailleur Cables and Housing

To lubricate the front and rear derailleur cables and housing, follow these steps.

- Shift the chain onto the largest rear cog by lifting the rear wheel off the ground and shifting while turning the cranks.
- To create slack in the cable move the rear derailleur shifter into the smallest cog setting.
- Pull the cable housing out of the slotted cable stop.
- Slide the housing up the cable and apply lubricant to the cable where it enters the housing.
- Remove excess lubricant and replace the cable housing in the slotted cable stop.
- Move the shifter back into the largest rear cog setting to pull the cable tight.
- Shift the chain onto the largest front chainring by lifting the rear wheel off the ground and shifting while turning the cranks.
- Move the front derailleur shifter into the smallest chainring.
- Repeat steps 3-5.
- Move the front shifter back to the largest front chainring.

Brake Cables and Housing

To lubricate the brake cables and housing, follow these steps.

- Open the brake (via the cable quick release as you do when you remove a wheel).
- Pull each section of cable housing out of each slotted cable stop. If your bike does not have slotted cable stops, you will have to pull out the entire cable.
- Slide the housing up the cable, rub lubricant with your fingers on the cable section that was inside the housing, and slide the housing back into place.
- If the cable still sticks, have it replaced by a qualified mechanic.

■ Pivot Points

A few other places on a bicycle require routine lubrication. Any parts that have pivot points should be lubricated, including derailleurs, brakes, brake levers, shifters, kickstands, and clipless pedals. Do not overlube. A drop in the right place is sufficient.

Make sure that all parts to be lubricated have been cleaned properly. Apply a drop or two of lubricant to each pivot point. Avoid getting lubricant on the brake pads or rims. Wipe off excess lube with a clean rag.

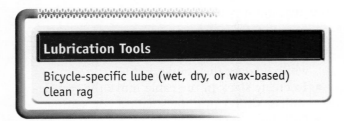

Lubrication Tools

Bicycle-specific lube (wet, dry, or wax-based)
Clean rag

Replacing or Repairing Tires and Inner Tubes

In order to replace tires and/or tubes, it is first necessary to remove and replace the wheels. Doing so requires knowledge of how to disengage and reattach the brakes and reseat the rear wheel so that the derailleur will shift properly.

■ Removing the Front Wheel

Removing the front wheel involves releasing the brake and opening the hub quick-release. Most brakes have a mechanism to release the brake arms so that they spring away from the rim, allowing the tire to pass between the pads. If yours does not, you will have to deflate the tire. V-brakes (also known as sidepull cantilevers) are released by pulling the end of the curved cable-guide tube (the "noodle") out of the horizontal link atop one of the brake arms while either holding the link or squeezing the pads against the rim with the other hand (FIGURE 12-10). Most cantilever brakes are released by pulling the enlarged head of the straddle cable out of a notch in the top of the brake arm while holding the pads against the rim with the other hand (FIGURE 12-11).

Most disc brakes allow the disc to fall away without releasing the pads, as the caliper is bolted to the fork and the disc slips in and out of it easily. However, models manufactured before the advent of disc-brake mounting tabs on the forks make wheel removal much harder. Releasing the old (mid-1990s) Dia-Compe cable-actuated hydraulic disc brakes requires opening a latch (under the caliper) that secures the caliper to the fork. The entire caliper can then be swung up and forward, allowing the wheel to come out. Do not squeeze the lever of a hydraulic disc brake when there is neither a disc

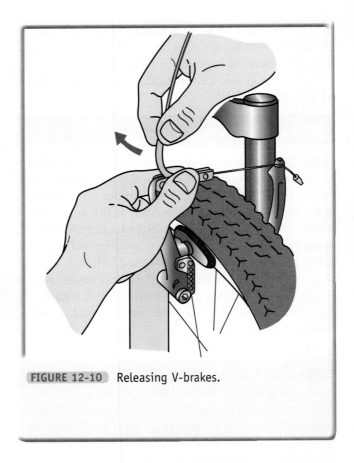

FIGURE 12-10 Releasing V-brakes.

nor a travel spacer between the pads, or else the pistons can pop out too far and you will not be able to get your rotor back between the pads without some extra work to push the pistons back into the caliper.

Detaching a wheel equipped with a quick-release skewer is easy and requires no tools. Pull outward on the lever to open it. After opening the quick-release lever, unscrew the nut on the opposite end of the quick-release skewer's shaft until both the nut and the head of the skewer clear the fork's wheel-retention tabs and pull off the wheel.

■ Installing the Front Wheel

With rim brakes, leave the brake open and lower the fork onto the wheel so that the bike's weight pushes the dropouts down onto the hub axle. This action will seat the axle fully into the fork and center the rim between the brake pads. If your fork or wheel is misaligned, you will need to hold the rim centered between the brake pads when securing the hub. With a disc brake, drop the slot in the caliper (the part attached to the fork) over the rotor (the big disc attached to the wheel). Make sure that the rotor does not dislodge either pad.

Continue with tightening the quick release

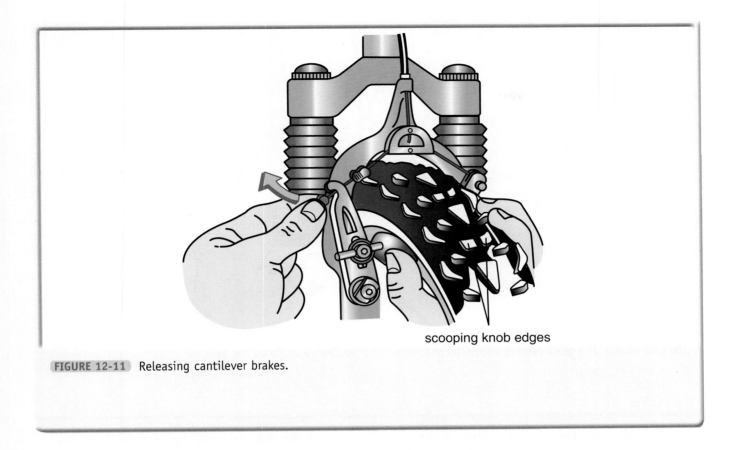

scooping knob edges

FIGURE 12-11 Releasing cantilever brakes.

skewer, remembering that the quick-release skewer is not a glorified wing nut and should not be treated as such. Hold the quick-release lever in the open position and finger-tighten the opposite-end nut until it snugs up against the face of the dropout.

Push the lever over (**FIGURE 12-12**) to the closed position (it should now be at a 90-degree angle to the axle). If done correctly, it will take a good amount of hand pressure to close the quick-release lever properly; the lever should leave its imprint on your palm for a few seconds.

If the quick-release lever does not close tightly enough, open the lever, tighten the end nut one-quarter turn, and close the lever. Repeat until tight. If the lever cannot be pushed down perpendicular to the axle, the nut is too tight. Open the quick-release lever, unscrew the end nut one-quarter turn or so, and try closing the lever. Repeat this procedure until the quick-release lever is fully closed and snug.

When you are done, position the lever pointing straight up or toward the back of the bike so that it cannot hook on obstacles and be opened accidentally. Double-check that the axle is tightened into the fork by trying to pull the wheel out.

■ Closing the Brakes

The steps required to close the brakes are the reverse of what you did to release them. With a V-brake (sidepull cantilever), hold the link in one hand, pull the noodle back, push the cable coming out of the noodle into the slot in the end of the link, and pop the end of the noodle back into the slotted hole (Figure 12-10 in reverse). With a cantilever brake, hold the brake pads against the rim with one hand and hook the enlarged end of the straddle cable back into the end of the brake arm with your other hand (Figure 12-11 in reverse). With most disc brakes, the brake is ready to apply as soon as the wheel is installed.

Check that the brake cables are connected securely by squeezing the levers. Lift the front end of the bike and spin the front wheel, gently applying the brakes several times. Check that the pads are not dragging, and re-center the wheel if necessary.

■ Removing the Rear Wheel

Removing the rear wheel is done in the same way as removing the front, with the added complication of the chain and cogs.

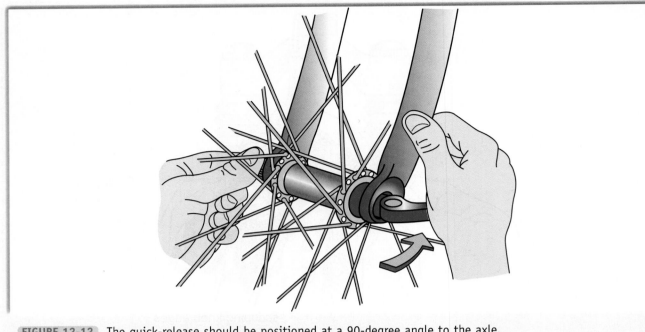

FIGURE 12-12 The quick-release should be positioned at a 90-degree angle to the axle.

First release the brakes as described above. Shift the chain onto the smallest cog by lifting the rear wheel off of the ground and shifting while turning the cranks. To release the wheel from the rear dropouts and the brakes, follow the same procedure as with the front wheel. When you push the wheel out, move the chain out of the way by grabbing the rear derailleur and pulling it back so the jockey wheels (pulley wheels) move out of the way, while pushing forward on the quick-release or axle nuts with your thumbs and letting the wheel fall as you hold the bike up (**FIGURE 12-13**). If the bottom half of the chain catches the wheel as it falls, jiggle the wheel while lifting it to free the cogs from the chain.

■ Installing the Rear Wheel

Make sure that the rear derailleur is shifted to its outermost position (under the smallest cog). Slip the wheel up between the seat stays and maneuver the upper section of chain onto the smallest cog (Figure 12-13). Set the bike down on the rear wheel, and as you let the bike drop down, pull the rear derailleur back with your right hand and pull the axle ends back into the dropouts with your index fingers. Your thumbs push forward on the rear dropouts, which should now slide over the axle

ends. If the axle does not slip into the dropouts, you may need to spread the dropouts apart or squeeze them toward each other to get them to fall between the quick-release ends and the axle ends. If you have a rear disc brake, guide the rotor in between the brake pads.

Check that the axle is fully seated in the dropouts, which should center the wheel between the brake pads. If the rim rubs on one brake pad, hold the rim in a centered position as you secure the axle. Tighten the quick-release skewer, bolt-on skewer, or axle nuts in the same way as explained for the front wheel. Reconnect the rear brake the same way as you did on the front wheel.

■ Removing a Standard Tire and Tube

Remove the wheel. If your tire is not already flat, deflate it. To deflate a Schrader valve (**FIGURE 12-14A**), push down on the valve pin with something thin enough to fit in that will not break off, such as a pen cap or a paper clip. Presta valves (**FIGURE 12-14B**) are thinner and have a small threaded rod with a tiny nut on the end. To let air out, unscrew the little nut a few turns and push down on the thin rod. To seal, tighten the little nut down again (with your fingers only!); leave it tightened down for riding.

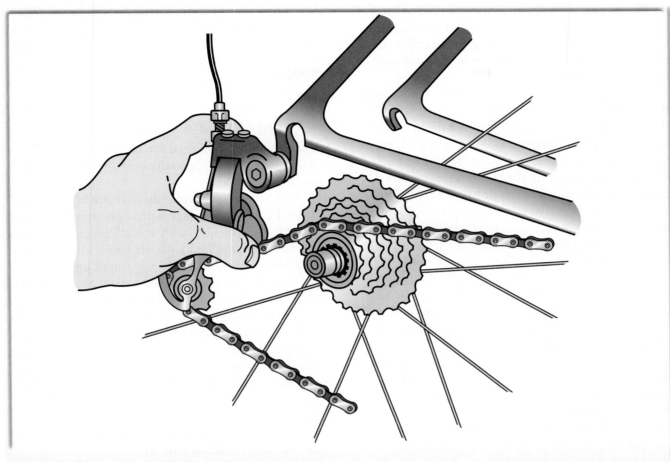

FIGURE 12-13 Removal and installation of rear wheel.

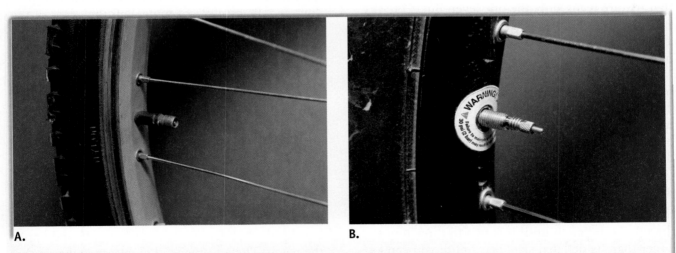

A.

B.

FIGURE 12-14A-B Inner tubes are equipped with either Schrader (A) or Presta (B) valves.

If you can push the tire bead off of the rim with your thumbs without using tire levers, do so, because there is less chance of damaging either the tube or the tire. It is easiest to start just one side or the other of the valve stem.

Removal of the tire is accomplished most easily by starting near the valve stem. The beads of the deflated tire can have fallen into the dropped center of the rim on the opposite side of the wheel, making it effectively a smaller-circumference rim off of which you are pushing the tire bead. If you try to push the tire bead off of (or onto) the rim on the side opposite the valve stem, the circumference on which the bead is resting is larger, because the valve stem is forcing the beads to stay up on their seating ledges opposite the side where you are working.

If you are not able to get the tire off with only your hands, insert a tire lever, then scoop the side up between the rim sidewall and the tire until you catch the edge of the tire bead. Again, this is most easily done adjacent to the valve stem. Pry down on the lever until the tire bead is pulled out over the rim (**FIGURE 12-15A**). If the lever has a hook on the other end, hook it onto the nearest spoke. Otherwise, keep holding it down.

Place the next lever a few inches away, and do the same thing (Figure 12-15A). If needed, place a third lever a few inches farther on, pry it out, and continue sliding this lever around the tire, pulling the bead out as you go (**FIGURE 12-15B**). Some people slide their fingers around under the bead, but beware of cutting your fingers on sharp tire beads. There are various "quick" tire levers on the market that require using only the one lever. But if the tire is really stubborn, the three-lever method outlined above may be the only way you will be able to remove the tire.

Once the bead is off on one side, pull the tube out. If you are patching or replacing the tube, you do not need to remove the other side of the tire from the rim. If you are replacing the tire, the other bead should come off easily with your fingers. If it does not, use the tire levers.

■ Finding Leaks

If the leak location is not obvious, put some air in the tube to inflate it until it is two to three times larger than its deflated size. Be careful; you can explode it if you put in too much air, especially with latex or urethane tubes. Listen and/or feel for air coming out, and mark the leak(s). If you cannot find the leak by listening and/or feeling, submerge the tube in water. Look for air bubbling out and mark the spot(s). Only small holes can be patched. If the hole is bigger than the eraser end of a pencil, a round patch is not likely to work. A slit of up to an inch or so can be repaired with a long oval patch.

■ Using Standard Patches

Use a patch kit designed for bicycle tires that has thin, gummy edges, usually orange, surrounding the black patches.

Dry the tube thoroughly near the hole. Rough up and clean the surface within about a 1-inch radius around the hole with a small piece of sandpaper (usually supplied with the patch kit). Do not touch the sanded area. Do not rough up the tube with one of those little metal graters that come with some patch kits; they tend to shred the tube.

Apply patch cement in a thin, smooth layer all over an area centered on the hole. Cover an area that is bigger than the size of the patch. Let the glue dry until there are no more shiny, wet spots (5 to 10 minutes). Oftentimes, the cellophane atop the patch is scored. If you fold the patch now, this cellophane will split at the scored cuts and be easy to remove after the patch is well affixed. Remove the foil backing from the gummy underside of the patch (but not the cellophane top cover). Cover the hole with the patch and push it down in place, making sure that all of the gummy edges are glued down.

Although there is no need to do so, the standard procedure is to remove the cellophane top covering. Be careful not to peel off the edges of the patch when removing the cellophane. If the cellophane atop the patch was scored and you folded it before sticking down the patch, it will split at the scored cuts, allowing you to peel outward and avoid pulling the newly adhered patch away from the tube.

■ Using Glueless Patches

There are a number of adhesive-backed patches on the market that do not require cement. Most often, you simply need to clean the area around the hole with the little alcohol pad supplied with the patch. Let the alcohol dry, peel the backing off, and apply the patch. The advantage of glueless patches is that they are very fast to use, take up little room in a pack, and you never open your patch kit to discover that your glue tube is dried up. The disadvantage is that they do not stick nearly as well as the

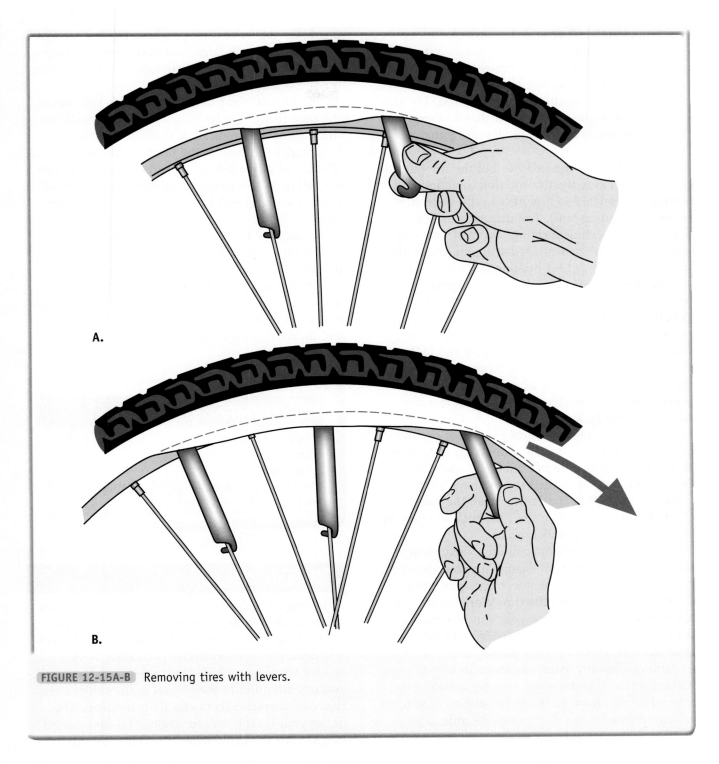

FIGURE 12-15A-B Removing tires with levers.

standard type. Glueless patches are suitable in emergencies, but they are not a long-term fix as is the case with standard, glued-on patches.

■ Installing a Tube and Tire

Feel around the inside of the tire to see if there is anything sticking through that can puncture the tube. This is best done by sliding a rag all the way around the inside of the tire. The rag will catch on anything sharp and prevent your fingers from being cut by anything stuck in the tire. If you find any sharp objects, remove them so they do not cause subsequent flats.

Replace any tire that has worn-out areas (inside or out) where the tread-casing fibers appear to be cut or frayed. Examine the rim to be certain that the rim tape is in place and that there are no spokes or anything else sticking up that can puncture the tube. Replace the rim tape if necessary. With an asymmetrically drilled rim, make sure the adhesive and/or the fit of the rim tape is very good. The rim tape only needs to slide over a little bit to expose the edge of one of the offset holes and puncture your tube.

By hand, push one side bead of the tire onto the rim, first checking the tire-rotation direction and orient the tire label so it is next to the valve stem for ease of finding both. Tire direction makes a difference for technical riding. On the front, you want the concave or v-shaped scooping edges of the tread blocks forward for braking (Figure 12-11), whereas on the rear you want the scooping edges oriented backward for propulsion traction. Some tires have an arrow indicating rotation direction for use either on the front or the rear. If yours does not, hold the tire up above your head and look at the tread as the ground sees it. Consider which way the wheel is rotating and what happens during braking and driving. The best way to orient the tread will then be apparent.

If you wish, smear talcum powder or tire talc around the inside of the tire and on the outside of the tube, so the two do not adhere to each other. Put just enough air in the tube to give it shape. Close the valve, if it is a Presta. Push the valve through the valve hole in the rim. Push the tube up inside the tire all the way around.

Starting at the side opposite the valve stem, push the tire bead onto the rim with your thumbs, making sure that the tube doesn't get pinched between the tire bead and the rim. Work around the rim in both directions with your thumbs, pushing the tire onto the rim (FIGURE 12-16A). Finish from both sides at the valve (FIGURE 12-16B).

You can usually install a mountain bike tire without tools. If you cannot, first try deflating the tube when you have gotten as far around as you can with your hands. You should now be able to push the tire on the last bit, as deflating the tube will allow the beads on the far side, opposite the valve stem, to drop into the lower center of the rim. If this does not allow you to complete the mounting by hand, use tire levers to pry the tire bead on, but make sure you do not catch any of the tube under the edge of the bead. Finish the same way, at the valve.

Reseat the valve stem and draw up any nearby folds of the tube stuck under the tire bead by push-ing up on the valve after you have pushed the last bit of bead onto the rim. You may have to manipulate the tire so that the entire tube is tucked under the tire bead.

Go around the rim and inspect for any part of the tube that might be protruding out from under the edge of the tire bead. If there is a fold of the tube under the edge of the bead, it can blow the tire off the rim either when you inflate it or while you are riding. It will sound as though a gun went off next to you and will leave you with an unusable tube.

Pump the tire up to within five pounds per square inch of its maximum recommended tire pressure.

Once you have inflated the tube fully, place the wheel back on the bicycle. Center the wheel and secure it with the quick release. Reattach the brakes and do another ABC Quick Check.

Flat Tire Repair Tools

Tire levers (three)
Patch kit
Spare tube
Air source (pump or inflator) compatible with tire valve type (Presta or Schrader) (Figure 12-14 A-B).

Cable Tension

Adjusting the cable tension is fairly easy once you understand how the cable works. Bicycle cables connect the brake levers and shifters to the brakes and derailleurs, respectively. The cables work against tension and housing friction, so the more you pay attention to the stretch of the cables over time and maintain them and their housings, the better your bicycle will function. The device used to fine-tune the cable tension is called the barrel adjuster. Each barrel adjuster on the bicycle serves as a threaded socket for the ends of the cable housing. The barrel adjuster is hollow, allowing the inner cable to pass to the brake or derailleur mechanism. The barrel adjuster threads in or out, allowing the rider to dial in the proper tension without tools. Once you understand the role that a bicycle cable plays, the barrel adjuster allows for a safer and more efficient ride.

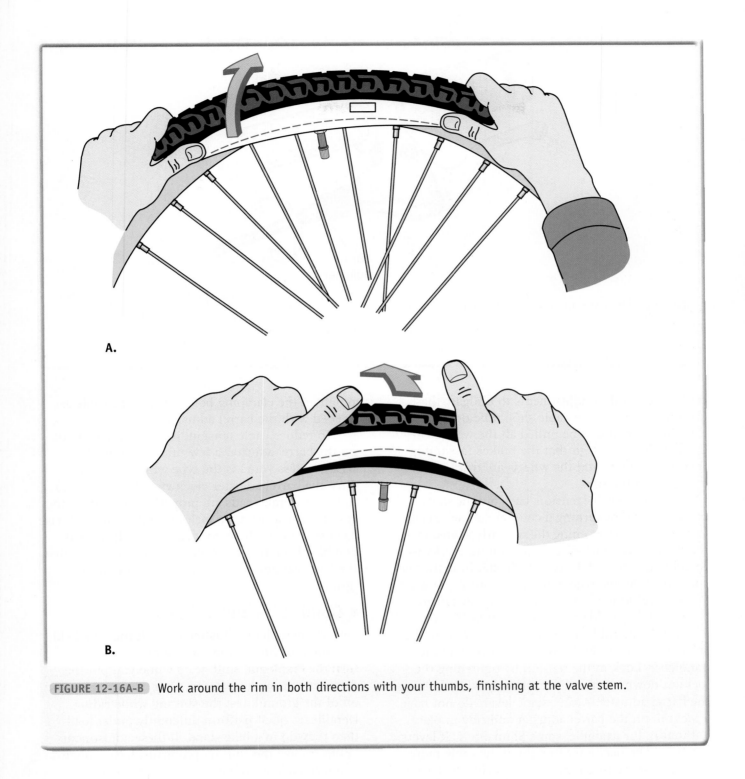

A.

B.

FIGURE 12-16A-B Work around the rim in both directions with your thumbs, finishing at the valve stem.

▪ Brakes

Given that cables transfer braking force from the levers to most brakes, proper installation and maintenance of the cables are critical to good brake performance. If there is excess friction in the cable system, the brakes will not work properly, no matter how well the brakes, calipers, and levers are adjusted. Each cable should move freely; have a mechanic replace any cable that has broken strands.

Cable Tensioning

As brake pads wear and cables stretch, the cable needs to be shortened. The barrel adjuster on the brake lever (**FIGURE 12-17**), through which the

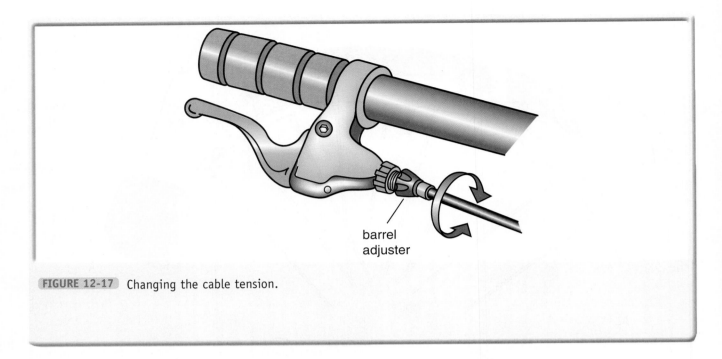

FIGURE 12-17 Changing the cable tension.

cable passes, offers adjustments to mitigate these kinds of changes. The cable should be tight enough that the lever cannot be pulled all the way to the grip, yet loose enough that the brakes (assuming they are centered and the wheels are true) are not dragging on the rims.

To increase cable tension, back out the slotted barrel adjuster by turning it counterclockwise (Figure 12-17) after loosening the similarly slotted locknut. Determine clockwise versus counterclockwise rotation direction of the barrel adjuster from the perspective of the end where the cable housing enters. Some barrel adjusters have no locknut; just turn them, and they hold their adjustment by friction.

Adjust the cable tension so that there is no less than a thumb's width between the lever and the handlebar. Lock in the tension by tightening the locknut down against the lever body while holding the barrel adjuster. Again, some levers do not have a locknut on the barrel adjuster and stay in place without it, for example, some Shimano XTR levers.

It may be necessary to tighten the cable more than is possible by simply fiddling with the barrel adjuster. If you need to take up more slack than the barrel adjuster allows, first, screw in the barrel adjuster almost all the way. This leaves some adjustment in the system for brake setup and cable stretch. Loosen the bolt clamping the cable at the brake. Check the cable for wear. If there are any frayed strands, have the cable replaced by a qualified mechanic. Otherwise, pull the cable tight, and

retighten the clamping bolt. Tension the cable as needed with the barrel adjuster.

To reduce cable tension, back out the locknut on the barrel adjuster a few turns (counterclockwise), unless yours is the type without a locknut. Turn the barrel adjuster clockwise (Figure 12-17) until your brake pads are properly spaced from the rim. If your lever has a locknut, tighten it clockwise against the lever body to lock in the adjustment. Double-check that the cable is tight enough so that the lever cannot be squeezed all the way to the grip.

■ Derailleurs and Shifters

Perform derailleur adjustments with the bike held in a stand or hung from the ceiling so you can turn the crank and shift gears while you put the derailleur through its paces. After adjusting it off of the ground, test the shifting while riding. Derailleurs often perform differently under load than they do in a bike stand. If these adjustments fail to resolve the shifting problems, have a qualified mechanic examine and repair the bike.

Limit screws control the derailleurs' range of motion. These are set by the manufacturer and should only be adjusted by a certified mechanic. Changing the settings of these screws could cause the chain to fall between the largest rear gear and the spokes of the rear wheel, which could result in the chain cutting through the moving spokes and causing the wheel to collapse.

Before starting, lubricate or replace the chain so that the whole drivetrain runs smoothly.

Indexed Rear Shifters

With an indexed shifting system (one that clicks into each gear), it is the cable tension that determines whether the derailleur moves to the proper gear with each click.

With the chain on the large chainring in the front, shift the rear derailleur to the smallest cog. Keep clicking the shifter until you are sure it will not let out any more cable (or it will not pull any more cable, if you have a Low Normal or Rapid Rise rear derailleur). Shift one click in the other direction; this should move the chain smoothly to the second cog. If the chain does not climb to the second cog, or if it does so slowly, the cable tension is off.

On a traditional rear derailleur, increase the tension in the cable by turning either the derailleur cable barrel adjuster (FIGURE 12-18) or the shifter barrel adjuster (FIGURE 12-19) counterclockwise (when viewed from the end of the barrel adjuster, where the cable housing inserts into it, as if it were

a screw viewed from the top). Turn the opposite way for a Low Normal or Rapid Rise derailleur.

If you run out of barrel-adjustment range and the cable is still not tight enough, retighten both adjusters clockwise, to one turn from where they stop, loosen the cable anchor bolt and pull some of the slack out of the cable. Tighten the anchor bolt and repeat the adjustment. Shimano Rapid Rise, some Shimano Low Normal, SRAM, and Sachs DiRT derailleurs have no barrel adjuster. For these, use only the barrel adjuster on the shifter.

If the chain overshifts the second cog or comes close to overshifting, decrease the cable tension by turning one of the barrel adjusters clockwise (or with a Low Normal or Rapid Rise derailleur, increase the tension by turning one of the barrel adjusters counterclockwise). Again, always determine clockwise and counterclockwise from the position of the end of the barrel adjuster where the cable housing inserts into it.

Keep adjusting the cable tension in small increments while shifting back and forth between the two smallest cogs until the chain moves easily in

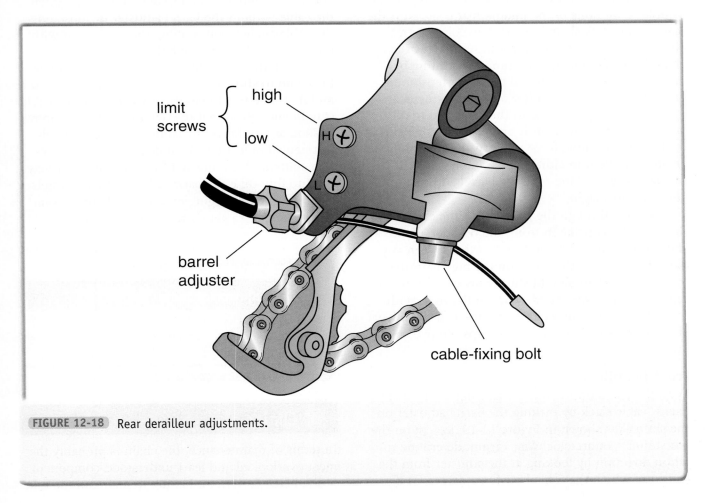

FIGURE 12-18 Rear derailleur adjustments.

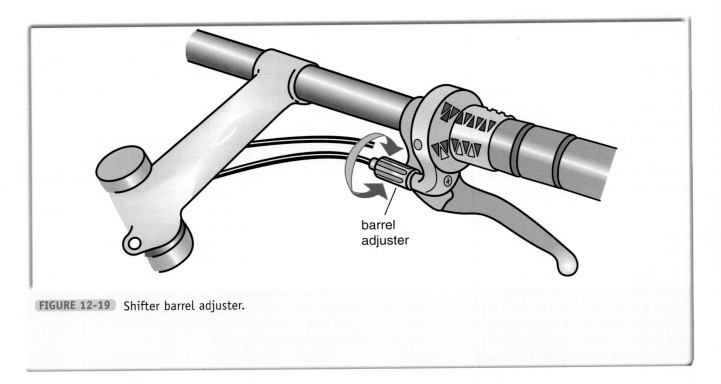

FIGURE 12-19 Shifter barrel adjuster.

both directions. Shift to the middle chainring in the front and onto one of the middle rear cogs. Shift the rear derailleur back and forth a few cogs, again checking for precise and quick movement of the chain from cog to cog. Fine-tune the shifting by making small adjustments to the cable-tensioning barrel adjuster on the shifter or rear derailleur.

Shift to the inner ring in the front and to the largest cog in the rear. Shift up and down one click in the rear, checking for symmetry and precision of chain movement in either direction between the two largest cogs. Fine-tune the barrel adjuster until you get it just right.

Go back through the gears. With the chain in the middle chainring in front, the rear derailleur should shift smoothly back and forth between any pair of cogs. With the chain on the big chainring, the rear derailleur should shift easily on all but perhaps the largest one or two cogs in the rear. With the chain on the inner chainring, the rear derailleur should shift easily on all but perhaps the two smallest cogs.

Front Derailleurs

With the chain on the inner chainring, remove any excess cable slack by turning the barrel adjuster on the shifter (as shown in Figure 12-19, except on the left shifter) counterclockwise (again, determine rotation direction by looking at the adjuster from the end from which the cable housing emerges, as if you were looking at the top of a bolt). Or, tighten the cable without the barrel adjuster by loosening the cable anchor bolt, pulling the cable tight with pliers, and tightening the bolt.

Check that the cable is loose enough to allow the chain to shift smoothly and repeatedly from the middle to the inner chainring. Check that the cable is tight enough so that the derailleur starts to move as soon as you move the shifter. This tension adjustment should work for indexed as well as friction shifters. With indexed front shifting, you may want to fine-tune the barrel adjuster to avoid noise from the chain dragging on the derailleur in some cross-gears, or to get more precise shifting.

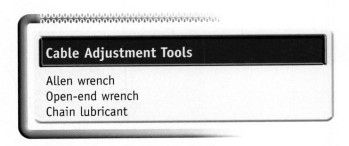

Cable Adjustment Tools

Allen wrench
Open-end wrench
Chain lubricant

Chains

In terms of maintenance, the chain is probably the most overlooked and least understood component of the bike's drivetrain. Failure to maintain the bike chain properly will cause sluggish operation of the bike, shifting problems, and chain breakage.

■ Chain Replacement

As the rollers, pins, and plates wear out, the chain lengthens. That, in turn, hastens the wear and tear on other drivetrain parts. An elongated chain concentrates the load on each individual gear tooth, rather than distributing it over all of the teeth that the chain contacts, causing the gear teeth to become hook-shaped and the tooth valleys to become wider. If such wear has already occurred, a new chain will not solve the problem. A new chain will not mesh with deformed teeth, and it is likely to skip whenever you pedal hard. To prevent the extra wear and tear, replace your chain regularly.

How long it takes for the chain to wear out will vary, depending on chain type, maintenance, riding conditions, and strength and weight of the rider. The chain should be replaced every 500 to 1,000 miles, especially for bikes ridden in dirty conditions by a large rider. Lighter riders riding mostly on paved roads can often extend replacement time to more than 2,000 miles.

■ Chain Elongation (Chain Wear)

The simplest method to determine the degree of chain wear is to employ a chain-elongation gauge. The gauge falls completely into the chain if the chain is worn out. If the chain is still in good shape, the gauge's tooth will not go all of the way into the chain.

Another way to measure chain wear is with an accurate ruler. Chains are measured on an inch standard and should measure a half-inch between adjacent rivets. There should be exactly an integral number of links in 1 foot—12 links, to be exact, where each complete link consists of an inner and outer pair of plates (FIGURE 12-20).

Set one end of the ruler on a rivet edge, and measure to the rivet edge at the other end of the ruler, 12 links away. The distance between these rivets should be 12 inches exactly. If it is 12-$\frac{1}{8}$ inches or greater, the chain must be replaced; if it is 12-$\frac{1}{16}$ inches or more, it is a good idea to replace it. (If you have any titanium or alloy cogs or an 11-tooth small cog, it is necessary to replace it.) Some chain manufacturers recommend replacement if elongation is 1%, or $\frac{1}{2}$ inch over 50 complete link pairs (50 inches), which is a little less than $\frac{1}{8}$ inch over 12 link pairs (1 foot). If the chain is off of the bike, you can hang it next to a new chain for comparison; if the used one is more than $\frac{1}{2}$ inch longer for the same number of links, replace it.

■ Chain Removal

The following procedure applies to all standard derailleur chains except those with a master link. Master link-equipped chains include all Wippermann and Taya chains, chains with Lickton's Super Link, Power Link-equipped SRAM or Sachs chains, and many KMC chains. All of these chains snap open by hand at the master link, although if necessary, they can also be opened at any other link by using a chain tool as described below.

Place any link over the back teeth on a chain tool (FIGURE 12-21). Tighten the chain-tool handle clockwise to push the link rivet out. Unless you

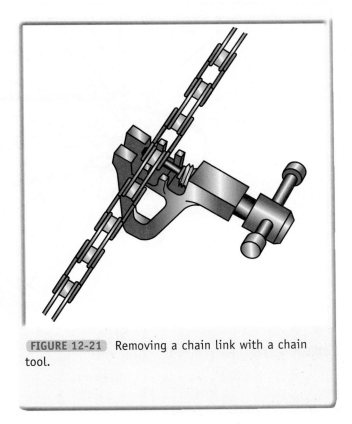

FIGURE 12-21 Removing a chain link with a chain tool.

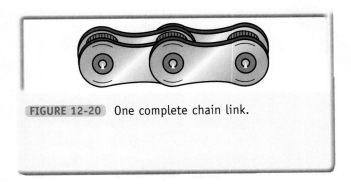

FIGURE 12-20 One complete chain link.

have a Shimano chain and a new subpin for it, be careful to leave 1 mm or so of rivet protruding inward from the chain plate to hook the chain back together when reassembling.

■ Chain Installation

Start by determining the chain length. If you are installing a new chain, determine how many links you will need in one of two ways: (a) under the assumption that your old chain was the correct length, compare it with the new one and use the same number of links; (b) if you have a standard long-cage mountain bike rear derailleur on your bike, wrap the chain around the big chainring and the biggest cog without going through either derailleur. Bring the two ends together until the ends overlap; one full link (Figure 12-20) should be the amount of overlap (**FIGURE 12-22**). Remove the remaining links and save them in your spare-tire bag so you have spares in case of chain breakage on the trail.

Routing the chain properly is the next step. Shift the derailleurs so that the chain will rest on the smallest cog in the rear and on the smallest chainring up front. Starting with the rear-derailleur pulley that is farthest from the derailleur body (this

will be the bottom pulley once the chain is taut), guide the chain up through the rear derailleur, going around the two jockey pulleys. Make sure the chain passes inside of the prongs on the rear-derailleur cage. Guide the chain over the smallest rear cog. Guide the chain through the front derailleur cage. Wrap the chain around the smallest front chainring. Bring the chain ends together so they meet.

Finally, connect the chain by using a master link, a Shimano subpin, or the existing pin you pushed out. Connecting a chain without a master link or a Shimano subpin is much easier if the link rivet that was partially removed when the chain was taken apart is sticking out toward you. Positioning the link rivet this way allows you to use the chain tool in a much more comfortable manner; that is, driving the rivet toward the bike, instead of back at yourself (**FIGURE 12-23**).

Connecting a Shimano Chain

Shimano chains have a special connecting pin, called a subpin, to ensure a stronger chain connection. On a new chain, insert the subpin through the outer plate holes Shimano left open, rather than through an outer plate from which you have re-

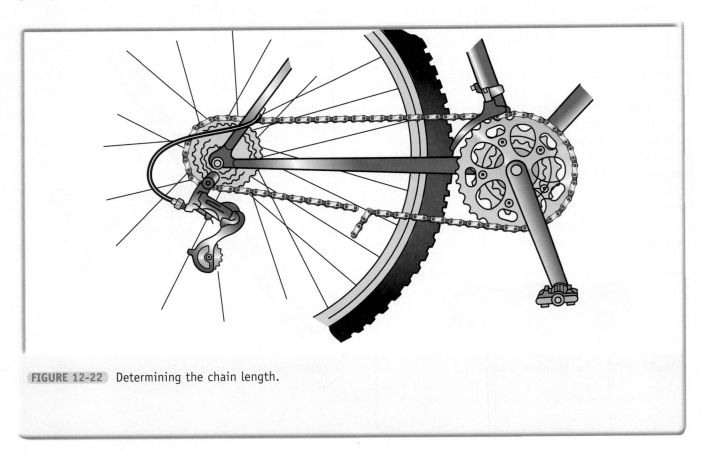

FIGURE 12-22 Determining the chain length.

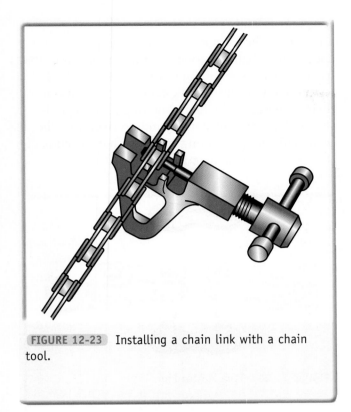

FIGURE 12-23 Installing a chain link with a chain tool.

moved a rivet. This will make for the strongest possible connection.

Make sure you have a Shimano subpin, which looks like a silver (for nine-speed) or black (for eight-speed) rivet with a second segment ending in a pointed tip. It is twice as long as a standard rivet and has a breakage groove at the middle of its length. Two subpins come with a new Shimano chain. If you are reinstalling an old Shimano chain, get a new subpin at a bike shop.

Remove any extra links, pushing the appropriate rivet completely out. As explained above, remove extra lengths at the end of the chain without a pair of open outer link plates (the right-hand end in Figure 12-22).

Line up the chain ends. Push the subpin in with your fingers, pointed end first. It will go in about halfway. With the chain tool, push the subpin through until there is only as much left protruding at the tail end as the other rivets in the chain. Break off the leading half of the subpin with a pair of pliers. The chain should move freely. If it does not, flex it back and forth at this rivet.

Connecting and Disconnecting a Master Link

There are several types of master links, all of which are connected and disconnected by a means other than a rivet.

Lickton's Super Link and SRAM (Sachs) Power Link
These links are the same; SRAM (which purchased Sachs) licensed Lickton's design. The master link is made up of two symmetrical link halves, each of which has a single pin sticking out of it. There is a round keyhole in the center of each plate that tapers into a slot on the end opposite the pin.

To connect the master link, put the pin of each half of the link through the hole in each end of the chain; one pin will go down and one up (FIGURE 12-24).

Pull the links close together so that each pin goes through the keyhole in the opposite plate. Pull the chain ends apart so that the groove at the top of each pin slides to the end of the slot in each plate.

To disconnect the master link, squeeze the master link plates together to free the pins and, at the same time, push the chain ends toward each other so that the pins slide out of the slot to the keyhole in each plate. Pull the two halves of the master link apart. In practice, this is often hard to do with an old chain. Try squeezing the link plates toward each other with needlenose pliers to disengage the link plate slots from the pin grooves while you push the ends toward each other.

Wipperman ConneX Link
The Wipperman link works much the same way as the SRAM Power Link, but unlike other master links, the edges of the link plates are not symmetrical. This means there is a definite orientation for the link, and you must ensure you do not install it upside down.

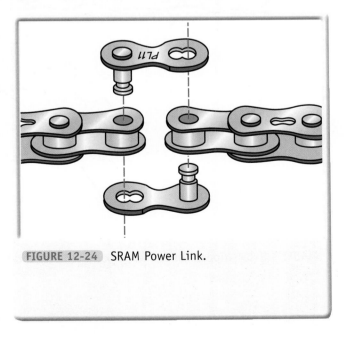

FIGURE 12-24 SRAM Power Link.

Orient the chain so the taller convex edge is away from the chainring or cog (FIGURE 12-25). The link is bowl-shaped, and if you have the convex bottom of the bowl toward the cog or chainring when it is on an 11- or 12- or even a 13-tooth cog, the convex edge will ride up on the spacer between cogs, lifting the rollers out of the tooth valleys and causing the chain to skip under load.

Install the ConneX link in the same manner as the SRAM Power Link, but make sure the convex edge is facing outward from the chain loop so that the long concave edge can run over the cog spacers on the smallest cogs without lifting the chain.

Taya Master Link
To connect the Taya master link, connect the two ends of the chain together with the master link that has two rivets sticking out of it (FIGURE 12-26). Snap the outer master link over the rivets and into their grooves. To facilitate hooking each keyhole-shaped hole over its corresponding rivet, flex the plate with the protruding rivets so that the ends of the rivets are close together.

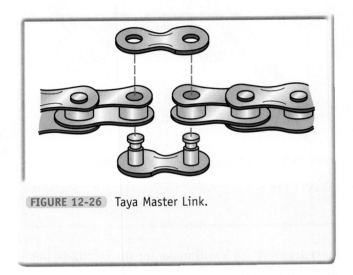

FIGURE 12-26 Taya Master Link.

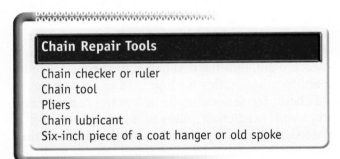

Chain Repair Tools

Chain checker or ruler
Chain tool
Pliers
Chain lubricant
Six-inch piece of a coat hanger or old spoke

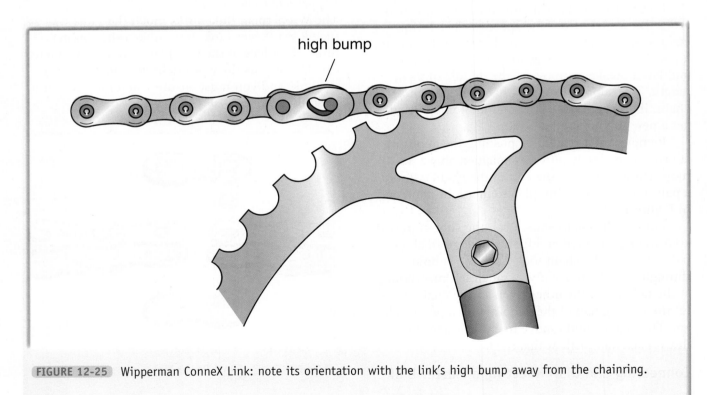

high bump

FIGURE 12-25 Wipperman ConneX Link: note its orientation with the link's high bump away from the chainring.

To disconnect the Taya master link, flex the master link so that the pins come closer together. Pull the plate with the oval holes off of the rivet.

Bicycle Replacement

Determining when to replace a bicycle depends upon a number of factors, the most important of which is the condition of the frame. Frames should be inspected for cracks several times a year by a bike mechanic. Usually, if the frame is in good shape, all of the other components can be repaired or replaced. If the frame is damaged, it should be replaced. Some brands offer lifetime warranties and will replace broken frames. Consideration should be given to the cost-effectiveness of replacing the components versus the cost of a new bike.

Preventive maintenance is the best way to ensure the longevity of the fleet. A bike mechanic (either in-house or at a bike shop) should maintain and inspect the bikes on an ongoing basis. Only properly trained bike mechanics should be charged with the responsibility of maintaining the bike fleet; if the bikes are to be cared for in the motor pool, the fleet mechanics should be cross-trained as bike mechanics.

Records of purchase, repair, and regular maintenance should be kept to ensure the bikes are in proper working order at all times and to determine when bikes should be replaced. These records can help guide the decision whether it is more economical to repair or replace a bike. As with an automobile, the costs of preventive maintenance and repair can eventually exceed the costs of replacement.

Conclusion

Proper maintenance and adjustment of public safety bicycles is important for many reasons. Primary among them are safety, comfort, and efficiency, although cost savings are also important. A well-maintained bike will last longer, reducing replacement costs, and will require fewer major repairs, resulting in maximized productivity. Therefore, all public safety cyclists must clean and lubricate their bicycles on a regular basis. They must also be well-versed in the basic adjustments and repair techniques addressed in this chapter. More complicated adjustments and repairs should only be completed by a qualified bicycle mechanic. Knowing the difference can save the department both time and money.

References

Zinn, Leonard (2005). *Zinn and the Art of Mountain Bike Maintenance*, 4th Edition. Velo Press, Boulder, CO.

13

Basic Nutrition

Introduction

Public safety personnel have a duty to maintain their bodies at a standard higher than that of the average citizen for two important reasons—short- and long-term survival. At any moment, an officer might become involved in a fight for his or her life, or a member of a rescue team may have to pull someone to safety and then provide life-sustaining care. Statistics have shown that public safety personnel have a 35% greater chance of contracting heart disease than the general public. While 70 to 90 police officers are murdered annually, more than 2000 die from heart disease. An emergency responder on a mountain bike must rely on his or her physical abilities to ride significant distances while carrying additional weight, and/or wearing body armor, for an entire shift, which may be 8 hours or more. Environmental conditions such as intense sunlight, heat, and humidity can likewise increase the amount of physical exertion and stress on their bodies. The very nature of public safety cycling demands a commitment to a healthy lifestyle.

In the 21st century, numerous technological advancements, such as elevators, televisions, comput-

ers, escalators, motorized vehicles, and microwaves, have all contributed to inactivity and overeating. Uniformed service professionals are not immune to this phenomenon. In fact, they may even be more prone to it. Statistics compiled by the North Carolina Justice Institute in 2001 reveal that:

- Despite being required to pass physical agility tests to enter and graduate from basic training, many public safety personnel abandon their fitness habits shortly after graduating, and many departments lack ongoing fitness requirements.
- On average, cardiovascular endurance decreases to pre-academy levels within 1 year, and body fat exceeds recommended amounts within 3 years.
- The average life span of a police officer is 15 years less than the average American whom he/she is sworn to protect.
- In the United States, 50% of all police officers will die from heart disease within 5 years of retirement, and heart disease is the single greatest cause of early retirement. It is also the second greatest cause of limited-duty assignments.
- Today's police officers are 25 times more likely to die from heart disease than from a bullet shot from a suspect's gun.

A multi-year screening (2003–2006) by the National Volunteer Fire Council (NVFC) Heart-Healthy Firefighter Program, which tested more than 12,000 career and volunteer firefighters, found the following:

- Six percent had Stage 2 hypertension, 24% had Stage 1 hypertension, and 47% were prehypertensive.
- The average Body Mass Index (BMI) of those screened in 2005 was 28.96, which is classified as overweight.

A National Fire Protection Association (NFPA) study conducted from 1995–2004 concluded that 440, or 43.7%, of fire fighters who died on the job experienced sudden cardiac death, and that three-quarters of them had known or detectable heart conditions.

Unique Factors

Public service personnel face a unique set of factors, which contribute to the risk of early death. Police officers often encounter threatening people and situations. Firefighters are exposed to carbon monoxide and other products of combustion. Critical incident stress is not uncommon. Emergency responders are often restricted by when, where, and how long they are allowed to eat, which makes it easier to succumb to the lure of fast food. Rotating shifts and extended tours contribute to poor sleep patterns and chronic fatigue. Working closely with those who are sick, injured, or suffering from infectious diseases is commonplace. All of these issues contribute to higher mortality rates for emergency services professionals.

Seven Major Risk Factors for Cardiovascular Disease

The seven major risk factors for cardiovascular disease (CVD) are high cholesterol, high blood pressure, smoking, diabetes, sedentary lifestyle, obesity, and family history. Other contributing factors include excess fat in the blood (triglycerides) and stress. Because emergency service professionals are more susceptible to CVD than the general public, they should know and understand these risk factors and take steps to avoid them. Even if a specific disease runs in one's family, steps can be taken to minimize the risk of acquiring that condition, usually through diet and exercise tailored to ameliorate the risk. In addition, a periodic physical exam and blood analysis will enable the early identification of detrimental health conditions and also will enable the professional to track his or her physiological conditions. Public safety cyclists can minimize the risk of developing CVD by practicing a lifestyle of sensible nutrition and adequate physical activity.

Seven Major Risk Factors for CVD

High cholesterol
High blood pressure
Smoking
Diabetes
Sedentary lifestyle
Obesity
Family history

Nutrients

There are several basic nutrients essential for good health and top performance. They include water,

vitamins, minerals, carbohydrates, protein, and fat. Fiber is also an important element of a healthy diet.

■ Dietary Reference Intake

From 1941 to 1989, the United States Department of Agriculture (USDA) published Recommended Dietary Allowances, or RDAs, of these nutrients. The primary goal of the RDAs was to prevent disease caused by nutrition deficiencies. In the early 1990s, the RDAs were revised by the Food and Nutrition Board of the National Academy of Sciences, which created Dietary Reference Intakes (DRIs) in 1997. DRIs have been established for life stage groups (infant, children, adult), both genders, and women who are pregnant or lactating.

DRIs have been established for water, carbohydrates, fiber, fat, fatty acids, cholesterol, protein and amino acids, vitamins, and minerals. The DRI report also provides recommendations for physical activity and energy expenditure to maintain health and decrease risk of disease. The DRI system includes Estimated Average Requirements (EAR), Recommended Dietary Allowance (RDA), Adequate Intake (AI), and Tolerable Upper Intake Levels (UL). A complete list of DRI reports is available through the USDA.

The USDA and the FDA established 2000 calories as the average daily caloric requirement. Actual caloric needs vary depending on a person's age, gender, weight, level of daily physical activity, and weight management goals. Individuals must monitor body weight to see if calorie intake should be adjusted.

■ Water

Water is essential to life. On average, half or more of an adult's body weight is made up of water. It is important to drink enough water to keep body fluids in balance and to help maintain proper temperature. Otherwise, dehydration can occur. Dehydration is indicated by thirst, fatigue, and weakness, and in extreme cases, it can be fatal.

The Centers for Disease Control and Prevention (CDC) define dehydration as a condition in which water or fluid loss exceeds fluid intake. The body becomes less able to maintain adequate blood pressure, deliver sufficient oxygen and nutrients to the cells, and rid itself of wastes.

Each day, an average person loses 12 cups of water (84 ounces) just by urinating, breathing, and sweating. That amount can triple or quadruple easily, when a person is riding a bicycle in hot, humid weather, carrying an additional 25 pounds of duty gear around the torso while wearing body armor, or hauling 30 to 40 pounds of emergency medical equipment in panniers. It is absolutely imperative for public safety cyclists to replenish the water they have lost and to supplement that amount to aid in recovery each day. The DRI for water is 91 ounces per day for women and 125 ounces per day for men; up to 20% of this can come from foods such as fruits and vegetables, and the other 80% should come from beverages. According to the CDC:

- Seventy-five percent of Americans are chronically dehydrated.
- Even mild dehydration will slow the metabolism as much as 3%.
- One glass of water ended midnight hunger pangs for almost 100% of the dieters studied in a University of Washington study.
- Lack of water is the number one cause of daytime fatigue.
- Preliminary research indicates that 8 to 10 glasses of water a day could significantly ease back and joint pain for up to 80% of sufferers.
- A mere 2% drop in body water can trigger fuzzy short-term memory, trouble with basic math, and difficulty focusing on a computer screen or printed page.

The opposite of dehydration is hyponatremia. Hyponatremia is a condition that occurs when an individual consumes too much fluid, diluting the body's sodium levels. It can also be caused by loss of sodium from sweating and inadequate sodium replacement during lengthy athletic events. According to the American College of Sports Medicine, exertional hyponatremia is relatively rare and may be avoided completely if fluid consumption does not exceed fluid lost.

■ Vitamins and Minerals

Vitamins are not a source of energy, but they regulate chemical reactions within the body and can contribute to perceived energy levels. Minerals regulate bodily processes (for instance, iron in the blood transports oxygen) and combine in numerous ways to form structures of the body, such as calcium and phosphorus in bones and teeth. They do not provide energy to the body, but they do contribute significantly to energy metabolism.

■ Fiber

Fiber is found in plants and cannot be digested by humans. Some types of fiber simply pass through the digestive tract. By doing so, fiber keeps the digestive tract healthy by preventing constipation, reducing chances of developing colon cancer, and toning the intestinal muscles. Fiber combines with and traps cholesterol in the intestines before it can be absorbed into the blood vessels where it does its damage. Water soluble fiber can help lower cholesterol amounts by as much as 15%, thus lowering the chances of CVD. Water soluble fiber is found in oats, beans, carrots, raisins, apples and prunes. The DRI for fiber is based on age and gender. Women between the ages of 19 and 50 should consume 25 grams of fiber per day, and men in the same age range should consume 38 grams.

■ Carbohydrates

Carbohydrates are the primary fuel for muscle contraction and the most important nutrient for physical activity, including cycling. Energy from carbohydrates is released much more quickly than the energy from fat. It is impossible to burn fat during highly intense activities such as a bicycle sprint to an emergency call, a foot pursuit, or a physical struggle; therefore, carbohydrates are the primary fuel for intense physical activity. Carbohydrates are made up of molecules of glucose and are stored in the body as glycogen, although these stores are limited. During light and moderate exercise, carbohydrates supply about one half of the energy requirements, although as time progresses the amount of energy provided by fat slowly rises and exceeds carbohydrates. Even during aerobic activity, the continual breakdown of carbohydrates is required to metabolize fat for use as fuel.

There are simple and complex carbohydrates. Simple carbohydrates, or sugars, are single and double molecules of glucose. Examples include refined sugar, hard candy, fructose (the sugar in fruit), and lactose (sugar in milk). Many energy bars and sports drinks contain simple carbohydrates as their energy sources because of the rapid availability of simple carbohydrates to the working muscles. Complex carbohydrates are longer chains of glucose molecules and are normally found in foods with additional nutrients, such as pasta, potatoes, rice, and bread. Complex carbohydrates are important to public safety cyclists, because they are digested quickly and available to the working muscles. Consumed carbohydrates restock the glycogen that has been used for physical activity by the muscles, and only after the muscles are "full" will excess carbohydrates be converted to and stored as fat.

All carbohydrates have an energy content of about 4 calories per gram. The recommended intake for carbohydrates is between 45% and 65% of total calorie consumption. This equates to 900 to 1300 calories, or 225 to 325 grams per day, based on a 2000 calorie total intake.

■ Proteins

Proteins are made up of long chains of amino acids. Muscles are made up of protein strands. The body is able to synthesize some amino acids (nonessential amino acids) but not others (essential amino acids), so it is important to ingest those that the body cannot produce. Among other physiological processes, protein is necessary for building and repairing muscles, blood cells, hair, fingernails, and other tissues. Protein is also essential for synthesizing hormones. It is not a significant source of energy for working muscles, but it can be used when carbohydrates are not available in adequate quantities, such as in a state of starvation or during exhaustive physical activity. Higher protein requirements are usually associated with weight lifting, body building, intense anaerobic training, and ultra endurance activities. The extra protein aids in repairing muscle tissue and provides an additional source of energy during prolonged endurance activity. Protein-rich foods include beef, pork, fish, poultry, dairy products such as milk and yogurt, tofu, beans, egg whites, peanuts, tree nuts, grains, dried peas, soy, whey, and lentils.

Protein has an energy content of about 4 calories per gram. The recommended intake for protein ranges from 10% to 35%, depending mostly on activity level and age. This range equates to 200 to 700 calories, or 50 to 175 grams per day, based on a 2000 calorie intake. A sedentary person requires much less protein and fewer calories than an active adult.

Simple and Complex Carbohydrates

Simple carbohydrates are single and double molecules of glucose. Examples include refined sugar, hard candy, fructose (the sugar in fruit), and lactose (sugar in milk). Complex carbohydrates are longer chains of glucose molecules and are normally found in foods with additional nutrients. Examples include pasta, potatoes, rice, and bread.

■ Fats

Even though excess fat can be unhealthy, the body needs a certain amount of fat for normal functioning. Fat is an essential part of the entire nervous system, including the brain. It aids in the transport of fat-soluble vitamins (A, D, E, and K) and is also used as a form of energy in physical exertion up to the anaerobic threshold, when it becomes possible for only carbohydrates to be used. Fat acts as padding to the internal organs and as insulation from the elements. A male requires a minimum essential body fat percentage of about 4% and a female about 12%.

Fats are categorized as saturated, monounsaturated, polyunsaturated, and trans. Saturated fats are usually solid at room temperature and are found in animal fat, butter, margarine, and coconut and palm oils. They may contribute to heart disease and some cancers and are therefore termed "bad fats." Monounsaturated fats are usually liquid at room temperature, for example, olive and canola oil. Polyunsaturated fats are also liquid at room temperature and comprise most vegetable oils such as safflower and corn oil. Trans fats are fats that have been altered by manufacturers to increase shelf life and stability of food products. Trans fats are to be avoided, as they have been shown to raise low-density lipoprotein (LDL), also known as "bad" cholesterol, and increase risk for coronary heart disease.

Fat has an energy content of 9 calories per gram, and the recommended intake ranges from 20% to 35% of total daily calorie intake. This equals 400 to 700 calories, or 44 to 78 grams per day, based on a 2000-calorie diet.

■ Daily Calorie Requirements

The basal metabolic rate (BMR), or metabolism, is the minimum amount of energy that the body requires to maintain itself at its current level. Many factors will determine BMR, such as the amount of lean muscle tissue, body fat percentage, height, surface area, gender, and age. Women tend to have a 5% to 10% lower BMR than men, because women generally have less muscle mass and a higher body fat percentage than men. Muscle is metabolically more active than fat and requires more energy to survive within the body.

To get an idea of how many calories the body requires each day at rest, use the simple formula shown next. Once you have calculated the BMR, calculate the activity factor to get a final approximation of actual metabolic requirements. This amount this will vary from day to day depending on physical activity, body type, age, and gender.

English BMR Formula

Women: BMR = 655 + (4.35 × weight in pounds) + (4.7 × height in inches) – (4.7 × age in years)

Men: BMR = 66 + (6.23 × weight in pounds) + (12.7 × height in inches) – (6.8 × age in years)

Your BMR = _____

Multiply your BMR by your daily activity level:

Harris Benedict Formula

To determine your total daily calorie needs, multiply your BMR by the appropriate activity factor as follows:

- If you are sedentary (little or no exercise): Calorie requirement = BMR × 1.2
- If you are lightly active (light exercise/sports 1 to 3 days/week): Calorie requirement = BMR × 1.375
- If you are moderately active (moderate exercise/sports 3 to 5 days/week): Calorie requirement = BMR × 1.55
- If you are very active (vigorous exercise/sports 6 to 7 days a week): Calorie requirement = BMR × 1.725
- If you are extra active (very vigorous exercise/sports, plus physical job or working out twice daily): Calorie requirement = BMR × 1.9

Your BMR (_____) × your activity level (_____) = _____calories/day

Dietary Guidelines

The *2005 Dietary Guidelines for Americans* provides science-based advice on food and physical activity choices for health. Throughout most of this publication, examples use a 2000-calorie level as a reference for consistency with the Nutrition Facts Panel (food labels). Although this level is used as a baseline, recommended calorie intake differs for individuals based on age, gender, and activity level. At each calorie level, individuals who eat nutrient-dense foods may be able to meet their recommended nutrient intake without consuming their full calorie allotment. The remaining calories—the discretionary calorie allowance—allow individuals flexibility to consume some foods and beverages that may contain added fats, added sugars, and alcohol.

The *Dietary Guidelines* provide key recommendations for nutritional intake, weight management, and physical activity. They describe a healthy diet as one that:

- Emphasizes fruits, vegetables, whole grains, and fat-free or low-fat milk and milk products;
- Includes lean meats, poultry, fish, beans, eggs, and nuts; and
- Is low in saturated fats, trans fats, cholesterol, salt (sodium), and added sugars.

The *Dietary Guidelines* are available from the USDA.

MyPyramid

In April 2005, the USDA released the MyPyramid food guidance system (**FIGURE 13-1**). The MyPyramid website offers tools for determining personal recommendations for daily intake from each food group and gives tips for selecting from these groups. The food groups include vegetables, fruits, milk, and meat and beans. The width of each band represents the percentage of one's diet that should be derived from that group, but the actual number varies among individuals. MyPyramid addresses fats, sugars, and salt as well; the point of the pyramid represents foods in each group that are high in these nutrients to emphasize that they should be consumed in moderation. Oils are included in the pyramid as a reminder to select them wisely and use them sparingly. Most liquid oils contain more unsaturated fats than saturated fats and are recommended, while solid fats such as butter and margarine should be limited. Trans fats should be avoided as much as possible. **TABLE 13-1** reflects the 2005 dietary guidelines for various levels of calorie consumption.

Food Labels

Monitoring one's caloric and nutritional intake can be challenging, especially when eating pre-

Anatomy of MyPyramid

One size doesn't fit all
USDA's new MyPyramid symbolizes a personalized approach to healthy eating and physical activity. The symbol has been designed to be simple. It has been developed to remind consumers to make healthy food choices and to be active every day. The different parts of the symbol are described below.

Activity
Activity is represented by the steps and the person climbing them, as a reminder of the importance of daily physical activity.

Moderation
Moderation is represented by the narrowing of each food group from bottom to top. The wider base stands for foods with little or no solid fats or added sugars. These should be selected more often. The narrower top area stands for foods containing more added sugars and solid fats. The more active you are, the more of these foods can fit into your diet.

Personalization
Personalization is shown by the person on the steps, the slogan, and the URL. Find the kinds and amounts of food to eat each day at MyPyramid.gov.

Proportionality
Proportionality is shown by the different widths of the food group bands. The widths suggest how much food a person should choose from each group. The widths are just a general guide, not exact proportions. Check the Web site for how much is right for you.

Variety
Variety is symbolized by the 6 color bands representing the 5 food groups of the Pyramid and oils. This illustrates that foods from all groups are needed each day for good health.

Gradual Improvement
Gradual improvement is encouraged by the slogan. It suggests that individuals can benefit from taking small steps to improve their diet and lifestyle each day.

MyPyramid.gov
STEPS TO A HEALTHIER YOU

U.S. Department of Agriculture
Center for Nutrition Policy
and Promotion
April 2005 CNPP-16

USDA is an equal opportunity provider and employer.

GRAINS VEGETABLES FRUITS OILS MILK MEAT & BEANS

FIGURE 13-1 The MyPramid food guidance system.

TABLE 13-1 MyPyramid Daily Intake

Daily Calorie Intake:	1600	1800	2000	2200	2400	2600	2800	3000
Grains (oz.)	5	6	6	7	8	9	10	10
Veggies (cups)	2	2.5	2.5	3	3	3.5	3.5	4
Fruit (cups)	1.5	1.5	2	2	2	2	2.5	2.5
Milk (cups)	3	3	3	3	3	3	3	3
Meat/beans (oz.)	5	5	5.5	6	6.5	6.5	7	7

Physical Activity At least 30 minutes of moderate to vigorous activity, 10 minutes or more at a time.

pared and packaged foods. Therefore, reading food labels is an important element in watching nutrient intake. The FDA requires that all food labels contain information on serving size, calories, proteins, fats, carbohydrates, sodium, and various nutrients (FIGURE 13-2). Paying attention to the servings per container and the percentages listed for nutrients is helpful for staying within the recommendations discussed in the nutrients section of this chapter.

Conclusion

Because of their increased risk of CVD, all public safety personnel should be aware of the risk factors and take appropriate steps to prevent them. Nutrition is a key aspect in preventing CVD, diabetes, hypertension, and other diseases as well as in maintaining a healthy weight. It is important for all public safety cyclists to educate themselves on the type and amount of food required each day for a healthy lifestyle, and tailor their nutrition accordingly. Nutrition, however, is just one aspect of a healthy lifestyle. The other, physical fitness, will be discussed in Chapter 14.

References

American Heart Association, www.americanheart. org.

Applegate, Liz (1991). *Power Foods: High-Performance Nutrition for High-Performance People.* Emmaus, PA: Rodale Press.

Blum, Jon (2001). *Promoting Fitness Adherence for Law Enforcement.* Prepared for the American Society of Law Enforcement Trainers, Annual Conference. North Carolina Justice Academy.

Clark, Nancy (1990). *Sports Nutrition Guidebook: Eating to Fuel your Active Lifestyle.* 2nd Edition. Champaign, IL: Human Kinetics.

Collingwood, Tom (1998). *Fit Force.* Salem MA: Fitness Intervention Technologies.

Cooper Institute. *Physical Fitness Specialist Manual,* The Cooper Institute, Dallas, TX.

Food & Drug Administration (2003). *FDA Consumer Magazine* September-October, Pub. # FDA04-1329C.

Gastelu, Daniel and Hatfield, Fred (1997). *Dynamic Nutrition for Maximum Performance: A Complete Nutritional Guide for Peak Sports Performance.* Garden City Park, NY: Avery Publishing Group.

McArdle, William; Katch, Frank; Katch, Victor (1991). *Exercise Physiology: Energy, Nutrition, and Human Performance.* 3rd Ed. Malvern PA.: Lippincott, Williams, and Wilkens.

Umeh, Davidson C. (1999). *Protect your Life! A Health Handbook for Law Enforcement Professionals.* Flushing, NY: Looseleaf Law Publications, Inc.

United States Department of Agriculture, www.usda.gov.

Nutrition Facts

Serving Size 1 Cake (43g)
Servings Per Container 5

Amount Per Serving

Calories 200 Calories from Fat 90

	% Daily Value*
Total Fat 10g	**15%**
Saturated Fat 5g	**25%**
Trans Fat 0g	
Cholesterol 0mg	**0%**
Sodium 100mg	**4%**
Total Carbohydrate 26g	**9%**
Dietary Fiber 0g	**0%**
Sugars 19g	
Protein 1g	

Vitamin A 0%	•	Vitamin C 0%
Calcium 0%	•	Iron 2%

* Percent Daily Values are based on a 2,000 calorie diet. Your daily values may be higher or lower depending on your calorie needs:

		Calories:	2,000	2,500
Total Fat	Less than		65g	80g
Sat. Fat	Less than		20g	25g
Cholesterol	Less than		300mg	300mg
Sodium	Less than		2,400mg	2,400mg
Total Carbohydrate			300g	375g
Dietary Fiber			25g	30g

FIGURE 13-2 Food label.

14

Basic Physical Fitness

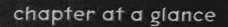

Introduction

The benefits of good physical fitness cannot be overstated. Being physically fit is important to any uniform patrol function, but it is essential for a person who functions as a vehicle engine. While patrolling on the bike, you are an athlete. Maintaining and/or improving your physical fitness can enhance your job performance and help prevent injuries. This chapter can be used as a foundation for developing a lifestyle that includes good fitness practices. This includes being attentive to new research results in the field of physical fitness.

Energy Systems of the Body

The body is an amazing machine. Through the use of three different and very complex systems or pathways, it can use fat, carbohydrates, and protein as energy to fuel working muscles. Carbohydrates are the fuel of choice for the public safety cyclist. When consumed, they are broken down into, or converted to, glucose, which can be used in all exercise, regardless of the intensity level. Once consumed, they can be used immediately by the muscles or stored in the liver and muscle tissue as

glycogen. Depending on the intensity of exercise, the body uses glucose in various amounts mixed with fat and protein. Protein is the last fuel of choice. If adequate fat and glycogen are available, protein accounts for only about 5% of the energy produced by the body.

■ The Phosphagen (ATP-CP) System

The phosphagen (ATP-CP) system is the body's first choice for providing energy. It is not critical to understand the complex chemical reaction within the muscle, but the phosphagen pathway fulfills the first 5 to 10 seconds of demand for all movement. It is like the lit match that starts the fire. The immediate resources required to fuel this process would be depleted quickly if used exclusively, but this rarely, if ever, happens; rather, the body uses all systems concurrently in order to keep ATP levels constant. As exercise continues, the body transitions energy production to the oxidative (aerobic) pathway until it relies on this pathway for the vast majority of its energy.

■ Glycolysis

Glycolysis is the breakdown of carbohydrates, whether it is glycogen stored in the muscle or glu-cose delivered in the blood. There are two types of glycolysis: fast and slow. Slow glycolysis, an aerobic system, allows for the use of carbohydrates through the oxidative system, and fast glycolysis is the primary source of energy for high-intensity activity that lasts up to about two minutes. It is not possible for sufficient oxygen to be metabolized at this very high intensity level; therefore, fast glycolysis is known as an anaerobic system, i.e., one that operates in the absence of oxygen.

■ Oxidative (Aerobic) System

While engaged in routine patrol at low to moderate intensity, the body uses both fat and carbohydrates as fuel. Because oxygen is required to metabolize fat, this is known as the aerobic system (with oxygen), and at lower intensities it can provide your body with a steady source of energy for hours. Slow glycolysis supplements the oxidative system at low and moderate intensities, as long as sufficient oxygen is available. As the intensity of exercise increases, as when responding to urgent calls, the body uses less and less fat until carbohydrates become the sole source of fuel, and fast glycolysis (anaerobic) becomes the primary pathway for energy.

Energy Systems Summary

Initial movement is fueled by the phosphagen system. Then, almost immediately, other systems begin contributing substantially to keep the phosphagen system replenished. If the intensity is low, experts suggest that as much as 85% of calories are supplied from fat. This changes to roughly 50% fat and 50% carbohydrates during moderate effort, when both the oxidative and slow glycolysis systems are at work. At high intensity levels, carbohydrates become the primary energy source and the aerobic systems (oxidative and slow glycolysis) are increasingly replaced by fast glycolysis.

Lactic acid is a byproduct of fast glycolysis. The point at which the muscle is not able to buffer the acid and clear it from the working muscle is commonly referred to as the lactate threshold, also referred to as the anaerobic threshold (AT) or onset blood lactate accumulation (OBLA). This accumulation of lactate has a detrimental effect on the muscles. It creates a painful burning sensation and will eventually force you to slow down. The available energy and the force of the muscle contraction decreases, and the muscle must slow down or stop the activity.

Because trained muscles can buffer and clear lactate faster than untrained muscles, it is beneficial for public safety cyclists to exercise at higher intensities for longer durations. For a police officer, this may mean the difference between him or the suspect becoming exhausted first.

Principles of Training

A competitive cyclist typically follows a personalized, structured training program. Although such a program would be much more complex than one required by the average public safety cyclist, the basic principles of training are the same. Progressive overload is a process in which the individual stresses working muscles by lifting weights, climbing hills, riding long distances, etc., and then provides sufficient rest and proper nutrition so the muscles can recover and adapt. Fitness is not improved during the activity; rather, it temporarily decreases. It is during the period of rest when muscles adapt to the stress through what is known as overcompensation. When the overload is gradually increased over days, weeks, and months, improved fitness is the result. The outcome of a fitness riding program is determined by many factors, including frequency, intensity, and duration.

Frequency

The term frequency simply describes how often you ride. A relative beginner would have to train at least three times a week in order to improve. A novice rider may need to ride five times a week. Your current fitness level will dictate how often and to what degree you must stress the body in order to improve. These training sessions must be spaced properly to provide sufficient recovery time.

Intensity

You must gradually and systematically increase your level of exertion, or intensity, during the training sessions. Intensity describes how hard your body is working. For example, if you ride the same 15-mile route at the same pace time after time, your body will adapt to the stress of that particular ride and will not continue to improve. You either have to increase your speed or distance. Which of those you increase depends on your training objectives.

Measuring intensity can be challenging for beginners. Some athletes choose to use a perceived rate of exertion scale on which "one" is nearly no effort at all and "ten" represents maximum effort. A more accurate method of monitoring your exercise intensity is with the use of a heart rate monitor as described later in the chapter. The intensity of your ride or workout should increase on a weekly rather than daily basis to ensure enough recovery time to allow the body to overcompensate.

Duration

How much time you spend on a ride is commonly expressed as duration. Increasing the duration of your rides can build your aerobic endurance. If you are among the many public safety cyclists who return to a more conventional patrol vehicle during the winter months, begin the season with a shorter ride than the one that ended the previous season unless you have maintained your workouts. Fitness can also be improved through increasing volume, or duration and frequency (volume = duration × frequency).

Performance Indicators

When the riding (or training) season begins, document your current state of fitness so you can monitor your improvements throughout the year. There are a number of standard terms and measurements used in exercise physiology to benchmark performance and related intensity levels. Those who are familiar with these common terms will be able to reap the benefits of modern training principles more easily.

■ VO2 Max

The term VO2 max describes an individual's aerobic capacity, that is, the maximum amount of oxygen the body can use during a given time. The test to determine VO2 max is conducted in a laboratory with specialized equipment that measures the volume of oxygen used during a maximal effort. VO2 max, measured in ml/kg/min, represents the volume of oxygen in millimeters used per minute, divided by the person's weight. Most people never know their VO2 max because of the complex procedure used to determine it. Most experts believe it is influenced to some degree by genetics and is limited by heart size, heart rate, heart stroke volume, muscle fiber type, and other physiological factors. The potential for improvement varies widely depending on the individual's current level of fitness, exercise intensity, and so on; but in general, it typically takes six to eight weeks of vigorous training to reach VO2 max peak values.

An average, fit, male athlete has a VO2 max of around 40-50 ml/kg/min. Three-time Tour de France champion Greg LeMond had a VO2 max of 92.5, one of the highest ever recorded.

■ Lactate Threshold

Lactate threshold (LT) is a more useful performance indicator than VO2 max because it is fairly simple for an individual to determine and it can be improved through training. LT is the highest intensity of exercise you can sustain before your body's ability to clear and buffer lactic acid is surpassed by the rate at which it is produced. It is generally considered the point at which the body transitions from aerobic energy to anaerobic energy and from using fat, oxygen, and carbohydrates for energy to using pure glycogen.

Lactate threshold typically is expressed as a percentage of maximum heart rate or VO2 max. An average person might reach his or her LT at 40% to 50% of the VO2 max, while a cyclist who has completed 8 to 12 weeks of proper training would reach his or her LT at 80% or 90% of the VO2 max. You can determine your own LT with only an hour and a heart rate monitor.

First, find a relatively flat stretch of uninterrupted road. After warming up for at least 15 minutes, ride at the highest intensity you can sustain for 30 minutes. Do not start out too hard or you will be fatigued before the end of the ride. Your average heart rate during the last 20 minutes of the ride will be very close to your heart rate at LT.

Understanding LT is of particular importance to public safety cyclists for two reasons. First, it can be used in designing an effective training program that can result in dramatic improvements for beginner and novice cyclists. More importantly, public safety cyclists, even those with high LTs, should not exceed their LT while on patrol. If, when responding to an urgent call, you begin to feel a burning sensation in your muscles and are gasping for breath, you have exceeded your lactate threshold and are now anaerobic. You have also created short-term fatigue and have compromised your safety because you will be unable to function effectively at the scene until you have recovered. Staying below your LT can help you maintain your ability to perform at a high level when you arrive at the call.

■ Heart Rate

Using a heart rate monitor to measure the intensity of your training efforts is an accurate and inexpensive way to ensure you are working hard enough to improve your fitness. Some cyclists use a power meter; however, compared to a heart rate monitor, a power meter is very expensive, and the data it provides is far beyond the needs of the average recreational cyclist.

Maximum Heart Rate

Many cyclists base their training programs on intensity zones that are described as a percentage of the maximum heart rate. The first step in creating such a program is determining your maximum heart rate, or the maximum heart rate you should achieve during physical exertion. The most accurate method of determining your maximum heart rate is during a medically supervised clinical evaluation such as the VO2 max or graduated stress test. You can estimate your maximum heart rate with reasonable accuracy by subtracting your present age in years from 220. True maximum heart rate may differ by plus or minus 20 beats per minute, but this formula serves as an adequate gauge for most people. There are also a number of sub-maximal tests and self-conducted field tests, some of which yield more accurate results. Maximum heart rate is specific to the individual, so the best approach is to research the method you feel best meets your needs.

Maximum Heart Rate

Maximum heart rate (MHR) can be estimated using the following formula*: 220−age in years.

*Results may vary as much as plus or minus 20 beats per minute.

Resting Heart Rate

Resting heart rate (RHR) is a good indicator of your state of fitness and recovery. This is the number of beats per minute while you are inactive. Many factors such as illness, medication, stress, and fatigue affect resting heart rate. Take your pulse for one full minute first thing in the morning for four consecutive days and calculate the average. The shriek of an alarm clock will raise your RHR, so after you've had your first urination of the day, return to bed and lie still for a few minutes before you record your daily RHR.

Target Heart Rate

To reap the benefits of training, including the effects of riding on patrol, you need to train at the right intensity to improve your aerobic and anaerobic systems. You will do so by monitoring your heart rate while you exercise to ensure it is elevated to a specific percentage of your maximum. That specific percentage is known as your target heart rate. As a public safety cyclist, you will benefit from training your aerobic endurance, your lactate threshold, and your aerobic capacity. Using the example in TABLE 14-1 , apply the same percentages to your specific heart rate data to determine your ideal training zones.

Weight Management

Whether you struggle with your weight or would just like to lose a few pounds, there is no secret to losing weight. No magic pill. No quick fix. It is simple math, but it takes discipline to achieve results. To lose weight, you must create a calorie deficit. Said another way, you must burn more calories than you consume.

There are about 3500 calories in a pound of fat. If you divide that into seven days a week, that is 500 calories a day. Therefore, if you have a calorie deficit of 500 calories a day, you would lose one pound a week. There are two ways to create a calorie deficit: Consume fewer calories by changing your diet, or burn more calories by increasing your activity level.

Obviously, the best results would be obtained from a combination of both methods. This is a rather simplified way to describe a very complex process, but despite what weight loss product companies would like you to believe, those are the facts.

Some people feel that they should try to lose weight before they begin cycling; however, cycling can be an extremely effective part of a weight loss program because it burns a significant number of calories, and in the case of a public safety cyclist, can be done on duty. Start riding and make good decisions about your nutrition habits as discussed in Chapter 13, and commit to a goal. If you maintain a healthy body weight and nutrition regime, you greatly reduce the risk of ailments like high blood pressure, high cholesterol, diabetes, osteoporosis, joint and back problems, stroke, heart disease, and certain types of cancer. Knowledge is valuable, but self-control is what stands between most people and a healthy body weight.

TABLE 14-1 Ideal Training Zones

This table illustrates the heart rate that must be attained to train a specific zone, assuming a MHR of 180 beats per minute.

Training Type	Improves	Practical Application	% of Max HR (MHR)	Example	Target HR
Recovery	Active Recovery	Slow patrol at low intensity	<65	180 x .60 =	108
Aerobic	Aerobic Endurance	Moderate steady patrols	66–85	180 x .80 =	144
Threshold	Lactate Threshold	Responding quickly to an urgent call	86–95	180 x .90 =	162
VO2 Max	Aerobic Capacity	You are in the fight of your life	96–100	180 x 1 =	180

Stretching and Flexibility

Cycling is a repetitive motion, and over time, it will shorten and tighten your muscles, reducing your range of motion and ultimately leaving you more prone to injury. Stretching improves your flexibility and will maintain and improve your range of motion. Make stretching a habit, and follow these guidelines for six easy stretches.

■ General Guidelines

- Take a short ride through the parking lot or around the building to warm up your muscles.
- Do the stretches in the same order each time to develop a pattern that will help ensure you do not forget any.
- Stretch the muscles slowly so to avoid triggering the stretch reflex, which will cause the muscle to contract suddenly and forcefully during the stretch, risking a muscle or tendon tear.
- Stretch to the point where the muscle is tight but not painful, and hold it for a minimum of 20 seconds.

■ The Basic Stretching Routine

Pectoralis

FIGURE 14-1A : Stand straight and grasp the wall at shoulder height. Twist your body and look in the opposite direction. Switch sides.

Quadriceps and Hip Flexors

FIGURE 14-1B : Grab one ankle with the opposite hand. Stand up straight and move the knee backwards. Switch legs.

Hamstrings

FIGURE 14-1C : Bend at the waist with one foot about 18 inches from your bike. Do not bend the knee. Keep your back flat and your arms straight. The other leg is directly behind the first. Lower your chest while your weight is on the forward leg. Slide your rear leg back for a greater stretch in the forward leg. Switch legs.

Upper Back

FIGURE 14-1D : Place the feet shoulder-width apart and bend at the waist. Support the weight of your upper body on the outstretched arms. Lower your chin to your chest, and focus on stretching the muscle that runs from below your shoulder to your low back.

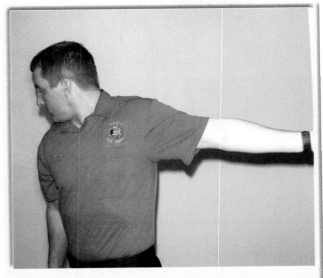

FIGURE 14-1A : Pectoralis stretch

FIGURE 14-1B Quadriceps and hip flexors stretch

FIGURE 14-1C : Hamstring stretch

FIGURE 14-1E : Back, quadriceps, and gluteus stretch.

FIGURE 14-1D : Upper back stretch.

FIGURE 14-1F : Calf stretch.

Back, Quadriceps, and Gluteus

FIGURE 14-1E : Using your bike to help you balance, place your feet shoulder-width apart and squat down. Keeping your heels flat, lower your buttocks towards the ground. Keep your back straight and try to slowly rock forward.

Calves

FIGURE 14-1F : Using your bike to help you balance, position one foot forward of the other with most of your weight on the forward leg. Make sure the toes of the rear foot are pointed forward and the heel is on the ground. Increase the stretch by moving the hips forward. Straighten the rear knee to stretch the gastrocnemius (calf). Stretch the soleus by bending the rear knee. Switch legs.

Proper Hydration

Proper hydration is important for everyone, but it is essential for a public safety cyclist conducting routine patrols. Proper hydration defends against fatigue, promotes efficient recovery, prevents muscle cramps and protects against heat-related illness. Blood is about 50% water and accounts for more than 35% of your total body weight. Your objective is to provide your body with an adequate supply of water.

It is generally accepted that one water bottle (650ml) per hour during patrol is a reasonable starting point, more in high temperatures. You should consume enough water to produce clear urine at least once a day. Do not ration your water. If you are on patrol and realize you are nearing the end of a bottle with no opportunity to refill, drink it.

If you are riding for less than an hour, water is sufficient. Sports drinks can be used to replenish certain minerals (electrolytes) and carbohydrates, but they can be expensive, usually contain dyes, and are unnecessary for short-term efforts.

Coffee, alcohol, and energy drinks with caffeine are all diuretics, which means they actually force water out of your body. Many people develop intestinal cramps from sugary beverages like soda, sports drinks, and fruit juice. Experts suggest that 75% of the general population is chronically dehydrated, so if these beverages encourage you to drink and the alternative is to drink nothing, then drink them. Staying hydrated is one of the least expensive and most effective methods of improving performance as well as general health and fitness.

Cycling Injuries

Cycling injuries can have a short- or long-term impact on a cyclist's well-being and performance. Although a more physically fit cyclist is less prone to injuries than one who is less fit, all cyclists should be aware of common cycling injuries and how to prevent and treat them.

In the year 2000, the International Police Mountain Bike Association (IPMBA) polled more than 300 police cyclists on several injury-related issues. It was discovered that 67% of respondents had been injured at least once during bike patrol train-ing, with 25% reporting serious injuries such as muscle sprains, tears, strains, dislocations, fractures, and broken bones. Time lost from work ranged from 1 day to 11 months. The numbers dropped significantly regarding on-duty injuries, with only 20% reporting injury. Half of those were minor scrapes and bruises while the other half were serious injuries such as those caused by being struck by motor vehicles, joint and muscle injuries, and broken bones.

■ Crash-Related Injuries

Because crashes are inevitable, it helps to be familiar with some common injuries and how to treat them. Seek medical advice if you are unsure of how to manage the injury. Road rash and acute injuries like minor sprains, strains, and bruises are common (FIGURES 14-2 AND 14-3).

Road Rash

Stop the bleeding, clean the wound properly, then apply an antiseptic ointment followed by a moist dressing. A modern approach to treating this common injury suggests that the wound should be kept moist. If it is more than just a minor scrape, change the dressing twice a day. Do not allow hard scabs to form. They can crack, easily become infected, and are more likely to scar.

Acute Injuries

A standard method of treating minor acute injuries, such as muscle strain, is the RICE formula: Rest, Ice, Compression and Elevation. Using this formula will help control swelling and promote recovery.

FIGURE 14-2 Road rash is a common result of bike crashes.

FIGURE 14-3 Use the RICE formula to control swelling.

■ Use Injuries

Use injuries are generally those caused by improper technique or lack of appropriate equipment. Proper bike fit and correct riding techniques, along with good fitness and nutrition habits, can dramatically reduce the risk of many use-related injuries.

Sore Muscles

When muscles are worked hard, they may feel sore and stiff over the next few days. This is usually due to microscopic tears in the muscles due to the increased workload. Warming up and stretching, adequate water intake, sufficient protein and carbohydrate intake, and adequate rest between riding sessions will help alleviate muscle soreness. Application of heat will feel good at the time; however, it may also result in swelling after the heat is removed. Ice is a better option, and an anti-inflammatory may help, as well as sports massage. A good practice is to warm the muscle before you use it and ice the muscle after you use it.

Muscle Cramps

It appears that there are many causes of muscle cramps, although they are not completely understood. They can be relieved by massaging and gently stretching the muscle that has contracted involuntarily. It is generally thought that fluid or electrolyte imbalances, being unaccustomed to intense efforts, poor flexibility, fatigue, and low blood sugar can contribute to these muscle spasms. Electrolytes are minerals that assist the body in balancing fluids and conduct electric currents between muscles. They are easily lost through sweat. If you sweat a great deal, are out in very high temperatures, or patrol for several hours on hot days, a sports drink that contains a small amount of electrolytes may prevent or lessen severity and frequency of muscle cramps. Eating and drinking foods that provide calcium, such as dairy products, leafy greens, and legumes, and foods with potassium, such as bananas, may also help alleviate cramping.

Sore Neck

Improper body position and a lack of stretching prior to cycling can cause a sore neck. Raising the stem height on the bike may help alleviate the problem as will keeping the elbows loose rather than locked while riding, to prevent shock transfer and fatigue. The shoulders and neck can be rolled, rubbed, and stretched frequently. When cycling in cold weather, keep the neck warm with layers of clothing.

Sore Back

Back and shoulder pain can sometimes be caused by a reach that is either too short or too long to the bars. However, in the vast majority of situations, back pain is due to poor core strength. Stretch the hamstrings and piriformis (a small muscle in each buttock) regularly. Spend plenty of time strengthening your abs and low back. A daily routine of strengthening and stretching will help alleviate back pain.

Sore, Numb, or Weak Hands

The ulnar nerve runs along the inside of the forearm and palm to the ring and pinkie fingers. Having a too-tight grip on the handlebars, not wearing padded palm protection, and improper body position (leaning too far forward) can lead to permanent injury to this nerve. Make sure the height and length of the handlebar stem is appropriate for body build. Check your saddle position, including height, fore/aft, and tilt. Finally, try to change your hand position frequently.

Saddle Sores and Saddle Soreness

These are two very different conditions. Saddle soreness is generally due to the fact that your behind is not used to riding. That is normal. Make certain your saddle is adjusted properly for your body. A saddle is designed to fit so the majority of your body weight rests on your ischium, or sit bones **FIGURE 14-4**. If your saddle is adjusted properly, the skin on your buttocks will adapt to the time you are putting in on the bike. However, the nerves that run between the front and the back will not adapt to the pressure. Pain caused by not being accustomed to riding can be alleviated somewhat by the choice of saddle. Ergonomically correct, gender-specific, and noseless saddles have made many tours of duty more tolerable.

A saddle sore is a painful infection caused by an irritation or chafing of the hair follicles. It typically starts as a small irritation or pimple and usually goes away in a few days. In some cases, however, it spreads to create larger and more painful boils, which may have to be removed surgically. To prevent saddle sores, wear chamois or synthetic-lined padded cycling shorts, and wear only cycling-specific underwear, if any. Wash the shorts after every ride, and wash the body with antibacterial soap. Sports lubricants are also an option if applied to the sitting area; consider chamois crème as a daily part of preparation for bike patrol. This provides a moisture barrier and reduces friction. Spend time off the bike while on duty and stand occasionally to air the area. If a saddle sore develops, take a few days off the bike and do not cover the sore with salves or ointments. Consult a doctor if it does not go away in a few days.

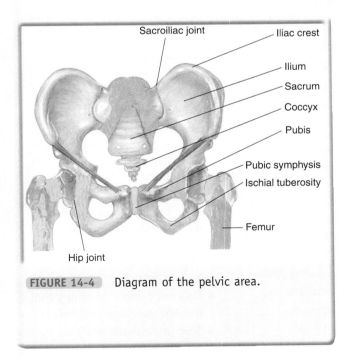

FIGURE 14-4 Diagram of the pelvic area.

Sore Knees

Patella tendonitis and chondromalacia are common cycling overuse injuries. Riding with a saddle that is too high or too low, and trying to ride in too high a gear are major contributors to these conditions. If clipless pedals are used, make sure they allow the foot to float a few degrees to reduce the stress on the ligaments in the knees. In cold weather, an additional layer, such as tights with wind-resistant front panels, can aid in keeping the knees warm. If pain is experienced on the outside and just above the kneecap, it may be the iliotibial band, or IT, which runs on the outside of the thigh, all the way up to the hip. Make sure the saddle is high enough and be sure to stretch the IT band before and after cycling. Follow RICE procedures as necessary.

Burning or Numb Feet

Burning or numb feet can be caused by shoes that are too narrow or that are laced too tightly. Loosening the tension on the laces or Velcro closures or wearing shock-absorbing insoles can help. Wiggle the toes when possible to keep them loose. Wear stiff-soled shoes to distribute the force over the entire bottom of the foot, not just the area that pushes on the pedals. Without appropriate shoes, the foot will bend over the pedal when force is exerted. This strains the plantar fascia, which is the tendon running along the bottom of the foot. Over time, a condition called plantar fasciitis can develop. Maximize the benefits of pedal retention by pedaling in a circle rather than only pushing down with your quadriceps, as this puts extra pressure on the sole of the foot. Pull up with the hamstrings as the foot reaches the lower half of the stroke.

Because their forefeet are under constant pressure, cyclists are also prone to neuromas, or nerves that are squeezed between tissue and metatarsal bones, the long bones behind the toes. Pain is usually felt on the ball of the foot, between the third and fourth metatarsal bones, behind the toes. Neuromas can result if the nerve has an extra branch, which makes it more likely to be pinched, or if the metatarsal bones are close together, leaving less room for the nerve. The first step in addressing neuromas is to change shoes. More cushioning or a wider toe box may be needed, and orthotics might help. Cortisone shots can shrink the nerve and reduce pain. Some doctors inject an alcohol solution into the foot to kill the nerve. Surgery, used in a few cases, removes the nerve, usually causing no serious side effects.

■ Other Conditions

Heat Exhaustion and Heat Stroke

When patrolling in high temperatures and high humidity, your core body temperature rises. The body's response is to release some of this heat by evaporating moisture on your skin, that is, by perspiring. When the air is dry, it is sometimes difficult to monitor how much water is lost, because it evaporates off the skin so quickly. When the air is humid, the body's evaporation system is hindered, because the ambient air is already saturated with moisture. When the body sweats, it loses water and electrolytes. When too much water is lost, the circulatory system can be severely impaired in its ability to deliver oxygen and nutrients and remove waste products. This deficiency can lead to heat exhaustion, heat stroke, and, if left untreated, even death. To prevent these conditions, drink plenty of fluids containing carbohydrates and electrolytes, ride at a moderate pace, and pay attention to both body temperature and sweating. Stay out of the sun during peak hours, wear light-colored clothing that wicks away moisture, and familiarize yourself with the symptoms and treatment of the most common heat-related illnesses (TABLE 14-2).

Intense Sunlight

Excessive exposure to and lack of protection from the sun can result in serious damaging effects. The tissue of the eye is especially susceptible to the damaging ultraviolet (UV) rays emitted by the sun, and skin can develop cancer from prolonged and unprotected exposure. Wear 100% UV-rated eye protection and sunscreen with a sun protection factor (SPF) of at least 15. Wear long sleeves where and when the sun is especially intense, but keep in mind that clothing does not block all of the sun's damaging rays. If possible, stay out of the sun at these times. All rules apply on cloudy days, too.

Riding in Cold Weather

Dress appropriately by wearing layers. Wear moisture-wicking clothing next to your skin, wool or fleece as the middle layer, and wind-resistant material on the outside. Cover the head underneath the helmet and be aware of wind chill. Familiarize yourself with the symptoms of frostbite and hypothermia, and know when to go inside. Drink plenty of fluids, avoid excess sweating, but keep moving, as the muscles generate heat while they work.

TABLE 14-2 Treatment for Common Heat-Related Conditions

Symptoms of Heat Exhaustion	Treatment of Heat Exhaustion	Symptoms of Heat Stroke	Treatment for Heat Stroke
■ Muscle cramps ■ Heavy sweating ■ Weakness ■ Headache ■ Dizziness ■ Nausea or vomiting ■ Pale skin color ■ Fainting ■ Cool, moist skin ■ Rapid, weak pulse	■ Stop any activity and take the person to a cool, shaded, or air-conditioned area. ■ Have the person rest with his or her legs elevated. ■ Apply cool towels to the person's skin. ■ Give the person a drink of a cool, non-alcoholic beverage. ■ Remove any extra equipment and helmet. ■ If not treated promptly, heat exhaustion will progress to heat stroke.	■ Throbbing headache ■ Dizziness ■ Nausea ■ Muscle twitching ■ Unusual behavior, such as irritability, confusion, emotional instability, and aggressiveness ■ Very high body temperature (above 103 degrees Fahrenheit) ■ Red, hot dry skin (no sweating) ■ Quick, strong pulse ■ Hallucinations ■ Unconsciousness	■ Stop any activity and take the person to a cool place, such as a shaded area or air-conditioned room. ■ Have the person lie down with the feet slightly elevated. ■ Place the person in a cool bath or shower. Spray the person with cool water from a hose, or sponge the person with cool water. ■ Wrap the person in a cool, damp sheet, and fan the person vigorously. ■ Apply ice packs to the groin and armpits. ■ Give the person something cool and non-alcoholic to drink. ■ Seek professional medical attention.

Pre-Selection Fitness Standards

The 2000 IPMBA survey mentioned earlier also revealed that at least three public safety officers had suffered fatal heart attacks while riding mountain bikes. These incidents happened either on patrol or during training. Yet only 23% of reporting officers were required to undergo medical pre-screening prior to engaging in bike patrol training or riding on duty.

Cycling requires the body and the heart to do strenuous work at times, and those who participate must be physically able to do so without placing themselves at risk. Proper screening will identify those who have pre-existing conditions and those who may not be healthy or fit enough to withstand the rigors of cycling on duty. At the very least, the screening process should involve a thorough medical exam, including a stress test, recovery heart rate, or other comprehensive cardiopulmonary exam. An orthopaedic exam with emphasis on the knees and back should also be conducted. A cycling-specific heart rate test, such as a short, uncomplicated time trial in which a certain time and heart rate recovery must be achieved, is also recommended. Cycle skill tests can also be conducted, but these might disqualify healthy, fit individuals who would be capable of learning the skills and becoming assets to the bike unit.

Conclusion

If you are not already a recreational cyclist, consider joining a local club or perhaps exploring a new cycling discipline. If you are a "roadie" or mountain biker, consider racing. Nothing pushes your fitness level like matching it against others. Whether it is in the context of bike-handling skills, taking a suspect into custody, or responding to a medical emergency, your fitness level is the cornerstone of officer safety. Remember, you are not only a public safety cyclist, you are an athlete.

References

Baker, Arnie M.D. (1998). *Bicycling Medicine.* Simon & Schuster, New York NY.

Burke, Edmund, M.D. (2003). *Optimal Muscle Performance & Recovery.* Avery Publishing, New York NY.

Earle, Roger W., Baechle, Thomas R., Triplett-McBride, Travis (2004). *NSCA's Essentials of Personal Training.* National Strength and Conditioning Association, Colorado Springs CO.

Friel, Joe (2000). *The Mountain Biker's Training Bible.* Velo Press, Boulder CO.

Hamblin, Lou Ann (1998). *Police Cyclist Anonymous Survey/Tactical Survey.* International Police Mountain Bike Association "Police on Bikes" Conference. Tacoma, WA.

Lynch, Tom (2006). *London Ambulance Service Cycle Response Unit Recruitment & Selection.* Ambulance Service Association UK (ASA), London, England.

Pavelka, Ed (2000). *Cycling for Health & Fitness.* Rodale Press, Emmaus PA.

Umeh, Davidson C. (1999). *Protect Your Life! A Health Handbook for Law Enforcement Professionals.* Looseleaf Law Publications, Inc. Flushing NY.

Vonk, Kathleen (1999). Police Mountain Bike Patrol: Policy, Training, and Tactics. *IPMBA News.* Volume 8, Number 1, pages 10-11.

Vonk, Kathleen (2000). Riding a Mountain Bike on Patrol: A Training Issue? *The Law Enforcement Trainer.* Volume 15, Number 5, pages 26-29, 38-39.

15

Funding

chapter at a glance

Introduction

Whether you are establishing your department's first bike unit, reinventing an existing one, or just trying to keep one running, the availability of funds will be a key element in your success. Public safety agencies do not usually have access to unlimited resources. Priorities change, and when they do, a previously well-funded program can find itself without the funds to sustain it. This chapter provides advice on getting started with fundraising, describes a basic fundraising process, and identifies typical funding needs and potential sources.

Whether the funds come from within the agency or from outside sources, it is imperative to attempt to diversify your funding sources and track your statistics. By diversifying your funding sources, you will minimize the risk of losing all of your financial support at once. Tracking your statistics will enable you to justify your program expenses by providing evidence of a positive return on the investment. It is also essential to recognize that funding is not usually available for bikes per se; rather, funders are interested in outcomes, and bikes are merely a means to achieve those outcomes.

Sources of funds are limited only by the imagination and the failure to ask. Do not be shy. Ask for

help, and accept as much as you can get, but do not accept items that you do not need. Ensure you are acting within the scope of your agency and not in violation of any regulations regarding the soliciting of funds or in-kind contributions. Finally, get organized. The most productive fundraising effort is one that is both well-planned and well-executed.

Getting Started

Before embarking on any fundraising efforts, you must first determine your needs. To do that, you should assess the uses and size of your bike team, your equipment needs and costs, and your training needs. This information will help you develop a realistic budget. Your budget will help you plan your fundraising effort, sell it to prospective funders, and measure its success.

Uses and Size of the Bike Team

The first step should be to define the uses and the size of the bike team, as the scope of the team will affect all other factors. Realistically, most teams can only cover a small- to medium-size geographic area effectively. Decide what you want the bike squad to

do, where they will work, and how many members you will need. Do not let the fear of asking for too much inhibit you, but avoid projecting more than you honestly believe you need. Prepare to be surprised with the generosity of some funding sources, but do not get discouraged by rejections.

Ask For What You Need

Do not let the fear of asking for too much inhibit you, but avoid projecting more than you honestly believe you need.

Equipment Needs and Costs

To determine equipment needs and project the cost of that equipment, ask established units what a bike team needs and how much that equipment costs. Conduct research, determine your needs, and devise a realistic estimate of how much it will cost to obtain and maintain the necessary equipment. Useful sources of information include IPMBA-affiliated vendors who specialize in outfitting public safety cyclists, bicycle publications, local bike shops, online suppliers, and established bike teams.

The first step is to gather information about the bike unit's needs, which means you have to know what the bike unit will be expected to do. Thus, it will be helpful to ask questions about how the unit will be used; how many members it will have; whether it will operate full-time or part-time; and whether each member will have his or her own bike, or whether the bikes will be shared.

In addition to the team members and the bicycles, there will be costs for team-specific equipment, including uniforms, helmets, gloves, eyewear, shoes, equipment for day and night operations and summer and winter operations, medical equipment, etc. Because the person reviewing your request may not understand the importance of certain pieces of equipment, be prepared to justify why you need it in your accompanying budget narrative. Try to identify items likely to be rejected by your agency, and focus your efforts on obtaining those items through your fundraising efforts.

Do not overlook the ongoing expenses of maintenance and repairs. Weigh the pros and cons of a service contract with a local bike shop against those of maintaining the bikes in-house. Replacement parts are an ongoing expense, especially frequently replaced items such as brake pads, tubes, tires, grips, and lights. Consider the amount and type of use the bikes are likely to experience. Experienced and established bike units are the best resource for this information.

■ Training Needs and Costs

Team members will have basic and ongoing training requirements. What type of training will your team members receive? How much does that training cost? Will the training fees be the responsibility of the agency or the team member? How many members will your bike team have? Is it more economical in the long run to have one or more individuals certified as IPMBA instructors than it is to send all members to a training course provided by another organization? What in-service training requirements are in place or will be established? An in-house instructor can continue effective in-service training and is prepared to develop training and policy. This must be weighed against the size of the bike unit, the important need for continual training, the anticipated team member turnover, and the availability and circumstances of outside training (**FIGURE 15-1**).

All successful fundraising efforts begin with a clear definition of the rules. Everyone involved in the process must know, understand, and adhere to the guidelines of both the agency and the committee responsible for the project.

■ Departmental Policies and Procedures

Familiarize yourself with any requirements and restrictions imposed upon donations of money and/or equipment by your agency or local governing bodies. Some departments do not permit fundraising or donations from the community. Others employ a grantwriter who is responsible for pursuing all potential grant and other funding.

■ Cash Donations

Establish a procedure for receiving, processing, and allocating financial contributions for specific purchases. If possible, save unrestricted funds to purchase equipment not donated by other sources.

■ Equipment Donations

Be prepared to approach donors with a list of specific equipment and the projected costs. Do not accept items that you do not need and cannot use. Make a firm policy of refusing any inadequate, improper, inapplicable, unrelated, and/or potentially unsafe items.

■ Benefits and Recognition

Be prepared to offer your donors something in return. Explain how their donation will ultimately benefit themselves, and put your plans for recognizing their contributions in writing. Make sure your plans are acceptable to your department and can be accomplished at no cost to you. Finally, ensure that all donors receive equal treatment for equal contributions, for instance, by establishing levels of recognition based upon contribution size.

All donors should receive a formal letter of appreciation whether the donation is monetary, equipment, or services. Also, consider special thanks to especially generous donors. These could either be donors who give especially high amounts or those who have demonstrated continued support over time. This special thanks can take many forms: engraved plaques, bike team photos showing donated equipment, or recognition of support through the media. Be respectful of donors who wish to remain

Raffle Ticket Sale

Win A Mountain Bike!!!!

The City of Bethlehem Community Services Unit is selling raffle tickets to raise money for officers to attend the Annual International Police Mountain Bike (IPMBA) Conference. This conference teaches officers many of the necessary skills including bike handling, suspect contact and apprehension, community policing, youth bicycle education programs, urban drug enforcement, and many more.

Win a GT Timberline 21-Speed Mountain Bike

**Date of Raffle:
April 1**

- British Racing Green
- 7005 Aluminum GT Triple Triangle™ design frame with Pro tapered downtube
- Gripshift shifters
- Aluminum cold-forged adjustable stem
- Suspension seatpost
- Plush Master saddle
- Valued at $500.00

**Ticket Price:
1 for $3.00
2 for $5.00**

Win This Bike

City of Bethlehem Police Department Community Services Division

10 E. Church Street
Bethlehem, PA 18018

Bicycle Provided By:
Action Wheels Bike Shop
530 W. Broad Street
Bethlehem, PA

FIGURE 15-1 Fundraising can help ensure access to initial and ongoing training.

anonymous. A gesture of good-faith recognition could have an unintended negative result.

Funding Sources

Equipment and funds can come from a variety of different sources, and it is essential to explore all avenues in both the public and private sectors.

■ Department/Agency

Agency funds include, in addition to the operational budget, funds from any auctions of unclaimed or seized property and already-awarded grants that may be used for bike operations. Some police bike units have received funds seized in drug arrests, especially if the bike unit conducts successful drug operations.

■ Department-Related Organizations

Many agencies raise funds through a nonprofit affiliate such as a foundation, citizens' police academy, or volunteer program. There may be an opportunity to obtain funding through one of these groups, especially if your unit will provide support for its goals.

■ Government Grants

Grants earmarked for local or national priorities may be available for a bike unit. The key to obtaining federal funds is to show how the bicycle unit will provide a solution to the priority problem or meet a need for services. Whether administered nationally or locally, federal grants often provide seed money for innovative programs. The grants are typically data-driven and require clearly defined objectives rather than broad goals.

Possible sources for federal funding at the time of publication include the United States Departments of Justice, Transportation, and Homeland Security. The availability of federal funding changes constantly, so it is important to research current grants opportunities regularly.

Government grants involve a highly structured application process, cost restrictions and limitations, and close monitoring. Typically, the most important thing to remember when responding to requests for proposals (RFP) is to answer the questions asked in the RFP. The RFP often provides the response format; and following the format, answering the questions thoroughly, and meeting all deadlines are essential. Most grantors receive numerous applications and immediately disqualify all that do

not adhere to the proscribed procedure. If your department has a grantwriter on staff, tap him or her as a resource. If not, apply yourself or find a willing member to attend a local class on writing grant proposals.

■ Foundations

A foundation is an entity that is established as a nonprofit corporation or a charitable trust, with a principal purpose of making grants to unrelated organizations or institutions or to individuals for scientific, educational, cultural, religious, or other charitable purposes. Foundations typically fund on a local level, and although their funds are often less restricted than grants, they still have clearly defined giving areas and procedures.

There are four basic types of foundations. Family foundations tend to be governed by the original donor and/or the family of the donor. Independent foundations may have been created by someone of great wealth, but are operated by unrelated trustees. Community foundations are hybrids in that they both solicit funding and make grants. Corporate foundations are legally separate from their parent companies and make grants from a pool of money set aside for the purpose of funding innovative programs. All of these are likely prospects.

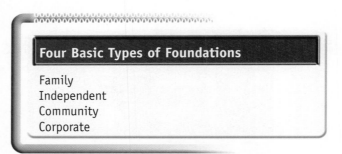

Four Basic Types of Foundations

Family
Independent
Community
Corporate

■ Businesses and Individuals

Some businesses give sizable donations to generate publicity and goodwill or to improve and support their communities. These funds may be available directly or through an affiliated foundation. Local outlets of national companies (retail stores, banks, etc.) typically have funds to be distributed within the community at the discretion of the manager. Large corporations often provide significant support to the communities in which their headquarters and/or other facilities are located.

Bicycle shops have been known to donate bikes and/or offer equipment at drastically reduced prices. They may also be willing to donate or reduce their labor costs for repairing the department fleet. Individuals who understand the positive impact of the bike unit on their lives may also become benefactors. Although it would not be appropriate to ask for or expect it, some agencies have received donations from grateful citizens and/or businesses who would like to see more public safety personnel on bikes.

■ Business and Community Organizations

Community and neighborhood associations, civic associations, and business associations (chambers of commerce, marketing co-ops, downtown partnerships) are often generous to bicycle units. When appealing to business associations, point out the positive impact of a bike patrol in terms of loss prevention and creating a safer environment for patrons. Statistics showing a decrease in retail-related crimes, for instance, can be extremely persuasive. Homeowners' associations and residential complexes can be encouraged to give using the same approach, tailored to their areas.

Some associations coordinate fundraising events because they recognize the positive impact the bike team has on their members. In Bethlehem, PA, the business association raises thousands of dollars for the bike team because the bike officers help keep their customers coming downtown. In Maryland in June 2006, merchants in Baltimore's Lexington Market purchased 14 Cannondale Pursuit bikes and donated them to the Baltimore City Police Central District. Also in 2006, the Rotary Club donated $8500 to the Bethesda-Chevy Chase Rescue Squad's medical bike team, which worked their many special events. Another civic association that frequently called upon their bike unit to conduct bike rodeos provided funds for the unit's members to attend training.

A department may be more comfortable accepting support from an association than an individual or business because the perception or fear that favored treatment is expected in return is not as great.

■ Recreational Clubs

Both police and EMS bike units have enjoyed the support of their local bicycle clubs, running clubs, golf associations, etc. The bike team is often deployed to support such events and, as such, is a logical beneficiary of funds raised for distribution within the community. Having a positive working relationship with these clubs has a potential added benefit—their members, who may represent companies, other clubs, and government agencies, can be influential in funding decisions.

■ Fundraisers

Traditional fundraisers still work and are limited only by imagination and energy. If a department permits this type of activity, it can be both fun and easy. Selling t-shirts, bumper stickers, or other items; sponsoring a race, bike rodeo, or bike wash and repair; throwing a pancake breakfast, spaghetti dinner, or auction; or holding the ever-popular bake sale can all be successful. Events should be heavily publicized to both the corporate and the residential communities and through civic and business associations.

Almost all communities have a fair or festival of some sort. A booth at such an event can bring in substantial donations and familiarize the community with the bike unit. Positive PR can be generated by offering bike inspections, registration, and/or bike safety literature at the booth. It is important to offer such services to the community without making it seem as though you are asking for donations for those services. The donations are so that your organization can begin or continue to serve the community.

Helping to properly fit bike helmets for children is possibly one of the most valuable services a bike unit can provide to the community. Having a fundraiser to provide items such as bike helmets for children and then providing the service of fitting those helmets to children in need can be a good way of getting positive exposure for your bike unit. Although these funds do not directly benefit your unit, this type of activity provides an example of the services your unit could provide with additional funds.

Fundraising Rules

Regardless of the type of fundraising in which you plan to engage, there are a few key elements to keep in mind as you build your proposal and prepare to solicit funds. First, consider the perspective of the potential donor. Try to see your agency through the eyes of the person you are asking for support. How has your agency benefited them in the past? How will your bike unit assist them in the future? Why do/should the potential donors care?

Second, focus on building relationships. Do not expect to meet your financial goals overnight.

City of Bethlehem

INDUSTRY • EDUCATION • RELIGION • MUSIC • RECREATION
AN EQUAL OPPORTUNITY EMPLOYER

DEPARTMENT OF POLICE

John Doe
A.E. Inc.
Main Street
Bethlehem, PA 18018

Mr. Doe:

The City of Bethlehem Community Police Bike Unit would like to thank you for your past support of our officers. Through the support received from A.E. Inc., our officers have been able to attend the annual International Police Mountain Bike Association (IPMBA) training conference. During the conference, officers attend classes on youth bicycle education, urban drug enforcement and police/community relations, just to name a few. The Bethlehem Police Department and its officers strive to maintain a high level of professionalism and service to the citizens and business community. The training the officers receive at the IPMBA Conference greatly aids in the goal of serving the community.

The IPMBA Conference provides the best training, resources and opportunities for bike patrol personnel from around the world. IPMBA offers a variety of courses that are relevant to the job of a Community Police/Bicycle Patrol officer that would assist in better educating and creating a well rounded police officer. The courses supply knowledge and information that can be used in conjunction with current programs as well as create new ideas on how to bring the community and police closer together.

The Bethlehem Police Department permits the officers to attend the conference as long as the funds are raised by the officers to cover the cost of the trip. The cost, which includes the conference fee, hotel accommodations, transportation, etc., is estimated at $1,150.00 per officer. There are eleven (11) officers interested in attending the conference. We would greatly appreciate any financial support extended from A.E. Inc. Any contributions can be addressed to the City of Bethlehem Wish Fund c/o Bike Unit. We are looking forward to using our schooling to better serve the community.

Thank you for your consideration in this matter. Please feel free to contact any of the following officers at (610) 865-7187 for further information:

Officer Jonathan Pesesko
Sergeant Jason Schiffer

10 EAST CHURCH STREET, BETHLEHEM, PENNSYLVANIA 18018

FIGURE 15-2 Building relationships with past and potential donors is essential to successful fundraising.

Fundraising is not necessarily a quick process. It can take years, so cultivating important relationships within the community is essential. Recognize all donors, no matter how small the donation; you never know the growth potential(FIGURE 15-2).

Third, develop a good, realistic story and stick with it. Be consistent in your needs, wants, and expectations. While it may be appropriate to tailor some of the details for a particular audience, do not change your story or provide different (or conflicting) rationales for the bike unit. Members of a community—especially a small community—belong to multiple organizations and talk to one another.

Fourth, highlight your successes. Paint a realistic picture of your bike unit. Describe how effective public safety cyclists are (or can be) in the community, provide samples of the type of media coverage you have received, and share your own heartwarming (or chilling) stories that will make it hard for potential funding sources not to support you.

Finally, recognize your supporters at every opportunity unless they prefer to remain anonymous. At minimum, be sure to deliver any publicity you have promised, but continue to show your appreciation both formally and informally, in appropriate ways.

Conclusion

In conclusion, here are important hints for fundraising success:

- Public safety cyclists work together—explore combined fundraising and group requests.
- Clear any fundraising efforts with your administration and always act within the scope of departmental regulations.
- Develop a "pitch" that is comfortable and effective, but be ready to adapt it according to your experience and your audience.
- When writing fundraising letters, avoid generic form letters; personalize each letter to its intended recipient.
- When applicable, point out that donations can be tax deductible.
- Tap all resources within your own organization. Find members experienced at soliciting donations who are advocates of your cause.
- Try several different types of fundraising options. Do not be overly optimistic, but do not get discouraged easily.
- When asked how much you need, be clear and explain your needs.
- When you receive a donation, always write a thank-you note and provide a receipt, if appropriate.
- Be certain that donated monies are earmarked for the bike unit.
- Ask for the money.

16
Bicycle Safety Education for Children

chapter at a glance

Introduction

For many people, the bicycle represents childhood. It conjures images of hours spent in playful exploration, and symbolizes a child's first taste of freedom. Many parents think teaching their child to ride a bike ends when they no longer have to run alongside the bike, but there is much more to learning how to bicycle. Children must also be taught how to control their bikes and ride safely on roads with heavy motor vehicle traffic. The better equipped they are to handle a bike, the more likely it is that they will ride for both fun and transportation.

As a public safety professional—and a cyclist—it is your responsibility to help keep young cyclists safe while still having fun. When asked to conduct bicycle safety education for children, you might find yourself interacting with parents, teachers, or the kids themselves in an informal setting or during an organized event, such as a bike rodeo.

As awareness of the need for bike safety education for riders of all ages has increased, there has been a proliferation of resource material. Organizations and agencies such as the League of American

Bicyclists, the Federal Highway Administration's Bicycle Safety Education Resource Center, the Pedestrian & Bicycle Infomation Center, the National Highway Traffic Safety Administration (NHTSA), and state departments of transportation offer a variety of programs and resources targeted to specific age groups. A search of the internet will yield numerous resources related to bike rodeos, bike safety, bike education, helmets, and injury prevention. Much of the advice in this chapter is from those sources. A highly recommended resource is the booklet *The Guide to Bicycle Rodeos*, written by John Williams and Dan Burden and available from the Adventure Cycling Association.

Teaching by Example

The first and most important thing to remember is that the easiest way to influence people, especially kids, is to practice what you preach. If you ride without a helmet, ride on the wrong side of the road, or go through a stop sign, you can be sure some kids will be watching. They will remember just how seriously you take the subject of bike safety, and most, if not all, of your credibility will be lost.

The Purpose of Bike Safety Education

The main purpose of bike safety education for kids is to minimize crashes and injuries. To be an effective educator, you must first recognize the most common causes of crashes involving children, and you need to learn which teaching methods are the most successful for various age groups. Most crashes are minor, involve only the child and his or her bike, and are caused by poor skills leading to a loss of control. Most serious injuries are the result of crashes with motor vehicles, and those crashes are frequently a result of the following rider errors:

- Mid-block ride-outs
- Failing to stop and look for traffic while entering the street from driveways
- Failing to stop for stop signs and traffic signals
- Making unexpected turns and swerving
- Riding on the wrong side of the road

The goal of all bicycle safety education programs should be to minimize these mistakes.

In designing or selecting a bike safety program, it is very important to keep in mind that kids are not small adults. They differ from adults in many ways that can affect their ability to learn how to ride a bike.

- They have physical limitations; they are unable to see over or around things as easily as adults.
- They have one third less peripheral vision.
- They have a poorly developed sense of danger.
- They cannot tell from which direction sound is coming.
- They have trouble judging speed and distance, so they cannot tell how quickly a car is approaching.
- They have a more limited attention span.
- They believe that if they can see you, you can see them.
- They overestimate their bicycling ability.
- They cannot multi-task in the way adults can, meaning that although they may be able to balance, watch where they are going, ride in a straight line, signal a turn, and talk to a friend, they need a lot of practice before they are capable of doing—and remembering to do—several of these actions at a time.

Bike Safety Education for Parents

Bike safety education for very young children begins with bike safety education for parents. The best way to begin is by encouraging parents to teach their children basic balance and coordination and instilling in their children an awareness of the importance of bicycle safety.

Helmets

A helmet is the most important piece of safety equipment for cyclists of all ages; therefore, parents must make sure their children wear properly sized and fitted, age-appropriate helmets (FIGURE 16-1). However, parents must also be taught that wearing a helmet does not prevent crashes; learning and practicing cycling skills does. The purpose of wearing a helmet is to decrease the chances of serious

FIGURE 16-1 All cyclists should wear properly sized and fitted, age-appropriate helmets.

injury during a crash. Finally, if parents expect their kids to be serious about wearing helmets, then parents need to be serious about wearing them, too.

■ Bicycles

Parents must also be taught what constitutes a safe—or an unsafe—bicycle. As with adult cyclists, the bike must fit the young rider (FIGURE 16-2). If the child cannot stand over a bike, it is too big and the child cannot ride it safely. The bike must also be maintained properly. Riding a poorly maintained bike can be likened to driving a poorly maintained automobile. If a car cannot turn or stop without proper air pressure in the tires, how can a bike? How can a child steer around a pothole if the handlebars turn independently of the front wheel? Are the child's small hands able to fit and work the hand brakes? As for a bike without brakes, most parents realize that a car without brakes could kill someone, but they often fail to see the danger in allowing their kids to ride bikes that are impossible to slow or stop.

■ First Lessons

Once they have provided their child with an appropriate bike and a properly fitted helmet, parents can begin teaching basic bike skills. They should start by having their child practice getting on and off the bike until it becomes easy. The next step, balancing, is best taught by letting the child coast down a slight hill while the parent holds onto the bike seat. The child can first balance with his or her feet near the ground, and then with the feet on the pedals. Stopping with the feet is acceptable to start, but children should be taught to use their brakes as soon as possible. They should also begin learning to pedal, using the ready or "blast-off" position—with the top foot at 1:00 or 2:00. This will make their riding much safer as they will be able to start riding without pushing the bike and looking down for the pedals. After mastering mounting, balancing, starting, pedaling, and stopping, they can start to practice turning.

These are all tips that you can give to parents to start on their own. Parents should also be reminded that kids should learn how to ride a bike in an empty parking lot, without any distractions, rather than on the road. In addition, when they are ready to ride, young children should ride with their parents, who should coach and encourage them. It takes awhile before kids remember everything they need to do.

The Bicycle Rodeo

At around age 10, most kids have developed the mental and physical capacity to learn the skills necessary for riding in traffic. The bike rodeo is designed to teach those specific skills, not the basics described in the previous section. If a child is struggling to start, stop, and balance, he or she will not remember to watch for traffic. The rodeo will teach children the skills they need to ride safely in the road, but in order to be safe, they need to put those skills into use each time they ride.

■ Preparing for the Rodeo

There are many resources available to help make your rodeo successful, including schools, businesses, government agencies, and civic organizations. A rodeo can be as simple or as involved as your time and resources permit. It can include education for parents

FIGURE 16-2 As with adult cyclists, the bike must fit the young rider.

as well as children, a helmet giveaway, contests and prizes, and/or refreshments. Many of these items can be solicited as donations from members of the community and local businesses.

Planning ahead is the key to success. Before selecting the location (park, school gym, parking lot, etc.), make sure it offers enough space for the planned activities and anticipated attendance. If the rodeo will include a helmet giveaway, arrange for helmets to be donated or purchased by your department in advance so that volunteers can be trained to fit them properly. Recruit plenty of volunteers, as the more help you have, the more you will be able to do. Make sure your volunteers know and understand what is expected of them; preparing and distributing written instructions in advance and providing a brief orientation and training will help ensure that your event goes smoothly.

Bikes

You may have the kids bring their own bikes, or you may keep your own supply. The advantage to having them use their own is that they will practice on what they will actually be riding. The disadvantage is the bike might not be a size that child can use safely, or it might not be in a safe condition. Be prepared for this by having one or more tire pumps, basic tools, and a mechanic on site. A local bike shop may be willing to send a mechanic to do a quick safety inspection and make the necessary repairs and adjustments. It is advisable to have extra bikes available for those children whose bikes do not fit or are beyond easy repair.

If you choose to keep your own supply, obtain a quantity of bikes in different sizes. Whether the bikes are from the property room, donated, or supplied by a bike shop, they must pass a safety inspection in advance. They should be well-lubed and easily adjustable. The advantage to supplying your own bikes is that you are guaranteed to have suitable bikes available, and although you may have to adjust some, you will save inspection time. The kids just have to show up and either bring or get fitted for a helmet. The disadvantage is that you have to procure, transport, and store the bikes. Despite this, providing your own bikes is often preferable to relying upon the children (and parents) to bring their own.

■ Setting Up the Rodeo

All of the information you need can be found in Adventure Cycling's *The Guide to Bicycle Rodeos*.

This book describes a variety of skills stations and cone courses, and also includes a list of supplies and equipment. The amount of supplies you need depends on the size and scale of the event.

Basic Rodeo Supplies and Equipment

Sidewalk chalk
Spray chalk and extended paintsticks
Crime scene or surveyor's tape
Twine or poly rope
Traffic cones
Poster board and paint or markers
Cardboard props (bushes, cars, trucks, fences, storm drains, etc.)
Signs (stop, yield, etc.)
Sponges or tennis balls cut in half
Tables and chairs
Bicycle tools and pump
Prizes and giveaways
Certificates of completion
First aid kit
Bikes
Helmets

■ Skills Stations

In order to learn, children need to do, not just be told. They also need repetition, but not to the point of boredom or frustration. Rather than requiring the kids to perform a skill to the point of mastery, have them repeat it a few times until they are comfortable doing it, and then use that skill to lead into the next one. Hold their interest by making it fun, but continue to maintain the control and structure necessary to achieve the desired goal.

ABC Quick Check

Begin with a bike check. Teach each child to do an ABC Quick Check of his or her bike to make sure it is safe to ride. Squeeze the tires, wiggle the seat, handlebars and front wheel, check the brakes, and instruct the rider to do the same each time he or she rides. As soon as they have completed their ABC Quick Checks, the children are ready to ride.

Basic Traffic Skills

Most rodeos include some or all of the following skills stations. These stations require several sets of lanes, each approximately 3 feet wide and 60 feet long. Each volunteer coach should be responsible for no more than 4 lanes.

Walk the bikes to the starting line. This simulates walking the bike to the end of the driveway, which can help prevent driveway ride-outs into traffic (**FIGURE 16-3**).

Mount the bike in the blast-off position. This will teach riders how to prepare to start pedaling without looking down, enabling the rider to focus on where he or she is going.

Look left-right-left for traffic. Instruct the child to look left-right-left, ride forward staying within the lane, turn, ride back in another lane, use the brakes to stop at the end of the lane, dismount, and walk the bike back to the starting line.

Start, stop, and ride. First have the children start, stop, and ride in a straight line with both hands on the handlebars. Then have them start, stop, and turn with both hands on the handlebars. Finally, have them practice letting go with one hand while riding in a straight line.

Check over the shoulder. While they are riding in their lanes, have them look back over each shoulder briefly on command, to learn how to do a rear scan, or shoulder check, for traffic.

Stop quickly. Have them practice stopping with their brakes, first on their own, and then on command, to simulate the need to stop quickly for unexpected traffic.

Rock Dodge. This exercise teaches riders how to avoid small objects safely, without swerving out into traffic when they do not have time to perform a rear scan. Place several tennis ball halves or wet sponges in the lane and teach riders how to just barely avoid them without going out of their lane.

Slow race. Have the children ride about 15 feet down the lane, as slowly as possible, to practice balance.

Bike Handling Skills

Turning and bike handling skills drills can involve cones and/or chalk circles.

FIGURE 16-3 Walk the bikes to the starting line to simulate walking the bike to the end of a driveway, which can prevent driveway ride-outs into traffic.

Serpentine. A fast, easy way to practice turning is the serpentine. Set up three rows of six or seven small cones. The cones in the first row should be spaced at 10 feet, the second at 8 feet, and the third at 7 feet or 6 feet. Have the children ride through the cones, following arrows chalked around the cones to keep them going in the right direction.

Turn and maneuver. For another good turning drill, draw 2 or 3 circles in a line, each approximately 11 feet wide, with the outsides of the circles touching. Within each circle, draw another circle approximately 9 feet in diameter. First have riders practice riding and keeping their tires between the lines, then have them ride figure eights.

Turn and communicate. Once the riders have mastered the figure eight, have four or more line up and ride figure eights. During this drill, the kids ride more slowly, balance more, and have to negotiate who goes first when they meet. When this exercise is done correctly, all riders should be able to time, communicate, and balance so that no one touches a foot to the ground.

■ Situation Scenes: Putting the Skills Together

Combination exercises help the kids apply skills in succession as they would in actual situations. These exercises require either a blocked off side street or a simulated street within the confines of the rodeo.

Road positioning. To emphasize the importance of road position, children are taught the basic rule of riding with the flow of traffic, not against it. They practice the "ride as far to the right as safe and practicable" rule by pedaling along the street (or simulated street) towards an intersection.

Intersections. At a simulated (or real) intersection, kids first cross like a pedestrian, i.e., dismounting to cross and remounting across the street. The next time, they stop at the corner, place their feet in the blast-off position, and ride across when traffic is clear. By using the blast-off position, they do not have to take their eyes off their surroundings when entering the intersection. During both exercises, they should check left-right-left for traffic when stopped at the corner.

Parked cars. Park several cars on the right side of the street. Demonstrate to the children how they disappear to traffic if they move to the right in between the parked cars, and have them practice riding a door's width to the left of the cars, in a straight line, until they have passed them all.

Driveways. Have the kids walk their bikes to the end of a simulated driveway, mount in the blast-off position, look left-right-left for traffic, then enter the roadway, either to turn right or cross the street to turn left. Have them repeat this with a parked car blocking their view to the left, to practice inching forward to ensure the road is clear.

■ Videos

Parents and kids can benefit from the inclusion of videos as part of the rodeo. The videos can be targeted towards children, such as an entertaining helmet video, or towards parents, such as one that debunks the myth that wrong way riding is safer for children. Several videos are available from the Safe Kids Coalition, NHTSA, state departments of transportation, and other sources.

■ Other Bike Safety Education Programs

One of the easiest programs for an agency to implement is the bicycle helmet giveaway. While helmet giveaways are often held during bike rodeos, they can also be a stand-alone program. Some agencies organize helmet giveaway events and advertise through local networks. Others distribute coupons while on routine patrol or during special events. These coupons can be redeemed at regularly scheduled times and locations. Helmets are available for free, or at a nominal price, from such resources as local children's hospitals, Safe Kids Coalition, and some helmet manufacturers. Other bicycle safety materials for the children and parents, available through state and federal departments of transportation, can be used to supplement the helmet giveaway.

A variety of education programs geared towards other age groups, including teenagers, adults, and seniors, are available from various sources. The League of American Bicyclists offers both *Kids I*™, whose purpose is to educate parents of young children, and *Kids II*™, a seven-hour course designed for upper elementary school-age kids. They also offer adult cycling education courses through their BikeEd program. The Pedestrian and Bicycle Information Center (PBIC) offers advice for teaching kids in all age groups, teenagers, adults, seniors, and motorists. The primary resource for cycling education in Canada is CAN-Bike, the education program of the Canadian Cycling Association.

There are many other formats, exercises and learning situations that can be tailored for different situations, presentations and age groups. When kids understand and follow the traffic laws early with their bikes, they often develop safer driving habits when they move to cars. Some enjoy their bikes so much that they keep using them as adults, replacing miles that otherwise would have been spent in their cars.

Providing statistical information can enhance your credibility. Ask your local hospital to start keeping statistics on emergency room visits for kids injured in bike crashes. You will need to document the statistics for several years, but you will find the hard numbers useful in justifying the investment of time and resources into conducting bike safety education programs for the community.

Conclusion

Even as bike officers and medics have taken on numerous roles, they are still an important component of public relations and community outreach. Education of the public about bicycle safety and awareness starts with those professionals who serve as peace officers and medical care providers. Public safety cyclists are in a unique position to both share their cycling expertise and strengthen their relationships with the children, youth, and adults of their communities.

Resources

Bicycling Street Smarts, Rubel BikeMaps, (617) 776-6567 or www.bikemaps.com.

Canadian Cycling Association, (613) 248-1353 or http://www.canadian-cycling.com.

Canada Safety Council, http://www.safety-council. org/info/child/bicycle.htm.

Federal Highway Administration (FHWA) Bicycle Safety Education Resource Center and Pedestrian & Bicycle Information Center (PBIC), (919) 962-2203 or www.bicyclinginfo. org.

Guide to Bicycle Rodeos, Adventure Cycling Association, 800-721-8719 or www. adventurecycling.org.

League of American Bicyclists, (202) 822-1333 or www.bikeleague.org.

National Highway Traffic Safety Administration (NHTSA), www.nhtsa.dot.gov.

Safe Kids Coalition, (202) 662-0600 or www. safekids.org.

Patrol Operations

Patrol Equipment

Introduction

Chapter 5 addressed clothing and personal protective equipment common to all public safety cyclists. However, police and security cyclists need specialized equipment to perform their duties. Modern technology and ingenuity have enabled the creation of duty equipment specifically designed to increase the officer's personal comfort level in all weather while reducing physical fatigue. Adopting equipment suitable for bicycle duty can help increase officer safety and effectiveness.

Equipment Carriers

Most bike officers use either a traditional duty belt or a vest carrier system to carry their weapons and other equipment. There are a number of factors to consider in selecting the most appropriate carrying system.

Duty Belt

As of the publication date of this manual, most United States-based bike officers used traditional duty belts. For most police officers, this carrying system is the most familiar and therefore often the most comfortable. Bike officers who use a duty belt have a choice between standard leather gear and

gear constructed of nylon or similar synthetic material. There are advantages and disadvantages to each system, and agencies must evaluate those considerations carefully. The trend, however, is to issue nylon duty gear to those assigned to bike patrol.

Standard leather equipment is considered professional-looking and is very durable, but it can be expensive. Despite its durability, it easily shows wear caused by the movement generated by cycling and from chafing against other equipment. Maintaining a polished finish is difficult to achieve, and the polish may bleed or run when exposed to rain and humidity. Moisture can also cause leather gear to shrink, hindering the drawing of weapons. Additionally, some chemicals and biohazardous materials are easily absorbed by leather, occasionally preventing decontamination of the belt and equipment holders. Finally, new leather may require a break-in period.

Synthetic duty belts, equipment holders, and holsters made of composites such as Accumold®, Kydex®, and Nytek are generally a more practical choice for public safety cyclists. These materials are less expensive, lighter in weight, and more pliable, moving with the officer as he or she rides. Synthetic web gear hides wear better than leather and can be cleaned up easily after exposure to biohazards and some chemicals.

Some synthetic gear use Velcro® closures for equipment holders rather than metal snaps. Such closures are easier to manipulate than snaps while wearing cycling gloves, especially full-fingered ones.

Holsters

Holsters come in various retention levels. Bike officers should use the highest level of holster retention with which they can become proficient, because the riding position leaves the weapon vulnerable. However, the retention level should not prevent an officer from drawing his or her weapon from the holster and firing one round center mass in less than 2 seconds, from 7 yards. Wearing cycling gloves can compromise the rider's ability to effortlessly operate any retention system. Therefore, the public safety cyclist should become proficient in manipulating the retention system and drawing his or her weapon while wearing any type of gloves that will be worn on duty. These skills should be practiced in a realistic environment, in various kinds of weather, and under both stress and non-stress conditions.

Regardless of the type of duty gear selected, the holster must be anchored securely to the duty belt, and the duty belt must be anchored to the inner belt. Officers should use the Velcro® keepers that are typically sewn onto bike uniform pants and shorts as well as additional keepers as they would with their leather gear.

Equipment Positioning

The positioning of the equipment on the duty belt is critical for bike officers. Equipment must be placed such that it is easily accessible to the officer but also so that it can be retained in situations such as riding in a crowd, which renders the officer vulnerable to an attempted weapon grab (FIGURE 17-1). Questions arise as to placing an impact weapon behind or in front of the duty weapon or on the opposing side; it may be necessary to try several different positions before deciding on the optimal placement.

Placement of the duty belt or other equipment should not compromise the pedal stroke and

FIGURE 17-1 A bike officer must be aware of the vulnerability of his weapons in order to guard against a weapon grab.

should not interfere with routine activity, such as dismounting from the bicycle. Although speed loads and magazine pouches are generally placed on the duty belt in a vertical position, some officers may prefer horizontal placement. Bike officers must also determine how many pairs of handcuffs to carry and whether they should be stored in separate holders or in a single, double-stacked model. If the handcuffs are not stored in a case, they can be offset from the small of the back and spinal area to reduce the risk of injury, or on the front of the belt for retention. The officer should follow departmental policies if the policies are applicable, but otherwise it is a matter of personal preference.

Many bike officers transition from leather duty gear to synthetic material for bike season; others choose their gear material depending on which uniform they are wearing. If personnel switch between two uniforms, it is of the utmost importance to achieve consistency in equipment placement on the gun belt. The equipment on both belts should be identically placed so the officer does not have to search for equipment when it is needed. If it is not possible to achieve identical placement, the most important factor in consistency is the holster. Regardless of the other equipment pouches, the holster and the retention system should be identical on both gun belts, because it is unrealistic and dangerous to expect an officer to remember a different position and/or draw technique in a high-stress situation.

Consistency

If personnel switch between two uniforms, it is of the utmost importance to achieve consistency in equipment placement on the gun belt. If it is not possible to achieve identical placement, the most important factor in consistency is the holster.

■ Equipment Vests

Police officers are required to carry a growing array of equipment: handgun, radio, impact weapon, chemical spray, conductive energy device (CED), such as a TASER®, handcuffs, flashlight, first aid pouch, and cell phone, for example. It can be difficult and uncomfortable to accommodate all of this equipment on a duty belt. For this reason, some agencies opt for equipment vests.

When the Chandler, AZ, Police Department adopted the TASER®, the limited space on their equipment belts caused some officers to remove their chemical spray (O.C.) and/or expandable batons. This led to the search for an alternative carrying method. The department adopted a system similar to the vest and equipment carriers used by tactical officers and by bike officers in the United Kingdom.

Vest carriers have been popular among bike officers because they can be designed and cut to be comfortable while cycling. The pouches and pockets can be customized to hold a CED, radio, O.C. spray, batons, magazines, handcuffs, and other equipment, although armed officers still need to wear a gun belt and security holster. Nevertheless, carrying equipment on the vest spreads the weight of the equipment across the shoulders, reducing the lower back discomfort that can result from cycling with a fully equipped belt. In addition, the ballistic panels between the officer and his or her equipment affords protection from the equipment should the officer fall (FIGURE 17-2).

Bike officers who use vest carriers should be aware of a few disadvantages. A bike officer is already at risk of being pulled off the bike by an attacker, and an external carrier could provide an assailant with a means to achieve this more easily. In addition, wearing the body armor externally negates any advantage gained by using a uniform shirt made of a high-tech wicking fabric. Most quality external carriers have a rubberized layer between the ballistic panels and the officer's body to keep perspiration from deteriorating the panels, which will render the moisture-wicking feature of the shirt ineffective. However, as discussed in Chapter 5, under no circumstances should bike officers patrol without some type of body armor.

Weapons

Bike officers carry the same weapons and equipment as their non-cycling counterparts. Because they are on bikes, however, they may consider different criteria when making their equipment selections. They must also determine the best placement of the equipment on the duty belt in order to maximize both their safety and their ability to access it. Finally, it is essential that they practice manipulat-

FIGURE 17-2 Equipment vests distribute the weight of equipment across the body and offer more storage options than a traditional duty belt.

ing their weapons under conditions unique to bike duty, such as while in the riding position and while wearing bike-specific protective equipment, such as padded cycling gloves.

■ Handguns

A majority of duty weapons, including both revolvers and semi-automatic pistols, are made of steel, either stainless or carbon, in their frame, barrel and slide or cylinder. These can be quite heavy.

If the agency offers a choice of weapons or allows officers to carry their choice of weapon as long as they qualify with it, armed public safety cyclists should consider some of the handguns with aluminum alloy or polymer/composite material frames. These handguns are available from a majority of the major manufacturers. Depending on the model and caliber, these weapons can weigh 25% to 50% less than their steel counterparts.

Because of the specialized bike equipment as well as the unique aspects of bike duty, all armed bike officers must receive bike-specific firearms training. This is addressed in Chapter 19.

■ Impact Weapons

Many public safety agencies issue their bike patrol personnel collapsible batons and impact weapons; however, some departments still issue long batons that are carried on the bicycle, held in a PVC sleeve or attached by zip-ties.

The benefit of carrying a collapsible impact weapon on the belt is that it is always with the officer, even when he or she dismounts from the bicycle for reasons such as initiating a foot pursuit or searching a building. If an impact weapon is attached to the frame of the bicycle, it will be inaccessible if the officer is separated from the bike or if the officer drops the bike on the side where the impact weapon is mounted.

Collapsible batons can be found in various lengths, from 16 to 29 inches, but consideration should be given to how length might affect the pedaling stroke or the ability to dismount the bicycle. The placement on the duty assembly and the ease of drawing the weapon is critical. A side-handled baton might be compromised by other equipment carried on the duty belt or by its position in relation to that equipment. Some manufacturers produce rotating or side-break scabbards for impact weapons that can help address some of these draw issues. Weapon retention concerns can be addressed by carrying the baton in a cross-draw fashion in front of the torso, rather than behind the handgun. Some bike officers may opt for impact weapons manufactured with aluminum alloy or polymer-based materials; however, these lightweight models are often less effective.

■ Chemical Spray

Finding a convenient place to put the spray on the duty belt is sometimes difficult. If the officer cannot remove and administer the spray easily, it is useless.

Finding the right place to position the chemical spray requires experimentation and practice. What works for one officer may not work for another.

■ Conductive Energy Devices

An electrical control device, such as a TASER®, is classified as a non-lethal weapon. It is used for subduing a person by firing something that administers an electric shock, which disrupts superficial muscle functions. Modern weapons of this type fire small dart-like electrodes propelled by small gas charges; the electrodes have metal wires that connect to the gun. The projectiles use a pulse or arc of electricity that disrupts nerve and muscle function. These pulse models are designed to bring down a subject wearing up to a Level III body armor vest.

The CED can be a practical choice for a bike officer. It is small and can hook onto the duty belt or into a pouch on an equipment vest, and it does not interfere with the operation of the bicycle.

Handcuffs

It is becoming standard practice to issue two or even three pair of handcuffs to bicycle patrol personnel. Handcuffs can be the typical linked model or the hinged variety, and they are manufactured in lightweight material, such as titanium, as well as stainless steel.

Whether using linked or hinged handcuffs, officers must practice manipulation skills, much as they do for the duty handgun, impact weapon, chemical spray or other equipment they carry. This includes practicing using the handcuffs with both half-fingered and full-fingered gloves. Officers should practice various handcuffing techniques (such as the FBI, COGA, or speed-cuffing methods), and double-locking and removing the cuffs while wearing gloves. A cuff key extender can be beneficial for this procedure.

The storage method of the handcuffs is also a consideration. A handcuff case protects the cuffs from the elements, whereas looping them on keepers attached to the duty assembly exposes them to weather extremes and increases the inspection and maintenance required. Handcuff cases can be found in single or double, but the latter can feel bulky on the duty belt.

Conclusion

Departments should evaluate their standard equipment and determine whether it is the most practical option for use by bike officers. It may be necessary to issue different equipment to the bike patrol or permit officers to supply their own equipment, within the agency's parameters. Regardless of the equipment issued, officers must become proficient in its use through proper initial and refresher training programs, and bike-specific practice.

Patrol Procedures and Tactics

chapter at a glance

Introduction

In the hands of a trained police cyclist, a bike is much more than a mode of transportation. It is a versatile law enforcement tool that can be used to achieve many different goals. Bikes can be incorporated into multiple aspects of policing, and for this reason, bike officers must know how to use the bike to gain a tactical advantage in a wide variety of situations. They must also know how to overcome the tactical disadvantages of the bike. This chapter addresses many of the considerations of operating a mountain bike in a police capacity, including safe patrol tactics and communication, effective rapid dismounts, stealth and plain clothes patrol, suspect contact, and traffic enforcement.

Communications

Communication is essential to the bike officer. Most police cyclists do not have vehicle locators, and if the officers become engaged in an enforcement situation or other incident, backup units may be unable to find them if they have not communicated their position to dispatch. Officers in patrol cars are accustomed to looking for other cruisers and may not notice a bike officer, especially after dark. Com-

pounding this is the fact that bikes often go where motor vehicles cannot. Therefore, prior to any enforcement action or contact, bike officers must always relay their precise positions, using both street names and landmarks.

Communication among bicycle officers working as a team is equally essential. Officers riding in pairs need to remain aware of one another's location, especially if they will be separated for any period of time. They should also develop a plan for any contact or arrest situation. In time, partners will be able to read each other's nonverbal cues, but until that familiarity exists, even the smallest things should be vocalized. If an arrest is going to be made, there should be a primary officer and a secondary officer. The primary officer should communicate what actions the team will take, such as "He's walking southbound on the sidewalk. I'll take the sidewalk and you take the street. I'll try to contact him near the set of cars so that you'll have cover." It takes very little time to develop a plan and communicate it. In the event of a higher risk contact or an arrest, it may be advisable for both officers to locate cover and then attempt to take verbal control of the subject, thereby minimizing the risk of injury to both officers.

While communication between partners and with the command center is essential, it is equally es-

sential that the communication remain private. Police cyclists should consider using an ear microphone attachment for their radios. Police radio sounds travel easily and can communicate an officer's location to a suspect, placing the bike officer in danger.

Dismounts

Upon arrival on a scene, officer safety normally dictates that a police cyclist dismount prior to contacting a subject. Officers should not attempt to control, handcuff, or fight a person while straddling a bicycle. There are times that the standard method of bringing the bike to a complete stop, placing the left foot on the ground, and stepping off the bike is fine; however, other situations demand more urgency. Consequently, police and security cyclists must know how to dismount quickly and safely while keeping their subjects in sight at all times. Dismounting skills must be developed to the point that they become second nature. These methods are suitable for use by peace officers only. IPMBA maintains that the only responsible way for an EMS cyclist who is carrying a heavy load that may be worth several thousand dollars to dismount is to stop with the left foot planted on the ground and step off the bike.

Any technique that suggests the officer physically contact or strike the suspect with the bike before dismounting may look dramatic, but such techniques place the officer at greater risk of being injured. In addition, such techniques may fall outside departmental guidelines on use of force and would be considered only as a last resort.

■ Pedal Retention

The first step of any dismount is to disengage the pedal retention devices. Regardless of the type of pedal retention used, cyclists should get into the habit of disengaging in anticipation of every dismount. This practice will better prepare the cyclist to dismount rapidly and safely and minimize the risk of a fall.

Cyclists who use toe clips and straps should be aware of a few issues unique to this type of pedal retention. Removing the feet and letting the toe clip or strap hang upside down beneath their pedals can cause a scraping sound on the ground that may eliminate any stealth advantage. If, when pulling the feet out of the toe clip or strap and placing the toes on the back edge of the pedal cage, the foot is not at least partially out of the toe clip, the twisting motion can cause even a loosened toe clip strap to tighten firmly enough to hold the foot in place. These potential problems can be alleviated through practice. Likewise, cyclists who use clipless pedals must practice and master the skill of rapidly disengaging from their pedals prior to using them on patrol, as an inability to disengage quickly and flawlessly can pose a significant officer safety issue.

■ Crossover Dismount

The simplest and most effective dismount is the crossover dismount, in which the cyclist crosses one leg over the back wheel, behind the saddle, and comes to a stop with both legs on the same side of the bike.

The first step in the crossover dismount is to disengage from the pedal retention devices. The next step is the maneuver that gives it its name. The cyclist crosses one leg behind the saddle and over the back wheel, resting it against the other leg and coming to a stop with both legs on the same side of the bike (FIGURE 18-1).

The cyclist exits the bike by stepping off the bike with the back, or dangling, foot first, and then, while still gripping the handlebar for balance, the cyclist carefully removes the remaining foot from the pedal. Once both feet are on the ground and the cyclist is balanced, the bike can be released. In normal circumstances, the kickstand can be engaged or

the bike placed carefully on its left side so the rear derailleur does not get damaged or knocked out of adjustment. In a pursuit or high-risk situation, however, the bike may fall to the ground unpredictably, thus it is wise to practice placing the bike quietly so that it becomes second nature. That said, under these circumstances, minimizing damage to the bike should not be a priority for the officer.

Crossover dismounts can be performed on both sides of the bike. Most people have more control standing on the left side of the bike, but it is important to master dismounting from either side in case a left-side exit is impractical or unsafe. When exiting the bike from either side, leave it resting 8 to 10 feet away from the subject. It can be dangerous to have a bike underfoot if the subject resists and a physical confrontation ensues.

The Crossover Dismount

1. Disengage from the pedal retention.
2. Cross one leg over the saddle and over the back wheel.
3. Rest it against the other leg and come to a stop with both legs on the same side of the bike.
4. Step off the bike with the back leg first and then step off with the other leg.
5. Engage the kickstand.

■ Rolling Crossover Dismount

The rolling crossover dismount enables the public safety cyclist to immediately walk or run upon dismounting. This maneuver is often used to apprehend fleeing suspects or achieve tactical deployments from the bike. It requires a good sense of balance and, as with most hand-eye coordination skills, mental preparation.

The cyclist prepares for the dismount by visualizing where and how he or she will actually leave the bike. With practice, this mental preparation narrows to a second or two, and the maneuver becomes automatic. It is advisable to first practice at slow speeds and gradually work up to higher speed dismounts. The dismount can be initiated at any speed, but the rider needs to be able to keep up the same speed and momentum (running or walking) as the bike after stepping off of it. Although it is important to master the rolling crossover dismount from both sides of the bike, dismounting from the left side of the bike is preferred because: (1) the kickstand is usually mounted on the left side;

FIGURE 18-1 In the crossover dismount, the cyclist comes to a stop with both legs on the same side of the bike.

(2) dismounting from the right side can result in injury from the chain rings, especially to the Achilles tendon; and (3) laying the bike down on the derailleur (right) side can cause damage to vital components, especially at higher speeds. Protecting the derailleur should be a priority and only disregarded in high-risk situations.

The first step in the dismount is to disengage from pedal retention. Keeping both hands on the handlebars and the brake levers engaged by at least the index and middle fingers of both hands, look at the place you want to stop the bike, not at the ground in front of the wheel. Next, decide from which side of the bike it is most advantageous to dismount, based on the reason for dismounting. Even if dismounting to the left side of the bike, you will either lay the bike down or use the kickstand, depending on the situation.

Once you have decided on which side to exit the bike, shift to a gear from which it will be easy to start after you have stopped, and move the pedal on that side of the bike to the 6 o'clock position.

Next, swing the other leg over the saddle and the rear of the bike. This will put you in a standing position with the pedal in the 6 o'clock position. The leg you have swung over the bike is the trailing leg and, in most cases, it will be the one that touches down first. Keep it close to the forward leg, because positioning it too far back can create balance problems, especially at higher speeds, and may cause you to do a split when you touch the ground, which usually results in a fall. You will have enough momentum that the bike will continue to roll. If you were attempting to apprehend a suspect fleeing on foot and this is no longer the ideal opportunity to dismount, you are not completely committed at this point. You can continue pursuing with the bike by simply swinging the trailing leg back over the bike and continuing to pedal.

As you stand on the down pedal, center your body weight over the bottom bracket along the seat tube, with the bike in an upright position. The bike should not be leaning left or right. Do not lean your body across the frame to the opposite of the bike to try to maintain balance, as doing so is likely to cause you to fall.

At this point, it is time to make speed and braking decisions. It is crucial to the success of this maneuver that you control the braking with a bias toward the rear brake. If you use too much front brake, your weight will shift forward (over the front wheel) as you stop. The momentum will either send you over the handlebars with the bike tumbling after you or cause you to trip over your forward leg after you step off the bike with the trailing leg. If you have positioned your body weight over the bottom bracket and seat tube, your fore/aft balance should be just right. Gradually begin to apply the brakes, using the amount of pressure necessary to stop at the desired speed while still maintaining fore and aft balance.

Keep your eyes on the place where you intend to dismount. Do not look at the front wheel, your feet, or the ground beneath the bike; this will throw off your equilibrium and impair your ability to control the bike safely. Once you have mastered the hand-eye-body coordination of this move and it has become instinctive, you can shift your focus to the person you are contacting.

When you have reached the speed at which you feel it is safe to dismount, apply the brakes harder, maintaining the bias towards the rear brake, and bring the bike to as complete a stop as possible. If you are traveling at a high speed, the bike may begin to skid, especially on loose surfaces; do not step off until you feel that you can keep up with the momentum of the bike as it continues to move.

You will normally step off with the trailing leg first and then the foot that was on the pedal, because at lower speeds this method causes less disruption of balance than just hopping off with both feet at the same time. Then, either lay the bike down or deploy the kickstand, making sure it has a solid footing.

If you dismount from the left side of the bike and intend to lay it down, let go of the left side of the handlebar first (releasing the front brake lever) while laying the bike on the ground (FIGURE 18-2). The right hand should lock the rear brake and lower the bike at the same time. This gives you control of the bike and can prevent it from bouncing up and hitting you, minimizing the potential for damage. The opposite will not work if you lay it down from the right side, because you would be locking the brake of the front wheel, which may not be touching the ground.

FIGURE 18-2 If you dismount from the left side of the bike and intend to lay it down, let go of the left side of the handlebar first (releasing the front brake lever) while laying the bike on the ground.

■ Hook (Power) Slide

The hook slide, also known as the power slide, is used to enable the cyclist to change direction and dismount quickly. It is useful when there is a need to make quick, face-to-face contact with subjects before they have a chance to make an evasive move. The first step is to pick an area to make the stop, leaving enough room to make a swinging arc of a turn toward, but in front of, the subject. This will create a safety zone between you and the bike in case you have to back up while on foot.

Before reaching the point at which you will perform the slide, decide from which side of the bike you will dismount. Stand on the opposite pedal (the outside pedal), with your buttocks off the saddle and straddling the top tube. You will be standing on the outside pedal, which will be on the "up" side of the bike after you lay it down.

As you stand on the outside pedal, your body weight should be biased toward the front of the bike and supported mainly by the outer leg. This will lighten the rear of the bike and cause the locked wheel to skid. If too much of your body weight is over the rear wheel, it will not skid when you try to make it slide with the bike leaned into a turn as in this maneuver. The tire will grab the pavement and the momentum will send you over the bike in the direction you were initially headed, not in the direction you chose to turn.

When you reach the point at which you will make the turn back toward the subject and dismount, lean the bike in that direction and counter-steer with the handlebars, that is, turn them in the opposite direction of where you want to go (FIGURE 18-3). This will assist in laying the bike down against its forward momentum. It may be helpful to lean the inside of the thigh of the out-side, weight-supporting leg against the top tube for leverage. Simultaneously, plant the inside foot as your pivot point for the turn/slide, and lock up the rear brake. Only practice will help you determine how far from the bike to plant your pivot foot. It must be far enough away to help lean the bike, but not so far that it causes you to lose balance as you step off the bike (FIGURE 18-4).

Locking the rear brake will cause the rear tire to slide in the direction you were going before you turned the bike. As the rear wheel slides away from you, lay the bike down so you can step off and away, unencumbered by the bike. If you dismount from the left side of the bike, you should try to employ the same handlebar control as in the rolling dismount: release the front brake first, and so on.

If you have trouble getting the bike to turn and lean over, try more counter-steering and pressure on the top tube with the outer leg. If the rear wheel does not slide, you probably have too much weight over it. Correct this by moving your weight forward. A good rule is to position your head and shoulders above or over the handlebars. This maneuver must be done with some speed because the rear wheel needs mo-mentum to slide. As with the other dismounts, it is helpful to first practice this move in a grassy area. Once you become proficient with the rear wheel slide, you will realize how quickly you can reposition your bicycle to gain a tactical advantage.

Cover and Concealment

Bike officers are among the most vulnerable officers on patrol; therefore, they must employ tactics to help reduce their risk. Knowing the difference be-tween cover and concealment, and employing them effectively, is essential. Cover is an object or barrier that stops, deflects, or substantially slows down projectiles, for instance, an engine block, telephone

FIGURE 18-3 Hook slide.

FIGURE 18-4 Plant the inside foot as your pivot point for the turn/slide.

pole, or concrete wall (FIGURE 18-5). Concealment is something that can hide a person from view but does not provide protection from projectiles, for instance, darkness, a bush, a fence, or a garbage can (FIGURE 18-6).

Although police officers are accustomed to seeking cover and/or concealment, bike officers must take their helmets into consideration. They must ensure their helmets can be accommodated by their cover/concealment choices. If the situation necessitates that you remove your helmet, position it such that it will be easy to put back on if you have to remount and continue on the bike. The helmet plays a vital role in the identification of the officer and should therefore not be removed except in situations when the officer is reasonably certain it will no longer be needed, such as a building search, or if it could pose a danger. Bike officers should accept the helmet as an integral part of their police uniform and learn to adapt their cover and concealment techniques accordingly.

It is impossible for a bicycle officer to have cover available continuously while on patrol; therefore, he or she must always be aware of the surroundings and the existence of potential cover

FIGURE 18-6 Using concealment.

FIGURE 18-5 Bike officers should constantly seek and use cover.

and concealment. Just as officers are taught in their basic training, the use of potential cover, concealment, and possible escape routes must be reassessed continually during all suspect contact situations.

Left-side bicycle dismounts are the most natural; therefore, bike officers should be especially mindful of potential cover to the left prior to making an arrest or contacting a suspect. When cover is not available, the bicycle officer should use concealment to limit the subject's opportunity to react to the bicycle officer's presence. However, there is no tactical advantage to remaining in an area that has no cover. If a suspect is moving through an area where cover is not available, you may choose to delay contacting the suspect until the surroundings are in your favor. The stealth-like capability of the bicycle can enable you to continue to observe the suspect undetected. As with all contacts, regardless of the type of patrol in which you are engaged, it is necessary to exercise good judgment and call for backup when appropriate.

Suspect Contact

Bike officers judge the risk associated with each contact and react accordingly, regardless of whether they are patrolling alone or with a partner. When resources permit, it is ideal to patrol with a partner; however, that is often not realistic.

When bike officers ride in teams of two, the concept of contact and cover should govern their actions. Contact and cover is a principle that allows multiple officers to control subjects during an encounter by clearly defining each officer's responsibilities, which can enhance officer safety. The contact officer is responsible for communicating with the suspect and dispatch, recording incident information, searching suspects, and issuing citations. The cover officer is responsible for scene safety, backing up the contact officer, controlling the suspects, and ensuring the integrity of the evidence. An officer who patrols alone obviously assumes the responsibilities of both cover and contacts and should call for a cover officer to assist with the contact if necessary. All arrests should be made in accordance with departmental policies and procedures.

The techniques described next categorize three levels of risk associated with public contact. Regardless of the risk level, most officers routinely unbuckle their helmet when they dismount to ensure that if they are involved in an altercation, they cannot be choked or controlled by an assailant who grabs their helmet. Some officers argue that the helmet may afford additional head protection during a fight and would likely only stay on if it were buckled, but that is not its purpose. Whichever option an officer chooses, he or she should be consistent to ensure the chosen technique becomes second nature.

■ Low Risk Contact

A low risk contact is one in which the officer perceives no immediate threat, for instance, an elderly couple that approaches to ask for directions or praise bike patrols. In such situations, both cover and contact officers may choose to stay on their bikes, stopping with the right foot in the power position. If they must dismount quickly, they can simply step to the left and lay their bikes on their non-drive sides. In doing so, they will create some time as well as position their bikes as an obstacle or hurdle between them and the suspect.

■ Medium Risk Contact

A medium risk contact is one that involves stopping an individual considered a potential suspect; for instance, someone who matches a description or whom an officer intends to question based on observation. The contact officer approaches and stops at a reasonable distance, speaks to the suspect, dismounts, and uses the bike as a barricade. During questioning, the suspect hands documents to the officer over the bike. This provides the officer with an advantage, because if the suspect reaches for the officer, he or she can kick the bike into the suspect while retreating, or grab and pull the suspect, causing the suspect to trip and fall on the bike. Throughout the contact, the cover officer stays mounted in the power position in case a chase ensues, and monitors the surroundings, ever mindful of crossfire (FIGURE 18-7).

■ High Risk Contact

A high risk contact is one in which the officer intends to take someone into custody. The situation and the environment at the time of a high risk stop are evaluated on an individual basis, but in general, the primary difference between a medium risk contact and a high risk contact is that the cover officer would likely take a position farther away from the suspect and be prepared to ride if the suspect flees. The officer will have evaluated the surroundings already and can become involved in the pursuit immediately. For the contact officer, a medium risk can immediately become a high risk stop if the suspect is going to be taken into custody, so little changes. The officers take the same precautions.

The contact officer may be able to use a stealth approach and effect an immediate apprehension, or may choose to dismount and use the bike as a barricade. If the suspect is cooperative, the contact officer has the option of backing the suspect up

FIGURE 18-7 The contact officer uses the bike as a barricade while the cover officer remains in the power pedal position.

against the bike (**FIGURE 18-8**) or using the bike to pin the suspect against a wall (**FIGURE 18-9**). If the suspect becomes uncooperative, the officer can pull the suspect backwards and down onto the bike. If the apprehension is made while ordering the suspect to the ground, the officer could immobilize the suspect with the bike while the subject is searched and cuffed (**FIGURE 18-10**).

■ A Tactical Approach

When contacting a suspect in medium or high risk situations, officers typically place themselves in the tactical L position, where the contact officer is in front of the subject and slightly offset. The cover officer is just outside the subject's peripheral vision. This enables both officers to observe the subject but avoids creating a potential crossfire situation (**FIGURE 18-11**).

It is the contact officer's responsibility to initiate the arrest. The cover officer approaches the suspect with the contact officer, but from a different angle, determined in part by the terrain. Because the cover officer can move more freely than the contact officer, the cover officer is responsible for positioning himself or herself to prevent crossfire situations. Typically the cover officer stays mounted until the threat of flight has been minimized. For their own safety, if a pursuit does ensue, the officers should attempt to stay within sight of each other.

Stealth Operations

Bicycles are a quiet mode of transportation that can enable officers to patrol without being noticed. This stealth enhances the officer's ability to conduct surveillance by affording access to unconventional lo-

FIGURE 18-8 The officer may choose to cuff the suspect over the bike.

FIGURE 18-9 The bike can be used to pin a suspect against a wall.

cations. By using a silent approach to crimes in progress, the bike increases the element of surprise, which makes it extremely effective in high-crime areas. Night patrols and plain clothes operations consistently illustrate the impact of a well-planned, covert project. The stealthy nature of bikes makes them ideal for a wide variety of crime-specific, area-specific, or suspect-specific enforcement programs.

Although most commonly considered in conjunction with night operations, stealth can be effective under any conditions. It not only means riding under the cover of darkness, it also means calming any noise created by the rider or equipment. In addition, police cyclists can use their surroundings to their advantage. Riding in shadows, against buildings, behind cars, or just simply blending in may help preserve stealth. Bike cops soon learn to use parking structures, alleys, walls, fences, trees,

dumpsters, shrubbery, landscaping, and buildings to conceal themselves from targeted persons.

■ Noise

Police officers need to be particularly aware of the sounds that they, their bikes, and their equipment make. Most public safety bikes are equipped with silent hubs to eliminate the sound of a coasting freewheel. These sounds can be minimized on bikes with regular hubs by pedaling slowly. Articles such as keys and tools can rattle around in a rack bag and should be quieted by wrapping them in cloth or other material. The bike should then be noise-tested by picking it up and dropping it a few inches, and riding it over a curb or other obstacle, listening for sounds that may give away your position. It is useful to incorporate this step into every pre-ride ABC Quick Check to ensure it is not overlooked. Finally, bicycle maintenance is important for more reasons than good performance: a poorly maintained bicycle makes unusual and unnecessary noises.

Bike officers must also be aware of the sound of their own voices and radio noises. When riding with a partner or in a group, the lead rider will

FIGURE 18-10 The officer could immobilize the suspect with the bike while the subject is searched and cuffed.

FIGURE 18-11 When contacting a suspect in a medium or high risk situation, officers typically place themselves in the tactical L position.

typically call out directions and warn of obstacles. To operate in stealth mode, riders must devise a series of silent signals to pass information back and forth. Radio traffic can be minimized through use of ear microphones and headsets.

Bike cops are not the only ones who may reveal their position because of the noise they create. Bike officers might hear breaking glass, gunshots, or cries for help that patrol car officers may not be able to hear. It is not uncommon for police cyclists to discover criminal activity in progress, after hearing noises and quietly following them to the scene.

Plain Clothes Patrol

Plain clothes bike patrol can be used effectively to address crime and unwanted conduct. Although it is similar in most respects to other plain clothes operations, there are several bike-specific considerations.

■ Clothing and Equipment

Select an inconspicuous bike for plain clothes patrol, but make sure it is mechanically sound and meets the legal requirements for lighting and other safety equipment. Painting some of the reflective parts, such as the crank arms and rims, flat black may be beneficial, especially for night operations.

Dress appropriately for the type of operation, but do not forgo personal protective equipment. Do not opt to patrol without a helmet in order to blend in; wear a plain helmet or a helmet cover over your police helmet. If you intend to use your equipment bag, be sure to remove or cover any police markings. A small backpack may be more appropriate in some situations, as many casual cyclists carry bags or backpacks rather than equip their bikes with racks and rack bags (FIGURE 18-12).

Do your best to conceal your body armor and duty equipment but do not forfeit any of your use-of-force options unless it is critical to the success of your project. And, as always, ensure you are in compliance with your agency's protocol.

■ Identification

Any plainclothes officer who makes contact with the public must be prepared to identify himself or herself with the proper credentials. This is especially critical on the bike, because the public are generally more skeptical about your identity when you have just hopped off a bicycle. Some may try to claim ignorance of the fact that you are a police officer if you do not identify yourself clearly.

Plainclothes bike officers may be called upon to perform regular police functions. Carry a retro-reflective vest with police markings in case you need to be visible for any reason, such as directing traffic at a crash.

Night Patrol

Bicycle patrol during darkness has distinct advantages over patrolling in a car; it is possible to see, hear, and smell things that would not be evident from the driver's seat of a cruiser. Bike officers in stealth mode typically patrol with minimal bike lighting in order to be less conspicuous. This emphasizes the importance of being familiar with your patrol area and its hazards, including obstacles, stairways, pavement flaws, and parking blocks. Night cycling is discussed in greater detail in Chapter 11; however, it is worth repeating that riding at night in traffic is exponentially more hazardous than riding during daylight hours.

Public safety cyclists must be cognizant of the effects of their lights, badges, and retro-reflective materials. Although some officers fear wearing any reflective material, placing retro-reflective material on the back of the uniform will help bike patrol members remain visible in traffic without compromising their safety. As explained in Chapter 11, retro-reflective material is designed to redirect a light source back in the exact direction from which it came. Therefore, if a car's headlights are pointed at an officer wearing retro-reflective material, the light returned to the driver of the car appears unusually bright, but a nearby suspect would not see the reflected light (FIGURE 18-13).

Because of its many shiny surfaces, a standard police badge poses a greater danger to the officer than does retro-reflective material. Bike officers are advised to use cloth or embroidered badges, especially for night operations.

An officer who is patrolling parks, trails, alleys, and parking lots may choose to do so without lights. The advantage in doing so is obvious. Patrols in these areas are conducted very slowly and are usually intended primarily for observation. The officer is essentially making an effort to hide. In addition, these areas are characterized by little or no vehicular traffic, and because they are not classified as roads, they are often exempt from legal lighting requirements. If you are unsure if it is legal to operate a bike without lights in these areas, check the local laws. When patrolling on the road in any circumstances, bike officers should ensure that they

FIGURE 18-12 Select an inconspicuous bike for plain clothes patrol, but make sure it is mechanically sound and meets the legal requirements for lighting and other safety equipment.

the first time, you will be introduced to an entirely new facet of police cycling. But your safety is of the utmost importance, and the research speaks for itself. Nearly half of all fatal cyclist collisions occur at night, and most of those crashes are because the driver failed to see the cyclist.

Traffic Enforcement

Bike officers can be very effective for traffic enforcement in specific situations, such as urban corridors and other settings where congestion is high and speeds are relatively slow. Officers can ride easily between lines of bumper-to-bumper traffic, looking down into the passenger compartments of the stopped vehicles as they pass. Numerous drunk driving arrests and open intoxicant tickets can be tallied in areas where cruising is popular or after

have both front and rear lights and are in compliance with the law. A public safety cyclist is at greatest risk while riding on the roadway after dark, and this risk can best be reduced through the use of proper lighting equipment.

In addition to equipping their bikes with front and rear lights, many bike officers attach a separate light to the rear of their duty belts. Not only does this create extra visibility in traffic, but if you were away from your bike and called for assistance, you would be more visible to back-up officers. Some believe that using a light in this manner could present a hazard if a suspect were to locate or target the officer because of the light. However, the importance of being located by your back-up or seen by motorists generally outweighs the risk of being assaulted because you are wearing a light. If the situation dictates, the flashing light can be switched off or easily discarded.

If you are patrolling on the bicycle at night for

FIGURE 18-13 Retroreflective material is designed to reflect light directly back to the source, not to all angles.

sporting events. These traffic stops often lead to other charges such as driving with a suspended license, open warrants, and drugs.

Bike officers are also effective in residential or downtown areas, where speeding, seat belt, and stop sign violations are common. The team approach is often used for such types of enforcement. For example, one officer might be positioned in a less conspicuous location with a radar unit or to simply observe. This officer reports speeds and descriptions to another officer (either on a bike or in a car) who is stationed a short distance up the street, ready to stop the vehicle, or waiting near the next stop sign to initiate contact.

Using bike officers for traffic enforcement raises a series of important questions: How does a police cyclist actually stop the vehicle while riding? What does the officer do for cover during the approach and duration of the contact? And what if the driver does not stop, either intentionally or unintentionally?

■ Traffic Stops

The first step in initiating a vehicle stop is capturing the driver's attention. Many drivers will be slow to recognize they are being stopped by a police cyclist; therefore, it is important for the officer to clearly identify himself or herself as a police officer. Without overhead lights or sirens, the bike officer requires an alternative signalling device. Several light/siren units have been designed specifically for police on bikes, although a whistle or verbal command can work just as well. A slow, exaggerated hand signal is one of the most effective methods of directing a driver to stop.

While still riding, the bike officer should stay behind the offending vehicle, as overlapping it would eliminate a potential escape route. If threatened, the officer would have to enter another lane of traffic on the driver's side or run up onto the curb or shoulder on the passenger side. If the driver does not stop and intentionally flees, officer safety must be the main priority. The police cyclist should provide the license number and vehicle description to the dispatcher, and rely on patrol cars to complete the pursuit and vehicle stop.

Once the driver has pulled over, the officer should always be aware of available cover. Care should be taken in placement of the bicycle to avoid damage to the bike by the vehicle and to allow for a rapid retreat to cover if necessary. Most traffic stops initiated by bike officers are conducted in urban settings, and if possible, the bike should be lifted onto the sidewalk next to the motor vehicle (**FIGURE 18-14**).

At this point, the officer approaches the driver in accordance with existing training and agency protocol. However, on a bike, a passenger side approach is preferred to the driver side approach for several reasons. Because the officer does not have the protection of a patrol car to offset from the target vehicle, approaching on the passenger side provides a certain measure of protection. Second, the passenger side approach is a surprise to the vehicle's occupants, who may not notice the officer immediately. This lag time puts the officer in a position to act rather than react, whether the choice is to retreat or engage. Again, it is critical that the officer clearly identify himself or herself to the driver, who will likely still be surprised at being stopped by a person on a bicycle.

Once the officer has made contact, the officer can increase his or her safety in several ways, such as asking the driver to activate the hazard lights for more rear visibility, or to turn off the engine to make it more difficult for the driver to flee.

To ensure safe traffic stops from a bicycle, remember the following:

- Do not ride next to or in front of a moving vehicle.
- Never make contact with a moving car.
- Position the bicycle to the rear of the vehicle, away from traffic, but not directly behind it.
- Do not position the bicycle in front of the vehicle in case the driver decides to flee.
- Approach the vehicle from the passenger side.

■ Vehicle Pursuits

In some instances, after considering the limited speed of bicycles, motorists have fled from police cyclists. While a police bike does not have the same equipment as a car, the cyclist can, at minimum, keep the vehicle in sight and report the direction of travel to the communications center. At times, however, bike officers can use their knowledge, training, and mobility to their advantage and catch up to the motorist.

Pursuing a motorist on a bicycle is exponentially more dangerous than simply patrolling on a bike. It places both the bike officer and the public at risk, and should only be undertaken as a last resort. Always consider the following:

- No one is faster than the radio. Call other officers to assist.
- Consider all factors. Do not disengage simply because the car is faster.
- The motorist may be forced to stop at the next traffic light or stop sign.
- Use bicycle-accessible shortcuts, such as alleys and vacant lots, to your advantage.
- A fleeing motorist's attention is usually not on the road, which may result in a crash with another car or object.
- Just as with a motorized pursuit, continually weigh the risks you are taking compared with the reason for the pursuit. Bike officers should adhere to departmental policy regarding vehicle pursuits, and seek clarification as to how that policy applies in situations involving bike officers.
- Pace yourself. If you are exhausted and out of breath when the driver does stop, you may

jeopardize your ability to use force if it becomes necessary.

Officers who engage in traffic enforcement on a bicycle increase the inherent risk of being injured. Officer safety is always the first consideration. Do not let the emotions associated with a fail-to-stop motorist cloud your judgement. Keep your enforcement effort in perspective. If a driver does not stop, under most circumstances you should let the motorist drive away. Do not compromise your safety for the sake of a speeding citation.

Responding to Urgent Calls

One of the many difficult skills a bicycle officer needs to learn is how to respond to an urgent, or "hot," call quickly, but not to the extent that the officer is exhausted upon arrival. Bicycle officers need to manage their energy so that, when they arrive at the call, they will still be able to respond to the situation effectively. A physical struggle with a suspect for any length of time demands an enormous amount of energy. Just speaking on the radio or concentrating on the scene of the event can be challenging if the officer is already exhausted. The worst scenario

FIGURE 18-14 Appropriately positioned bike and officer making passenger side approach.

would be arriving at an urgent call nearly incapacitated because of fatigue, thus becoming a liability for your colleagues or a victim yourself.

Bicycle officers must also exercise caution while moving into the area, using whatever cover and concealment is available. They must be alert to their surroundings and mindful of any limitations placed on their vision by the helmet; for instance, it may impede their ability to observe activity on balconies or rooftops. Again, as is the case with any type of patrol, they must use good judgment and wait for other units to arrive when appropriate.

Conclusion

Bike officers can and should engage in everyday police patrol functions, such as responding to calls. They will build credibility with their colleagues, who may still be skeptical about the value of bike patrol, when they are seen performing their share of the duties. In the case of low-priority calls, the extra time it may take a bike officer to arrive on the scene is often immaterial. However, depending on the area, officers on bicycles often arrive on scene earlier than those in cars because of their ability to maneuver around traffic congestion and use shortcuts only accessible to bikes. If the geographic patrol area is large and staffing issues prevent the officer from riding a bicycle for the entire shift, a bike rack can be mounted on the patrol car for a park and ride. It is also possible to remove the front wheel and put the bike in the back seat of the car.

Criminals often choose to commit their deeds where police cruisers cannot follow, and bike cops often patrol such areas quite successfully. Bikes are so quick and stealthy that criminals usually do not have a chance to conceal evidence or flee. If a suspect does run, the police cyclist is able to utilize the mechanical advantage of the bicycle, increasing the chances of apprehension.

Police cyclists will always play a role in various community policing and education initiatives; however, many law enforcement agencies integrate them into a wide variety of operations. Whether it is plainclothes patrol or traffic enforcement, conducting business from the saddle of a bicycle offers unique advantages but also requires a new approach to patrol tactics. By thinking tactically and strategically, bike officers can reduce their own risks and enhance their effectiveness in a wide variety of situations.

References

IACP (2004). *Model Bicycle Patrol Policy*, August.

Vonk, Kathleen (2002). Beyond Community Policing: The Crime-Fighting Effectiveness of the Police Cyclist. *Law and Order* magazine, Volume 50, Number 4, pages 92–96.

U.S. Consumer Product Commission (2001). *Night Bike Riders at Risk*. Document 5003.

19

Firearms Training

Introduction

The first documented bike officer-involved shooting in the modern era of police cycling occurred in 1989. Two bike officers in Seattle were investigating an alcohol-related open container offense. During the course of their investigation, the confrontation escalated and both officers were shot. Over the years, many police cyclists have been involved in shootings and other deadly force encounters. These encounters have taken place in a variety of settings, including military installations, hospitals, and university campuses. This comes as no surprise: while on patrol, bike officers frequently ride into narcotics transactions and other crimes in progress. The officers themselves are often surprised, which can make them vulnerable. As a result, experienced public safety cyclists have recognized the need for specialized firearms and tactical training specific to the duties of the armed public safety cyclist.

Training Mandates from the Higher Courts

Historically, the higher courts, including the United States Supreme Court, have unintentionally guided the development of police deadly force training. Courts have dictated to federal, state, and local

agencies what type of deadly force training should be implemented for law enforcement. In some cases, courts found agencies liable for failing to train and prepare officers for firearms-related use of force incidents properly.

In *Young v. City of Killeen 775 F. 2d 1349 (5th Cir. 1985)* the court found the agency negligent in training, tactics, and procedures because the officer failed to use back up; failed to use the police radio; placed his patrol vehicle dangerously close in relation to the suspects; ordered two men out of the vehicle at once rather than keeping them somewhat immobilized and with hands in plain view; and chose to abandon a cover position and advance into the open where the odds of overreacting would be greater. It was the court's opinion that if the officer had stayed behind cover, he may have not caused the situation to escalate or may not have had to use deadly force.

In *Popow v. City of Margate 476 F. Supp. 1237 DNJ 1979,* the court described the agency's training and supervision as "grossly inadequate" because training did not reflect the environment in which officers worked (e.g., dim light, moving targets, "shoot-don't shoot" decisions, and shooting in populated areas), and the officer's training was not ongoing and therefore was not recent.

In *Zuchel v. Denver 53 Cr L 1327,* July 21, 1993,

the court deemed that the officer's deadly force training was inadequate because the officer's training consisted only of one "shoot-don't shoot" video; therefore, instruction in "shoot-don't shoot" situations, as well as how to avoid them, was inadequate.

These cases also align firearms training with the proper use of tactics, as in *Killeen. Popow* elaborated on the types of activities to be included in range exercises and mandated that training be ongoing throughout an officer's career. *Zuchel* and *Popow* emphasized the concept of decision making and discriminating between "shoot" and "don't shoot" targets.

The Three R's

These landmark cases apply to all police specialty units, including police cyclists. Thus, the three R's—realism, recency, and relevance—must be integral to the design and implementation of firearms training for the police cyclist. Such factors as the officer's available equipment, environment, and ability to use weapons both effectively and safely must be considered to ensure that the training meets the three R's rule. The training must be current with trends, including available technology, meaning that a refresher course of live fire training that simulates real-world conditions should be implemented on a regular basis. Finally, firearms training should incorporate lessons learned from documented deadly force encounters. Collaborating with firearms and use of force instructors for instructional design is one of the best methods of providing effective and defensible training for bike officers and their agencies.

Research indicates that the conditions in which a police cyclist typically operates include outdoors, darkness, secluded areas, and exposed areas. The environment often lacks the immediate cover and concealment afforded to an officer operating a motor vehicle. For these reasons, bike officers may need to fire their sidearms accurately from considerable distances. Firearms training should capture these issues along with physical factors associated with riding a bike, such as the physiological effects of riding aggressively to a call. Providing the officer with an opportunity to experience those effects in the training environment before experiencing them on the street is of paramount importance. Officers engaged in live fire exercises should also train as they patrol, i.e., on their bikes and wearing their full bike uniforms, including gloves, helmet, and eye protection.

The Three R's

The three R's—realism, recency, and relevance—must be integral to the design and implementation of firearms training for the police cyclist.

■ Deadly Force Encounters

Data on other officers' experiences is one of the most logical and valuable tools to consider when designing training. Training should be based on what could happen because it *has* happened, and should recognize that the likelihood of such occurrences may be based upon the mission and duties of the public safety cyclist. Incorporating these considerations can help satisfy the three R's.

Training should reflect the conditions that the officer will most likely encounter in the scope of his or her duties. The circumstances of 32 police cyclists involved in deadly force encounters have some elements in common. The information in TABLE 19-1 has been provided by the actual officers involved, their partners, police reports, and press releases, as well as published articles and the *Complete Guide to Police Cycling,* 1st edition. An overview of incidents, locations, number of officers, number of suspects, time of day, etc., highlights the common factors among the situations.

Many of these encounters occurred while police cyclists were on general patrol. Therefore, it is reasonable to believe that public safety cyclists are likely to have spontaneous encounters. Foot pursuits and motor vehicles also appear be hazardous to the public safety cyclist. As national studies of law enforcement officers assaulted and killed in the line of duty show, evening hours continue to dominate in terms of when such incidents occur. Police cyclists often ride in pairs; the data indicates that multiple officers were usually present in encounters where deadly force was used. It also indicates that alcohol and narcotics play a part in a significant number of police cyclist-involved shootings. This information will help determine relevance for designing and developing range training as well as reality-based training for the public safety cyclist.

■ Equipment Considerations

As discussed in Chapter 17, public safety cyclists use clothing and equipment specific to the conditions under which they operate. They lack access to equipment readily available to officers in cars. These factors must be considered in the design of firearms and other use of force training for bike officers.

Gloves

If the police cyclist wears gloves on duty, as IPMBA recommends, training with all force options while wearing the same gloves is likewise recommended, whether the glove is full-fingered or the fingertips are exposed. This is essential because the barrier created by the gloves between the skin and the object may cause the object to feel different. In the case of firearms, the typical cycling glove has padding in the heel of the hand; this could adversely affect the grip and trigger indexing, causing the officer to shoot abnormally. For example, a right-handed officer may find his or her point of impact shifting up and to the right due to the heeling effect on the weapon caused by the padding. Conversely, some shooters prefer shooting with gloves because the padding helps to minimize the perceived recoil of the weapon. The padding can also cause difficulty during reloading. Officers may

TABLE 19-1 Deadly Force Encounters

Police Cyclist-Involved Deadly Force Encounters (as of December 2006)

Of the 32 encounters studied:

Daytime versus nighttime

19 encounters occurred during evening hours. Eight occurred during the daytime; five are unknown.

Number of officers present

22 involved more than one officer. 10 were single officer incidents.

Number of suspects present

In 16 incidents, multiple suspects were involved.

General patrol versus dispatched calls

26 incidents occurred when officers were on general patrol, four were dispatched to the area for a complaint, one involved cooperative narcotics operations, and one is unknown.

Narcotics and alcohol factors

13 of the encounters involved narcotics, alcohol, or a combination of both.

Foot pursuits

In eight of the incidents, officers pursued suspects on foot.

Weapons

17 of the deadly force encounters involved guns.

14 involved motor vehicle assaults.

One involved an edged weapon.

In one incident, no weapon was used.

Location

Two occurred on college campuses.

Two occurred in hospital settings.

Six occurred in known drug areas.

26 occurred in an urban environment.

Nine occurred in parking lots.

Other

Two incidents involved identified emotionally disturbed persons.

One was found to be a "suicide by cop" mission.

Compiled by Officer L. A. Hamblin.

---

experience a different "feel" when they draw and seat the magazine. If the glove is too loose or the padding is too thick, it may catch in the magazine well. Therefore, live fire range exercises should include drawing and firing as well as stoppage clearing and magazine exchanges while the officer is wearing the same cycling gloves that will be worn on duty.

Helmets

The helmet might be an impediment while the officer is in a prone position. It may cause the officer to contort his or her body to obtain a good sight picture, which may reduce shooting accuracy. If the officer fires from a prone firing position, he or she can remove the helmet if there is time. However, most real-world spontaneous encounters will not allow for the removal of helmets.

■ Weapon Retention

In 1998, the IPMBA membership survey indicated that vulnerability is a significant officer safety concern; 48% of the respondents believed the chance of being assaulted was greater while patrolling via mountain bike than via automobile. As stated in Chapter 17, the riding position leaves the weapon exposed. There have been several documented weapon grabs involving bike officers, including one resulting in officer injury (Boone County, Kansas City, MO, 1994), one resulting in a suicide by a student using the officer's sidearm (Our Lady of the Lake University, TX, 2002), and one in which the officer was not injured and the suspect died of a cocaine overdose (Dayton, OH, 2004).

Weapon retention for police cyclists can be improved by carrying the baton in a cross-draw fashion in front of the torso, rather than behind the handgun; by positioning weapons and other control devices towards the front of the body, forward of the hips; and by using security holsters for both the handgun and any conductive energy device.

Weapon retention can also be improved through weapon retention training specific to the bike officer. Such training should include on-bike exercises such as the gauntlet (FIGURE 19-1). In this exercise, which simulates a crowd situation, one cyclist at a time rides through a gauntlet of people, offering no resistance as items are removed from the cyclist's gun belt. Open-ended baton holders and level one holsters are easily defeated. In the next part of the drill, only one member of the crowd attempts a pistol or baton grab. The cyclist dismounts from the bike quickly while maintaining his or her weapons and then handles the threat in

an appropriate manner. This enables the officer to experience the difficulty of disengaging from the bike and gain a sense of the weapon's vulnerability. The officer must become intimately familiar with his holster's built-in retention measures and what it takes for an attacker to defeat them. The officer needs to tailor his or her weapon retention tactics to those that do not negate the retention of the holster. Any tactics that lessen the retention of the holster should be regarded as last resorts.

■ Secondary Weapons

The configuration of police cyclist uniforms, especially polo-style uniform shirts, can limit back-up weapon carrying options. Department policy may dictate where an officer can carry a secondary weapon, as well as the weapon's caliber, which may limit an officer due to the physical size of the

FIGURE 19-1 Gauntlet training can help an officer become less vulnerable to a weapon grab.

weapon. Because shorts are a part of the standard public cycling uniform, ankle holsters are not a carrying option. The design of most duty cycling pants, which are cinched at the ankle or equipped with a stirrup, also eliminates ankle holsters as an option. Some carrying options for back-up pistols for the public safety cyclist are a body armor holster, a holster inside the cargo pocket, or a retrofitted bike jacket holster.

Regardless of the carry mode, the officer must train in producing and firing the back-up weapon; training should include shooting from awkward positions as a result of falling or crashing the bike, e.g., lying on the ground or in a fetal position.

■ Long-Distance Shooting

Police cyclists are limited by their lack of access to shoulder-mounted weapons. A public safety cyclist should therefore understand his or her pistol's capability and his or her ability to deliver deadly force in a controlled fashion, especially at greater distances. Because of the lack of immediate cover and the speed afforded by a patrol car, the police cyclist may not be able to quickly catch up with an armed suspect. Simply stated, a speeding bullet will beat a pedaling officer to the scene every time. On June 30, 1994, Airman Andrew Brown pedaled aggressively to the medical facility located on the Fairchild Air Force base in Spokane, Washington. There he was faced with an active shooter wielding a MAK-90 assault rifle. Brown dismounted his bicycle and effectively delivered deadly force from 71 yards away with his 9 mm semi-automatic pistol. This ended a shooting spree that left 4 people dead and 23 wounded. Although this is one of the more memorable incidents, there have been other documented police cyclist-involved shootings that have occurred from greater than 20 yards. Officers should be required to test their marksmanship capabilities in a training environment that encourages the development of an extended range of handgun performance.

Range Exercises

A basic course of firearms usage should be part of any police or armed security cycling unit training program. Some variations may be necessary depending on the range and training facility availability; however, the following exercises represent fundamental functions of the police cyclist and should be addressed when developing range exercises.

■ Indoor Ranges

Indoor ranges have limitations because they do not capture the environment in which the bike officer typically rides, with some exceptions, such as shopping malls and airports. Even so, there are many relevant exercises that can be performed on the indoor range. Here are some examples of typical indoor range drills that can be conducted under the supervision of a qualified range officer.

- Stationary dismounts facing toward and away from the target.
- Slow roll dismounts to engage turning targets.
- Weapon transitioning drills deploying all control devices on the gun belt individually; multiple weapons, e.g., O.C. and baton; and escalating or de-escalating using all force options.
- Relative shooting positions, on and off the bike, sitting and lying on the ground (FIGURE 19-2A–D).
- Shooting while moving around the bike, keeping track of the bike relative to the shooter (FIGURE 19-3).
- Use of FATS and other simulators.
- Weapon manipulation drills while wearing cycling gloves, e.g., clearing stoppages, magazine exchanges, deploying O.C., etc. (FIGURE 19-4).
- Use of a stationary trainer to simulate riding hard to a call, using a heart rate monitor to determine level of exertion, followed by dismounting the stationary trainer and shooting with elevated heart rates.
- Low-light shooting conditions using bike lights.
- Using smaller targets to simulate distance shooting.

■ Outdoor Ranges

Outdoor ranges can provide multiple fields of fire depending upon range design. They typically offer the possibility of increased speeds prior to dismounting and can test a shooter's marksmanship ability at greater distances. The following exercises can be performed in any outdoor range facility with a qualified range officer.

- Relative shooting positions, on and off the bike, sitting and laying on the ground. (Figure 19-2, A–D).
- Higher speed rolling dismounts.
- Moving/aggressive targets and simulated foot pursuits.

FIGURE 19-2A–D Shooting from relative positions.

- Weapon transitioning drills and practice deploying all control devices.
- Moving around the bike when upright or positioned on the ground (Figure 19-3).
- Simulated foot pursuits using drop, spin, or pneumatic target systems.
- Stationary dismounts facing towards and away from the target.
- Weapon manipulation drills while wearing cycling gloves, e.g., clearing stoppages, magazine exchanges, deploying O.C., etc. (Figure 19-4).
- Use of cover.
- Firing from increasing distances.

◼ Tactical Considerations

There are several tactical considerations that are unique to bike officers. These should be integrated into firearms training by discussion or practice as appropriate and feasible within facility limitations.

Dismounts

Officers should practice moving dismounts during live fire range exercises, including dismounts at varying speeds to experience the physiological effects of riding, exiting the bike, and identifying and engaging a deadly threat. Both

FIGURE 19-3 The officer must be aware of the bike's position at all times while engaging the suspect.

crossover dismounts and hook slide dismounts (Chapter 18) should be incorporated into range exercises.

Knowing how to dismount the bike is a fundamental of public safety cycling, and knowing when to dismount rapidly is essential to officer safety (FIGURE 19-5). The use of moving target systems teaches and tests the officer's ability to disengage from the bike and address the advancing target. The target is stationary until the officer moves into its path. The target is then put into motion, creating urgency for the officer to clear the bike and engage the advancing suspect.

Cover

Seeking cover should always be emphasized to the public safety cyclist. During range exercises, officers are encouraged to use points of cover when they are available, including telephone poles, cars, buildings, fire hydrants, and mailboxes (FIGURE 19-6). This point becomes especially clear when the firearms training incorporates reality-based training using force-on-force scenarios. Exercises should simulate situations in which no cover is available, causing the bike officer to shoot while moving towards cover and creating a moving target for the adversary. The training

FIGURE 19-4 Potential negative effects of gloves on weapon manipulation can be mitigated through practice while wearing the gloves.

should also emphasize the importance of staying with the bike as long as possible to maintain the mechanical advantage, as well as how to recognize when the bike is no longer an advantage. These tactical decisionmaking skills are important for officer survival.

Exertion

Because bike officers are self-propelled, an understanding of how exertion level affects performance is valuable. Therefore, it is imperative that bicycle officers maintain a high level of cardiovascular fitness, as Chapter 14 discusses. They should also have an understanding of how to monitor and control their own physiological responses. Drills that incorporate various levels of physical exertion can educate officers and training staff about physiological effects of exertion on performance.

Exertion can inhibit an officer's ability to exit the bike safely, shoot accurately, secure suspects, communicate with loud and clear verbal direction, etc.

Shooting from the Saddle

IPMBA has established that there are no tactical benefits in engaging in a firefight while on a moving mountain bike. The 1998 IPMBA survey posed this question to respondents: Do you think you could fire effectively from a moving mountain bike? Of the 145 responses, 37% responded that they could, but only under unrealistic conditions, while 63% stated they could not perform this task well even if it were not against department policy.

Just because it is possible to do something on a mountain bike does not mean that it should be

FIGURE 19-5 Dynamic dismounts are an important component of bike-specific firearms training.

FIGURE 19-6 Bike officers should seek points of cover to reduce their vulnerability to injury.

done. There are major safety considerations involved with shooting from a bicycle; therefore, it is recommended that, when possible, the officer should dismount, preferably to a position of cover, prior to engaging the suspect with a firearm. This is supported by extensive scenario-based training involving police cyclists and by documented deadly encounters in which bike officers report having dismounted the bike prior to engaging their adversaries.

Compared to running, the bike offers greater speeds; however, an officer's movements are more nimble off the bike. In high threat situations, being unpredictable is more important than being fast. On the bike, the officer's movements are very predictable, similar to those of a gliding duck in an arcade game. Off the bike, the officer can be a quick, moving, and unpredictable target. For these reasons, IPMBA does not advocate shooting from the saddle of a moving bike.

Conclusion

In part as a result of September 11, 2001, police agencies have not only become more specialized but have been forced to provide a broader range of services. Training must meet growing public demand and must be relevant to the duties of officers and their missions. It should mirror the environment in which the officer works, promote problem solving, and develop critical thinking skills. It must also be current in order for it to be effective and defensible in any court. Not only should training include relevant live fire drills, it must also incorporate the type of threats and situations the officer is likely to encounter on the street. Using existing research available through IPMBA creates a foundation on which to develop a solid firearms training program specific to public safety cyclists and their agencies.

References

Hamblin, Lou Ann (2002). Firearms Training for the Police Cyclist. *Law and Order* magazine, April 2002, pgs 105–109.

chapter

20

The Bicycle Response Team

chapter at a glance

Introduction

The Bicycle Response Team (BRT) is a useful tool for public order, especially for tasks such as controlling and managing crowds. Whether at demonstrations, sporting events, or large street parties, a BRT can provide a police presence that is quick to respond to trouble but can also interact positively with the crowd. During demonstrations, a BRT can function as a quick response unit. At sporting events or street parties, a BRT can be deployed inside the crowds, preventing problems or stopping them before they escalate. Bicycle response teams were introduced with great success during the 2000 Democratic National Convention in Los Angeles and Republican National Convention in Philadelphia. Since then they have proven to be an effective tool for many departments, both large and small. The BRT works as a physical barrier as well as an effective tool for communicating with crowds, with the goal of achieving compliance with police instructions.

Member Selection

Officer selection is crucial to the success of a bicycle response team. BRT members must possess

superior cycling skills, above average stamina, the ability to stay in line and obey commands, the ability to work in a team environment, and the ability to learn, remember, and perform various maneuvers. They must be willing to practice team maneuvers repeatedly and to work long hours without hesitation. Above-average bike maintenance and repair skills are also helpful. Many bicycle response teams comprise personnel from throughout the department, not just the bike unit, who bring relevant skills and experience to the unit. This makes more personnel available during large-scale events, but ideally, these officers will have some degree of bike patrol experience. Regardless, adding officers from outside the bike unit underscores the importance of frequent training and practice, because those officers will not have the opportunity to hone their skills while on patrol.

Training

In order to be effective, a BRT should spend hours training together. All members and supervisors need to be trained in the basic concepts and movements. They need to practice throughout the year and just prior to any large event. This is essential to unit cohesiveness and effectiveness.

Bicycle Response Team Uses

Bicycle response teams can be deployed in a wide variety of situations. The following are some of the circumstances in which BRTs have been effective.

■ Riots

A riot is a major unrest caused by specific parties, generally for a cause, resulting in the breaking of laws. Rioters often destroy property and cause injury to participants, observers, or targeted persons. BRTs can be used on the outside perimeter to arrest small groups, prevent uninvolved persons from entering the area, and provide police services. The ability to move a team or multiple teams of bikes to any point rapidly is a great asset.

■ Demonstrations

A demonstration is a public display of group opinion, such as a rally or march. Demonstrations often occur during meetings involving political leaders. They can be peaceful or violent. The number of response team members required is based on the size and nature of the event and predictions of crowd behavior based on past, similar events. BRT members can communicate with demonstration leaders, explaining where they are allowed to march or rally or both. They can also ride and walk parallel to or behind the crowd to keep them moving in the desired direction (**FIGURE 20-1**). Equipment and transportation vans follow the event.

■ Street Parties

Street parties, although usually peaceful, can become problematic, especially when they involve alcohol and people of diverse backgrounds. Deployment of bike officers depends on the size of the crowd, the size of the bike team, and the potential for violence. All officers respond together for disruptions, and patrol vehicles are kept in a secure environment.

■ Sporting Events

Bicycle response teams can be ideal for the crowds attracted to large-scale sporting events. Many of these events are peaceful; however, some, such as football games in the United Kingdom, attract instigators of violence, and others ignite deep-seated rivalries. Victory or defeat can be used as an excuse to engage in riot-like behavior and cause property damage. BRT officers can patrol quadrants and parking lots, monitor tailgaters (partiers), support EMS personnel, and assist in traffic control and crowd dispersion after the game.

■ Fairs

Depending on the size of the fairgrounds and the number of people in attendance, two to four team members can usually patrol the crowd at these events. Responsibilities may include locating lost children, responding to calls for service, keeping track of suspicious groups or gang members, and helping to clear the fairgrounds after the fair closes.

■ Search and Rescue

Team members are needed to cover large areas, especially areas that vehicles have trouble patrolling. Bike officers are able to hear and see better than officers in motor vehicles. Many urban search and rescue scenarios involve searches for lost and missing children and elderly people.

■ Natural and Manmade Disasters

BRTs can be useful in situations in which normal transportation systems are disrupted. Bikes were used effectively following the 9/11 terrorist attacks: by bike messengers who were able to deliver blood and supplies to rescue workers, and by the Pentagon police whose automobiles were largely stymied by traffic evacuating Washington, DC. They have also been used in the aftermath of hurricanes to search for victims and protect

FIGURE 20-1 BRT members can move demonstrators in the desired direction.

against looters in areas where roads are blocked and visibility is limited by downed tree limbs and other debris. Bike officers can also provide assistance to medical personnel, and by using GPS or marking street corners with spray paint, they can identify gas leaks, power outages, and downed power lines.

Bicycle Response Team Deployment

The size of the bike team will determine how and in which situations the team can be deployed. Size of the crowd and potential for violence are two important considerations. With the proper equipment, the BRT can be deployed day and night. The BRT is flexible and can change formations at any time. For specific situations, such as preparing to arrest an individual, the team supervisor can prearrange the formation to be used during that arrest. Proper deployment of the bikes has to be decided prior to the actual deployment of the bike team.

When planning for deployment, various factors must be addressed, including the mission; authorized use of force and arrest procedures, including

the level of force the department equates with using the bike as a shield or impact weapon; the role of bikes within the department's overall policing strategy; transportation of suspects; equipment requirements (flex cuffs, mace or OC spray, less lethal weapons, first aid supplies, tool kit, etc.); medical background cards on all team members and medical support (tactical EMS team, hospital location, etc.); and hydration and food.

Uniforms and Equipment

A heavy-duty riot control uniform is not bike friendly, but BRT members can and should be equipped with appropriate protective equipment (FIGURE 20-2). BRT officers typically wear long-sleeved shirts or jackets, long pants, full-fingered gloves, boots, or leather-sided shoes; forearm guards, chest and shoulder protectors, wraparound eye protection, shin guards, and appropriate foul weather gear. Officers often carry a large OC canister, flex cuffs, gas mask in a carrying bag, and a water bottle for personal use. Large-capacity personal hydration devices can prevent hydration problems and also be used to carry smaller

FIGURE 20-2 Bicycle Response Team members can be equipped with full riot gear, including riot helmets and shields.

equipment such as cuffs, OC, first aid kits, and food. However, as indicated in Chapter 4, officers must be aware of and prepared for the possibility of the straps being used against them in an altercation. Team members may also be equipped with a riot helmet and face shield, if the helmet is lightweight and rider-friendly. Bicycle helmets can be used if bike-friendly riot helmets are not available; however, if circumstances dictate, officers should be provided with rain covers to protect their heads from fluids thrown by protesters.

■ Gas Masks

Wearing a gas mask provides bike officers with the offensive capacity of deploying gas and the defensive capacity of protecting themselves from gas, noxious fumes, and other airborne hazards. For their own safety, officers equipped with gas masks must be trained to use them properly.

The gas mask should fit comfortably under the bike or riot helmet. The officer should practice removing the gas mask from the carry bag, putting it on, and buckling the helmet over it. It is important for the officers to get accustomed to the masks. This can be accomplished by riding in columns and practicing squad movements and formations while wearing the masks. The officers will then become familiar with the restrictions placed upon their peripheral vision by the masks and learn to compensate by turning their heads more frequently. Gas masks also affect depth perception, so it is important to practice such drills as braking, instant turns, and cone courses, as well as curb and stair ascents and descents. The training can be enhanced further by practicing these skills in a simulated gas environment, using a smoke generator, gas simulators, and a darkened area such as a parking garage (FIGURE 20-3).

Finally, fitness tests should be conducted. Wearing the masks, riders should ride up hills, sprint, and ride until winded enough to require recovery. This will familiarize team members with the effects of the gas mask on their cardiovascular capacity so they can compensate for it in the field.

Squad Maneuvers

Bicycle use in crowd situations can generally be broken down into two types: static and moving. The most effective use of bikes for public order requires a careful blending of both techniques.

FIGURE 20-3 Training exercises in simulated gas environments enable officers to get accustomed to wearing gas masks while on bike.

■ Static Maneuvers

Static refers to using the bike in one small geographic area. The two most common assignments are post and barrier. In the post position, the bike unit is assigned to maintain a high-visibility presence in a particular location, such as one corner or an entire city block. In the barrier, or fence, position, the bikes are used to block or fence off a street, entryway, or other large area.

The post technique is the simplest, but is often the most difficult to accomplish. The squad is assigned to a high-visibility patrol of a small area simply to maintain order. The officers must maintain a professional demeanor, project an aura of control, write tickets, and make arrests for any violations they observe. Pairs are used instead of large groups in order to make the police presence appear greater than it is.

The barrier technique involves lining the bikes, front wheel to rear wheel with chainring towards the crowd, across the area to be blocked or protected (FIGURE 20-4).

The barrier can easily become a moving tactic called mobile fencing if the team leader determines that the crowd needs to be moved. Upon command, the bike team readies itself to move forward by holding the bikes by the stem and seat post. At the order, the squad members lift their bikes to chest level and, pressing them toward the crowd, take one step forward and order the crowd to move back.

■ Moving Maneuvers

Moving maneuvers include most standard crowd control movements used by foot and horse-mounted teams, such as columns, lines, diagonals, wedges, crossbow, and leapfrog. These techniques are employed to move the crowd in the desired direction, take ground away from the crowd, effect an arrest or rescue, and otherwise manage the situation.

These movements should be performed at a moderate pace to enable the team to stay together and prevent overexertion, and to allow as much intimidation factor as possible. If a crowd is intimidated by the presence, demeanor, and skill of the bicycle response team, no other force may be needed.

Typically, the BRT members ride in a single or double column. It is easy to move into the other positions from either type of column. There are several ways to move from a single column to a line formation; the option selected depends on where the unit is riding and where it is to be set up. All of them are simple in theory but take practice to make them look and feel smooth and professional. It is therefore essential that all bicycle response team members be exceptionally proficient in group riding, including various transitions. The better the team rides together as a group, the more impressive it will be to the public.

FIGURE 20-4 A Bicycle Response Team uses the barrier technique to provide parameters for the crowd.

■ Limited Contact Uses

Although the BRT works extremely well with other units on the front lines, it also works well on the periphery of an incident. The speed and mobility of the BRT allow it to quickly outflank a crowd if the crowd moves in an undesirable direction. A squad or two of bicycles positioned several blocks away from the action can be moved in a fraction of the time required to move a foot squad or even a vehicle squad, as bikes are not hampered by stairs, traffic, or a lack of roads. This mobility makes the bike squad the ideal backup unit for the interior officers. In addition, the strong flanking presence provided by the bikes can discourage people on the outskirts from joining the main group. The bike squads also function as crime suppression units left on the periphery to deal with those who would take advantage of the diverted attention of the other officers.

■ Conclusion

Successful crowd management and control is best achieved through a joint operation of department units into which the Bicycle Response Team can be integrated. Although it may seem that this type of bike deployment is suitable only for large departments, the concept can be adapted for smaller agencies operating independently or in multiple-agency BRTs under mutual aid agreements. The principles of bicycle response are applicable to most crowd management situations, from demonstrations and parades to high school football games, college parties, and politically charged speaking events. The escort, blocking, diversionary, and dispersal techniques utilized by the BRT may be scaled to fit departments and crowds of all sizes.

■ References

Goetz, Mike (2002). Police Bicycle Use in Crowd Control Situations. *Law and Order* magazine, April, pages 102–104.

Hudson, Don (2002). LAPD's Bicycle Rapid Response Team. *Law and Order* magazine, April, pages 97–99.

Raulerson, Gary (2005). Hurricane Season Is Busy One for Bike Cops. *IPMBA News*, Summer, pages 33–34.

21

Campus and Private Security Operations

chapter at a glance

Introduction

The same qualities that make bikes a practical choice for policing make them ideal for campus and private security operations. Whether they are police or security, public safety officers in academia face a unique set of circumstances and challenges. The bicycle can help them overcome some of those challenges. Private security officers operate in extremely diverse settings, ranging from shopping malls, airports, and casinos to campgrounds. In most of these settings, the bicycle can be an effective tool for ensuring the safety and security of residents, visitors, and employees.

Academic Campus Public Safety Operations

Like their counterparts in towns and cities across the country, many campus-based public safety departments have created mountain bike patrols to serve the unique needs of their communities. And like their counterparts, they have been tremendously successful.

Campus law enforcement is unique because public safety professionals in an academic setting interact with a specialized community, one com-

prised of a diverse population of temporary residents who come together for educational purposes. There is usually a high percentage of young people, many of whom are experiencing independence for the first time. These students intermingle with the permanent campus population, including members of the faculty and staff, as well as community residents. These interactions, though often positive, can be negative, and campus police officers often find themselves preventing or defusing "town vs. gown" conflicts. Like their non-campus colleagues, campus officers must be mobile, easily accessible, and personable. Bike patrol is remarkably well-suited to the academic environment, and there are many different ways the bike can be used to benefit the public safety department as well as the diverse community it serves.

The mobility of a bicycle is an asset on the academic campus. Most campuses are self-contained, either within the confines of a town or city or in a rural area. Many contain or abut open or wooded areas and have secluded foot paths between buildings or residence halls. Some sprawl through urban centers and demand quick response to noncontiguous locations, often on traffic-choked streets. In addition, the typical campus contains numerous areas designed to be off-limits to motor vehicles. If these

pedestrian-only areas are patrolled by officers in cars, the officers appear to be above the law. If they are not patrolled, they tend to attract illegal activity. Bike officers can easily traverse such areas, as well as various types of non-motor-vehicle-friendly terrain, and as a result are often the first to arrive on a scene. In some cases they are the only ones who are able to respond.

Bike patrol can be used for routine purposes, such as patrolling parking lots, garages, catwalks, walking and bike paths, trails, athletic fields, and other areas as well as for many of the tactical purposes described in Chapter 18. The bike officer can effectively patrol high crime areas or be assigned to specialized crime details such as vehicle break-ins, vandalisms, and underage drinking violations. Because campus officers generally patrol a smaller area, bike officers are likely to cover their patrol areas frequently, thus discouraging would-be criminals with their presence and unpredictability.

Bike officers can also be very beneficial at campus-based special events. They are frequently deployed at sporting events, often patrolling parking and tailgate areas for alcohol and disorderly conduct violations. They can be used for crowd management and control, helping to disperse fans and avert post-game disturbances. The bike patrol can be also be used indoors at events like games and commencement ceremonies, during student move-in, at block parties, and at student gatherings, festivals, and demonstrations. Despite the congestion associated with such events, bike personnel retain the ability to respond quickly to emergency situations.

From a community relations perspective, the benefits of bikes are numerous. The citizens of the university community get a more approachable officer. Students often relate well to bike officers and will approach them to discuss the bike, equipment, or uniform. In addition, on most college campuses bicycles are the main mode of transportation for many students, and there are few better ways to form a bond that will create an air of acceptance and build relationships of trust. Finally, bike officers interact readily with parents, faculty and staff, and permanent residents, who, as tax- and tuition-paying citizens, are important members of the academic community. Because of their frequent and often friendly interactions with all members of the community, bike officers are perhaps the best ambassadors for a campus public safety department (**FIGURE 21-1**).

Private Security

Private security is a diverse and growing segment of public safety. Security officers typically operate on private property and are employed by a variety of private or quasi-public entities. They both actively patrol and respond to calls for assistance within the boundaries of their assignments. They are often referred to as the eyes and ears of the police, because they are typically in close communication with local police agencies. Their primary purpose is to help create a safe and secure environment for residents, visitors, employees, and other clients of their employing agencies, and the bike is an extremely practical tool for helping them achieve this goal.

FIGURE 21-1 Bike officers frequently interact with students, encouraging an atmosphere of trust and respect.

As is the case with law enforcement, bikes can be deployed in most situations involving security officers. Shopping centers, malls, zoos, amusement parks, parking facilities, casinos, business compounds, and corporate campuses have all found uses for mountain bikes. Bike-mounted security guards are often hired to patrol special events, concerts, festivals, and street fairs. The popularity of bikes in the private security sector can be attributed to their mobility, low operating cost, stealth capability, and effectiveness in engaging the public. Through their efforts, many facilities have reported reduced crime and increased positive contacts. They have also noted higher motivation and a more proactive attitude among bike officers.

A Positive Impact

Through the efforts of private security, many facilities have reported reduced crime and increased positive contacts. They have also noted higher motivation and a more proactive attitude among bike officers.

■ Security Cyclist Operations

Security officers, both armed and unarmed, patrol in many different settings. Much of the information pertaining to academic campus patrol is equally relevant to security cyclists who patrol shopping centers, casinos, corporate campuses, parking facilities, and more. This section describes just a few of the areas frequently patrolled by bike-mounted security officers employed in the protection of a wide variety of facilities.

Corporate, Hospital, Residential, Sports, and Entertainment Complexes

Private security officers often patrol complexes that include numerous buildings, parking facilities, and open space. These complexes can be the size of several city blocks or cover many acres. The complex is patrolled for the protection of all of the employees, patients, residents, visitors, and others who use the complex. The presence of bike patrols can impart a sense of security as well as reduce crime. Patrolling such a complex is similar to patrolling an academic campus; however, access by the public is often more restricted, especially on corporate campuses.

Shopping Centers and Malls

Shopping centers and malls are other locations in which bike officers can be very effective. Retail centers need a high volume of shoppers in order to survive. Bikes can operate inside and outside of the shopping center as a deterrent to crime and to create a safe environment (FIGURE 21-2).

Because all people come to and from a shopping center from the exterior, whether by transit, auto, foot, or bike, exterior security patrols often are one of the most important aspects of a shopping center security program. Bike officers can be very effective in ensuring both actual and perceived safety of access and egress routes. While this is important year-round, many shopping centers supplement their regular patrols with highly visible bike patrols during holiday shopping season to prevent theft from vehicles and generate goodwill.

Many urban shopping centers are in proximity to low-income housing, schools, and public transit stations (bus, subway, or light rail). Although these circumstances are desirable from a mall management point of view because of the potential customers, they may cause issues that must be managed by the proprietary or contract security team, for instance, "grab and runs," theft, alcohol violations, congregating youths and others, fights, drug use/dealing, loitering, and shoplifting.

Effectively deployed bike officers can help mitigate the negative aspects of these situations through such actions as apprehension of shoplifters and trespassers and dispersal of loiterers. They can also address such risk management issues as skateboarding on mall property.

Parking Facilities

Private security departments in almost every setting are often responsible for one or more parking facilities. Crime in such facilities can have a negative effect on business. If customers feel that either they or their vehicles are not safe, they will often seek an alternative. Sometimes facilities are equipped with video surveillance or a guard in a booth, but often they have no security at all. Deploying security in parking facilities demonstrates to members of the public that measures are being taken to ensure their safety. Properly deployed high-visibility bicycle patrols in these areas can and should be designed to make the customer feel safe and the potential criminal feel uncomfortable (FIGURE 21-3).

Some surface lots, such as those at amusement parks, casinos, and shopping centers or malls,

FIGURE 21-2　Bike-mounted security officers are an effective crime deterrent in and around retail complexes.

stretch on for acres, and parking garages can be several blocks long and many stories high. For this reason, bikes are often the most practical patrol vehicles. Security officers riding bikes can cover more ground and in less time than their counterparts on foot. They can respond quickly to calls for assistance. They can use their stealth advantage to look for suspicious activity during day or night-time hours, increasing their chances of witnessing crimes in process. Therefore, awareness, communication, and intimate knowledge of the facility layout, barriers and obstacles, and egress points are essential for officer safety.

Bike patrol in parking facilities also has public relations value. In most settings, bike patrol officers create a visible presence and interact with both children and adults prior to their entering the facility. This positive interaction can often defuse a potentially upset customer who has circled the parking facility in search of a convenient parking stall. This

positive interaction with a bike officer can be reflected in the customer's behavior and actions within the business. In addition, bike officers can assist people who have forgotten where they parked their vehicles or who have mechanical problems.

Enforcement

The degree of enforcement action undertaken by security officers is dictated by company policy. Some security officers are responsible only for patrolling and reporting suspicious behavior while others engage in nearly every suspect contact method used by the police. Some have arrest powers within the confines of their patrol area. Some are armed; many are not. The ability of the officers to take the expected enforcement actions depends upon their training, which must be relevant to the expected tasks.

Security cyclists must always keep their company policy and training in mind when determining

FIGURE 21-3 By helping ensure the safety of patrons in parking facilities, bike officers can contribute to the continued success of local businesses.

the degree to which the bicycle should be used in a tactical manner. In potentially dangerous situations, the security cyclist should call the police. The security cyclist can be a good witness by keeping the suspect under surveillance, looking for weapons, watching suspects' actions, and staying in communication with the police.

Conclusion

Using bikes for campus and a wide range of private security operations can result in improved enforcement of laws, rules, and regulations. Because bike officers are so mobile, they can increase interactions with staff, residents, patients, guests, students, and visitors. Officers riding bikes have a better vantage point, and will see, hear, and smell more than someone walking or driving around in a vehicle. Bike officers also convey a positive image to the public. Regardless of the setting in which they operate, bike patrol personnel must be provided with a clearly articulated policy manual and the appropriate level of training to perform their duties safely and effectively.

Reference

Trout, Mike (2002). Police Cyclists and Campus Law Enforcement. *Campus Law Enforcement Journal,* November/December, pages 15–17.

EMS Operations

EMS Bike Teams

Introduction

Bicycles are used by a wide variety of EMS providers in many types of situations. Bikes are used by paid and volunteer fire departments, third-service EMS agencies, collegiate (student-staffed) EMS providers, hospital-based and private ambulance services, and search and rescue teams. While some operate on a full-time basis, most operate part-time or for special events only. There are many reasons for establishing an EMS bike unit, but the common goal is to get medical assistance to those who need it as quickly and safely as possible. The mobility of a bicycle in areas with heavy pedestrian and/or vehicle traffic can literally mean the difference between life and death.

Uses for EMS Bikes

Most EMS bike teams in the United States operate on a part-time basis, usually during special events. Some patrol busy areas at peak times, for instance, in an entertainment district during weekend nights. Some ride part-time throughout the year, while others operate only seasonally. In some settings, such as airports and amusement parks, EMS cyclists are deployed on a full-time, year-round basis

(**FIGURE 22-1**). Similarly, a number of cities in the United Kingdom have addressed growing congestion problems and strict response time mandates by implementing full-time EMS bike operations.

Bicycles have many advantages over other means of delivering emergency medical care. They are quiet, maneuverable, efficient, and small. They provide access to areas that larger vehicles cannot.

FIGURE 22-1 The London Ambulance Service Cycle Response Unit patrols parts of London on a full-time, year-round basis.

When necessary, a bike can be ridden or carried over obstacles or terrain that would stop other forms of transportation. Bikes can be maneuvered through crowds of people and around heavy traffic (FIGURE 22-2). They offer many of the advantages of foot travel, but are much faster. All of this makes them ideal for EMS work in many venues, including shopping malls, tourist areas, entertainment districts, sports complexes, pedestrian-only zones, city centers, convention and trade show facilities, amusement parks, airports, train stations, parks and trails, golf courses, beach and resort communities, boardwalks, race tracks, and academic and corporate campuses.

Bikes can also be deployed at nearly any type of event, large or small. EMS bike teams have proven effective during concerts, political rallies and public speaking events, trade shows, sporting events, run-

ning, cycling and other participatory athletic contests, golf and tennis tournaments, and fairs, festivals, and parades. In addition, bicycles are often a practical choice for proactive patrol in congested areas, service delivery in wilderness areas, urban and wilderness search and rescue, disaster response and mass casualty situations, public safety outreach

FIGURE 22-2 Bike medics are able to maneuver swiftly through crowds to reach those in need of emergency medical treatment.

and education, and tactical medical support of law enforcement bicycle response teams.

There are probably countless other ways in which to incorporate bikes into service delivery; the possibilities are limited only by the imagination.

■ Special Events

There are numerous success stories involving EMS cyclists and special events. Because they are so mobile, EMS cyclists are often the first to arrive on a scene. Many of the people they treat are suffering from minor ailments, but others' lives depend upon a rapid response by EMS personnel. The cyclists need to hear the call for assistance, maneuver to the scene, evaluate the patient, provide treatment, and communicate with other members of the event team. To do all this effectively and efficiently requires planning. Planning for an event of any size includes surveying the site, determining equipment needs, establishing communications, and writing an operations plan that addresses all aspects of event logistics.

Site Survey

The first step towards a successful event is the site survey. The entire event site and the immediate surroundings should be examined in great detail. Maps and/or floor plans should be generated, identifying permanent features and structures as well as temporary ones that will be present during the event. The plan should locate all entrances and exits, designate EMS transport unit pickup points, and identify staging areas such as casualty clearing stations and helicopter landing points. An appropriate location for a command post should be selected. Many times these can be shared with other public safety agencies.

Operations Plan

The response team must consider all event logistics carefully and devise appropriate plans. Logistics include, but are not limited to, a plan for transporting all personnel and equipment to and from the event site, food, hydration, proper attire, staff scheduling, equipment storage, equipment security, command post operations, and areas of assignment.

The operations plan compiles all the details of the event into a useful format. It should include the event dates and time, the personnel assigned, the event location, a list of key personnel, their contact information, and their areas of responsibility; a detailed staffing plan, schedule, and assignment sheet; and a list of equipment and where it will be located. It should designate the command center location, outline the communications procedure, contain specific staging and transportation information, and detail the uniform policy and personal bike bag inventory. The operations plan should contain a grid map of the event area marked with the command center location, ambulance pick-up points, resupply locations, break areas, and other relevant locations. It should also contain a mass casualty incident response plan and information on all area hospitals and EMS agencies that may be involved. The plan should be shared with all bike medics and other EMS personnel, event staff, and other public safety agencies. A reference copy should be kept at the command post. Here is an example of a response plan:

> ### Example Response Plan (Abbreviated)
>
> The EMS personnel and equipment assigned to the event consist of four advanced life support (ALS) bikes, one ALS ambulance, one ALS golf cart and an Incident Commander (IC). Each bike team shall comprise one paramedic and one EMT. Operational procedure consists of communicating on a designated channel with the IC, who is in contact with the EMS dispatch center, police, and event security. Upon receiving an emergency call, the IC notifies the bike team patrolling that area via radio. The teams confirm information and the first team responds. The second bike team moves in the direction of the incident to compensate for the temporary unavailability of the first team and offer better area coverage. An ALS-equipped golf cart is also dispatched. Police and event security are notified so they can assist with securing the scene and enabling rapid treatment and transport.
>
> When the bike team arrives on scene, the paramedic assesses the patient and determines the course of treatment. The EMT is responsible for taking command of the incident: advising command of precise location; requesting additional resources; and

assisting with patient care. This requires outstanding communication and teamwork among the bike team members.

When the ALS golf cart arrives on scene, personnel assist with patient care. If possible, care is turned over to the ALS cart. If not, the bike medics continue care according to pre-hospital protocol. If the patient's condition warrants, the bike team may assist with moving the patient. The bike team restocks from the ALS cart and returns to available status as soon as possible. The patient is transported by the ALS crew to the appropriate designated ambulance access point, on-site treatment facility, or hospital.

Equipment, Supplies, and Communications

All bikes should be inspected prior to the event to make sure they are in good working order and are properly equipped, including lights if there is any potential, planned or unexpected, that the bikes will be operated at night or in low-light conditions. Any battery-operated equipment should be checked to ensure adequate power level. Each rider should carry emergency bike tools, and spare parts should be brought to the event site by designated personnel.

The panniers should be packed with routine and event-specific EMS equipment, and the plan should designate an area or areas for resupply. In some situations, it is possible for teams to resupply from the ambulances that respond to transport patients. However, it can be more practical to stock the staging area, on-site treatment facility, or command post with frequently used items and resupply from there. This is advantageous because there are times when a bike medic treats numerous patients, none of whom requires transport. Supplies of such items as band-aids, ice packs, and patient care reports (PCRs) can be exhausted quickly. Also, many EMS cyclists carry specially sized oxygen cylinders that are not typically carried on ambulances. Stocking spares at the command post will eliminate the need to leave the event to refill them.

Event communications may be different than those used for day-to-day operations. A communications system for event staff and EMS should be established, preferably a dedicated dispatcher at the command post or dispatch operations center. En-

sure that all radios and microphones are in good working order and can be used in all areas of the event site. Everyone should be briefed as to dispatch protocol and the event Incident Command System (ICS).

Day of the Event

On the day of the event, team members should arrive early, especially if the event and/or the venue is unfamiliar. All bike medics should conduct a ride-through to familiarize themselves with the event site and plan potential response routes. These response routes may include surrounding streets, which may be less congested than the event grounds. Bike medics should familiarize themselves with the answers to the most frequently asked questions: restrooms, food, water, and program details. They should carry a program guide and be prepared to provide information.

It is important for bike medics to plan rest breaks, eat properly, and stay hydrated throughout the day. End-of-shift activities include restocking, charging batteries and completing reports, and preparing the bikes for their next ride.

■ EMS Bike Patrol

Although it is not the most common use of EMS bike teams, proactive patrol can be very effective in certain situations, such as pedestrian zones, crowded business or entertainment districts, and airports. In addition to providing medical care in these settings, bike medics can also distribute health information and advice easily when appropriate.

In the early 2000s, a number of cities in the United Kingdom responded to the implementation of national response time mandates by integrating bike teams into their full-time operations. Cities such as York, London, and Manchester began deploying teams of medics to patrol pedestrian-only zones and other crowded areas, responding to incidents in both a proactive and reactive manner (FIGURE 22-3).

In York, the Tees East and North Yorkshire Ambulance Service's (TENYAS) Life Cycle, which began in 2001, attended 1432 incidents in its first two years and was estimated to have potentially saved 3 lives every day. Like other agencies, they discovered that using bikes not only lowered their average response time, but enabled them to realize

FIGURE 22-3 Cities in the United Kingdom deploy bike medics in pedestrian zones in order to meet stringent national response time mandates.

significant savings from cancelled medical calls. Likewise, in 2000, during their first 6 months of operation, London Ambulance Service (LAS) reported an average of 22 ambulance cancellations and 22 not transported per week, saving 250 hours of ambulance time. This translated to a savings of approximately £80,000 (in 2007, US $157,000) in ambulance non-dispatch and £2000 (in 2007, US $4000) in fuel.

Airport medical bike units operate in similar fashion. Established in 2004, the LAS Heathrow Cycle Response Unit recorded nearly 400 calls within its first 4 months of operation, 75% of which were handled by the bike medic, enabling the ambulance that would have been dispatched to be deployed elsewhere. The average response time was only 2 minutes. Similarly, in 2005, Fort Lauderdale International Airport's medical bike unit responded to 236 calls within its first 3 weeks, with an average response time of 2.5 minutes. This was significantly less than the airport rescue's average time of 4.37 minutes and the mutual aid average response time of 9.0 minutes.

Public Relations

Any discussion of EMS bikes must include the public relations aspect. There are few more effective ways to generate positive publicity and encourage positive community interaction than to operate an EMS bike team. As they ride amongst the members of their community, EMS riders soon discover that people want to talk with them. A person may want to thank a team member or ask a question about EMS response. They may be interested in the bike, the equipment, or job opportunities. Each of these interactions is an opportunity to convey a professional image of the agency.

More importantly, each citizen contact is an opportunity to educate. This education can take a variety of forms. EMS cyclists are often involved with bicycle safety education, both formally (as in a bike rodeo) and informally (as when they teach a child how to wear a helmet properly). They can teach citizens about how the EMS agency functions and how they relate to other public safety agencies. They can distribute educational material about a health hazard, disease prevention, or safety. They can provide informal health information and advice on how to or when to call an ambulance. Finally, EMS cyclists can promote the agency and its services by distributing literature and items such as pens and stickers. If a hospital has a booth at a public event, for instance, a fully equipped bike and medic is an excellent way to attract attention and start conversations about the available services. Public interaction is most effective in less crowded situations. Smaller events and public venues such as parks and trails encourage more interaction than extremely crowded areas in which the medic is totally focused on response and patient care.

Nick Gatlin of Williamson Medical Center in Franklin, TN, once compared the costs of advertising in local business publications and contracting for exhibit space at local events to that of deploying bike team members. The cost of paying bike team members was not only lower, but they encountered more people, interacted with them personally, distributed educational information, and provided a necessary service—medical care.

During the 6-month pilot program of the Cycle Response Unit (CRU), Tom Lynch of London Ambulance Service noted an increase in cross-organizational partnerships due to positive interactions among CRU members, LAS and other health care agencies, and the police and fire departments. The CRU placed a high priority on informing the press of their success, generating more than 70 instances of positive media coverage in the local, national, and international press, including coverage in print radio, television, and Internet sources.

Although patient care is always the first priority for bike medics, the public relations value of operating a bike team should not be underestimated. The effectiveness of your public relations can help determine whether or not your program will survive (FIGURE 22-4).

FIGURE 22-4 EMS cyclists interact with members of the public, offering general advice and generating positive public relations.

Conclusion

EMS agencies of all types have discovered that bicycles are an effective mode of transportation for providers of emergency medical services. Bike medics can be deployed full-time or part-time in a variety of settings, including pedestrian zones, downtown business districts, amusement parks, and airports. They are extremely valuable during special events of all kinds, ranging from sporting events to fairs, festivals, and other celebrations. The ability of trained bike medics to maneuver through crowds and around obstacles puts them in a position to respond swiftly to emergency situations in a variety of circumstances. Their agility, mobility, and speed can transform a potentially fatal medical emergency into a life-saving victory.

References

Fried, Drew (2003). EMS: Back to Basics. *fireEMS*, September/October, pages 34–38.

Gatlin, Nick (2002). What's a Bike Team Worth? *IPMBA News*, Fall, pages 13–14.

Lindsay, Dave (2006). Wheeler Healers. *IPMBA News*, Spring, page 21.

Lorenzi, Darrell and Youngsma, Jeffrey (2003). Fremont's Bike Medic Program. *fireEMS*, September/October, pages 40–43

Lynch, Tom (2003). London's Life-Saving Team. *IPMBA News*, Fall, pages 6–7.

Morris, Ray (2004). Sunshine and Rowdy Golf. *IPMBA News*, Spring, pages 5 & 10.

Robinson, Gerard (2005). Treating Travelers in the Terminal. *IPMBA News*, Spring, pages 7–8.

Tees, East and North Yorkshire Ambulance Service (2003). A Statistical Overview of the Tees, East, and North Yorkshire Ambulance Service Life Cycle, May 2001–May 2003. http://www.tenyas.org.uk/Documents/lifecyclestatistics.pdf. Retrieved January 8, 2007.

EMS Equipment and Load Placement

Introduction

There are two phases to being a bike medic—getting to the scene and rendering medical aid. In contrast to the police bike, which is used as a tactical tool, the EMS bike is primarily a mode of transportation. Its primary purpose is to transport the medical care provider and equipment to the scene. The most important actions take place after the EMS cyclist arrives on the scene; therefore, it is essential that the cyclist carries the appropriate type and amount of equipment and supplies to provide patient care effectively.

Equipment Selection

Deciding how and where the bike team will be deployed determines what equipment will be carried. This should be done both when setting up a bike team for the first time and for individual events and situations. There may be circumstances in which the bike team needs the full complement of equipment and other events that have more limited requirements. The planning process for each situation needs to be thorough. There is nothing more devastating than the realization that you do not have the right equipment to perform your duties. The liabil-

ity, bad public relations, and psychological effects can have long-range negative effects, both on the individual and the agency.

When choosing medical equipment to carry, there are several factors to consider, all of which center around the question of the best way to use bikes to provide medical support in a particular situation (FIGURE 23-1).

Factors Affecting Equipment Selection

- Level of care
- Environment
- Type of assignment
- Access to emergency vehicles
- Budget
- Jurisdictional licensure mandates

■ Level of Care

The level of care to be provided is determined by many things: licensure level of personnel, departmental mandates, medical control options, the event planner's and/or incident commander's expectations, and the need for Basic Life Support (BLS) or Ad-

vanced Life Support (ALS) care. There may be circumstances where ALS care on bicycles is not feasible and alternatives must be provided, such as having an ambulance on scene or a medical tent. Many departments are only BLS-equipped. Some areas may be so large or have areas of terrain so challenging that carrying ALS equipment is impractical due to additional weight and resulting rider fatigue.

■ Environment

Environmental conditions can affect equipment choices, particularly when there is a high risk of environment-related illnesses, such as heat exhaustion, heat stroke, or hypothermia. It may be necessary to adjust quantities of items such as IV fluids, emergency blankets, and ice packs for these conditions. EMS personnel will also need room for personal gear such as sunscreen, extra clothing, and a raincoat or jacket.

■ Type of Assignment

Some EMS bike teams work on a patrol basis. They usually operate in specific areas—for instance, a downtown area, airport, or entertainment district. What they carry depends on various factors, including length of shift, typical calls for service, and population served. Those who work

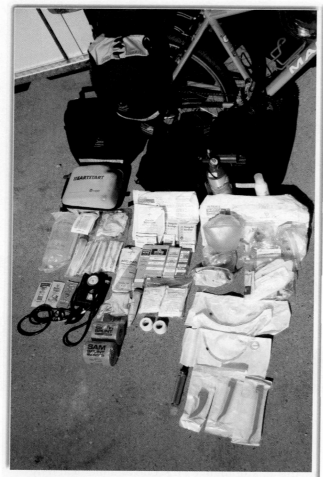

FIGURE 23-1 EMS Cyclists carry a full complement of medical supplies and equipment on their bikes.

the same area on a routine basis will quickly begin to identify patterns and tailor their pannier contents accordingly.

Many EMS bike teams work at a variety of special events, including festivals, sporting events, charity walk/runs, and bike rides. The type of event will dictate the type of equipment needed. Sporting events may require more bandaging and splinting equipment. Child-oriented events may require extra pediatric equipment, while events that attract mostly adults may not. A large concentration of senior citizens or an event like Special Olympics will have its own unique demands. The expected attendance also has an impact upon the amount and type of equipment to be carried. The area layout, size, and opportunities for restocking equipment also play a role.

Search and rescue operations may require personal survival gear, extra water and food, and basic first aid supplies. Because the primary goal is locating the missing individual or individuals and communicating to rescuers, GPS, maps, compasses, search pattern instructions, radios, and other communication equipment may be necessary. First aid equipment should be geared toward managing immediate life threats such as respiratory distress, cardiac arrest, dehydration, and hypothermia.

■ Access to Emergency Vehicles

If the area is not easily accessible to a fully-equipped emergency vehicle due to traffic, distance, or other conditions, a bike medic may need to sustain care for an extended period. If an ambulance will take more than 20 minutes to respond, the bike medic will require more supplies to sustain medical care than one whose ambulance is just around the corner. It is good practice to plan to render medical care long enough for the second-closest ambulance to arrive on scene, as the closest ambulance may be on another emergency call.

■ Budget

After the organization has assessed its needs and determined what is appropriate to carry, it must weigh these needs against its budget. For instance, the budget may not allow an ALS provider to equip every bike with a cardiac monitor/defibrillator or an automatic external defibrillator (AED) and ALS medications. It may be necessary or even preferable to eliminate some redundancy and reduce quantities of medical gear by equipping only one bike with the ALS equipment and cardiac monitor/AED if the riders work in pairs. The other bike(s) can be equipped with BLS gear that complements the equipment on the ALS bike. BLS-only units are likewise constrained by the financial realities and will choose their equipment and supplies accordingly.

■ Jurisdictional Licensure Mandates

Some local EMS licensure mandates require certain equipment to be available on any response unit regardless of its size. Several North American states and provinces require such minimum equipment levels. U.S. cities with federally and regionally administered counter-terrorism programs, such as the Domestic Preparedness Plan, have equipment mandates that include additional drug regimens and specialized personal protective equipment.

■ Other Considerations

Other factors to consider when selecting medical equipment include terrain, staffing levels and deployment (teams vs. solo riders), crowd composition, and projected number of calls for assistance. It can be helpful to examine statistics from comparable situations during the planning process.

Carrying Options

Once you have determined what to carry, the next step is determining how to carry and pack it. The first step is to weigh everything. An EMS cyclist who will be carrying less than 20 pounds and nothing bulky should be able to operate using only an expandable rear rack-mounted bag or backpack, while an EMS cyclist who will carry more than 20 pounds or bulky items will need rear panniers. Once you have determined what to carry, what to carry it in, and how to pack it, subject it to a field test before deploying it in the field. Like anything else, it may need some adjustments. Constantly evaluate your load as you gain experience. Do you really need each of the items you are carrying? Are you missing anything? Investigate newer and alternative products to find lighter or more practical versions of the same items.

■ Rear Rack Bag and Panniers

Most EMS cyclists carry their equipment in a rear rack bag with panniers attached to the rear rack. This is ideal for roads and flat, open terrain, and is the preferred setup for special events, especially those with long hours or patrol shifts.

There are several advantages to rear panniers, and these advantages should be maximized. The weight of the medical gear is carried on the bike, which allows for more options when choosing the type and quantity of medical gear. The panniers ride low to the ground, lowering the center of gravity and thus minimizing the added difficulty of riding with additional weight. The panniers are also deep, and can accommodate small oxygen tanks and/or monitors or defibrillators and other items that do not fit in the standard rear rack bag.

The panniers have yet another advantage. They are designed for quick removal. Therefore, if it is necessary to enter a building or any other place where taking a bicycle would be difficult, the panniers can be removed from the bike and carried by the rider. In addition to ensuring that medical equipment is easy to reach, this can also mitigate the risk of theft in situations in which the bike may be left unattended. In addition, the panniers offer a convenient storage space for jackets, gloves, snacks, and other necessary personal items.

There are a few disadvantages to panniers. The weight is disproportionately allocated to the rear of the bike, which makes handling and maneuvering more difficult; however, this is easily overcome through training and experience. Carrying the gear on the rear of the bike makes it less suitable for off-road single track or rough terrain where the rider is required to climb or negotiate obstacles. Having the weight in a fixed position reduces mobility and the ability to compensate for such trail conditions. The medical equipment also bears the bumps, vibrations, and jolts normally caused by riding conditions and may get damaged. Front panniers can provide additional space; however, they should be used to carry only lightweight items as they can affect balance and the steering of the bike.

Pannier Selection

When choosing panniers and a trunk bag, there are various options available. Generally, EMS teams use rear-mounted panniers and a rear rack bag. These bags attach to a rack that is mounted at three or four points on the bike, typically the seat stays, seat tube, and the rear dropouts of the bike. There are racks designed to attach to the seat post for full suspension bikes; however, the weight is supported at only one point, on the bike frame at the seat tube. These types of racks can cause early bike frame failure because of the weight of the medical gear, and they are often restricted to a carrying capacity of 25 pounds. A hardtail or rigid mountain bike is more suitable for use with panniers and rear rack bags. (Chapter 4 provides more information on racks.)

During the early stages of EMS cycling, the bicycle touring industry served as the primary resource for panniers and rear rack bags, and often still does. These bags are typically not compartmentalized, and access is usually limited to a top-zippered opening. While these touring panniers are not designed for EMS use, they can and do work. To facilitate organization of and access to supplies, many EMS cyclists have learned to place their equipment into small color-coded bags that can slide into touring-style panniers easily. However, even well-organized gear tends to settle and can become mixed together in the bottom of the bag,

FIGURE 23-2 EMS-specific panniers enable easy organization and protection of medical supplies.

FIGURE 23-3 The LAS CRU trunk is designed to carry a significant amount of equipment.

causing the rider to have to search for specific equipment or supplies.

In more recent years, both bike and medical bag designers have recognized the need for EMS-specific bike bags. These bags provide compartments for easy access to equipment. The compartments are often transparent to enable quick identification of equipment. In some cases, the entire bag can be opened and folded out flat to eliminate the need to rummage for gear. Many bags have compartments designed to hold oxygen cylinders and AEDs, which help prevent them from shifting around and causing frictional wear on the bag or being subject to damage (FIGURE 23-2).

Panniers and rear rack bags are often designed to work together as a system; therefore, it may be beneficial to select the same brand or follow the manufacturer's recommendation. Some bags are designed to work with a brand-specific proprietary rack. These bags attach to the rack using a different locking mechanism than the traditional hook-on type. Because proprietary systems can limit your product choices, the long-term implications of selecting this option should be considered.

The United Kingdom's London Ambulance Service (LAS) designed a trunk that combines the pannier and rack bag into a single unit, and equips riders to patrol long hours in heavy congestion while carrying a significant amount of equipment. It is constructed of nylon and is flame-retardant and

antibacterial/anti-fungal. Lights attach directly to webbing, and the fabric has reflective markings. The weight of the equipment is supported by a plastic/alloy frame insert, and the bags sit high enough to prevent the feeling of towing a trailer (FIGURE 23-3).

The trunk is attached to the rack by a bolted plate system and full-length, heavy-duty Velcro® fastenings. There are four compartments: a main trunk accommodates one slim grab bag slotted down each side, with space on top for a defibrillator; a document pouch, an A4-size envelope space with a Velcro® opening, located inside the top flap; a storm flap on the top, which opens a see-through pocket map holder, has room for paperwork, and serves as a good desktop in the field; and a half-moon shaped, under-seat personal storage area.

Front panniers are also used to distribute equipment evenly. All panniers are highly visible and have reflective markings to enhance the unit's visibility and to make it identifiable as an operational medical unit.

Guidelines for Load Placement

When using a rear rack bag and panniers, it is extremely important to keep the bike balanced. This cannot be done without knowing the weight of everything to be carried and dividing it according to weight, function, and frequency of use. For optimal performance, medical equipment should be packed into the panniers and rack bags in accordance with the following rules:

- Bicycles should be laterally balanced for maximum operational safety.
- Heavier items should be placed in panniers to lower the center of gravity.
- Equipment that is breakable/sensitive should be placed on the power (drive) side of the bicycle or in the rack bag.
- The most commonly used or most critical equipment should be easily accessible.

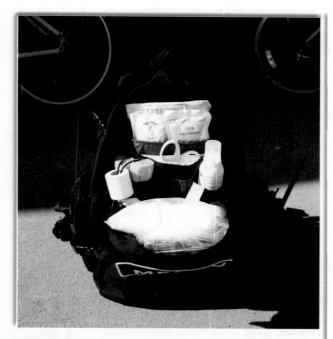

FIGURE 23-4 Backpacks can be used to carry medical equipment, either alone or in conjunction with panniers.

■ Backpacks

Some EMS cyclists prefer backpacks, especially off-road or in situations that require the rider and bike to be nimble (**FIGURE 23-4**). Like panniers, backpacks have their advantages and disadvantages. Backpacks offer greater maneuverability in off-road and technical riding situations. Because they do not require a rack, a full-suspension bike can be used easily. The weight is on the rider's back, close to the body, and moves with the rider. On rough terrain, bumps and vibrations are absorbed by the rider, reducing the impact transferred to fragile medical equipment. The medical equipment stays with the EMS provider, both on and off the bike, which is particularly important when controlled drugs are carried. One notable disadvantage is that because the rider shoulders the weight of the gear, fatigue may set in more quickly. In addition, if backpacks are to be kept to a reasonable size and weight, the amount of equipment that can be carried is limited.

Medical Equipment Packing Guidelines

- Bicycles should be laterally balanced for maximum operational safety.
- Heavier items should be placed in panniers to lower the center of gravity.
- Equipment that is breakable/sensitive should be placed on the power (drive) side of the bicycle or in the rack bag.
- The most commonly used or most critical equipment should be easily accessible.

Backpack Selection

When choosing a backpack, comfort, fit, space, and price should be considered. The backpack should fit well, particularly in the riding position on the bike. Many backpacks have grooves and contours that allow for air flow and ventilation between the pack and the back. Shoulder straps should be well-padded and adjustable. Many models have ergonomic shoulder straps that are wide at the shoulders and narrow as they approach the torso. These allow for better range of motion, particularly with outstretched arms on the handlebars. Attachment points on the straps for a radio microphone, whistle, or other equipment are also desirable features.

Compartmentalized backpacks work best to prevent settling and clutter from mixing of different groups of medical equipment. They are easier to use and organize than those with a single chamber. To carry the same gear as would fit into a rear rack bag and panniers, 1800 to 2400 cubic inches of space is needed; however, backpacks are only recommended if your needs assessment shows that you require less equipment.

Guidelines for Load Placement

Correct load placement in backpacks is as important as load placement in panniers. Heavier objects should be placed towards the bottom of the pack and central to the midline of the body. This balances the weight and lowers the center of gravity. Fragile objects need to be placed at the interior, while items such as bandages can be packed toward the exterior of the bag. This provides better cushion for the rider and fragile equipment in the case of a fall. Gear with hard or angular edges and narrow points, such as an O2 regulator, should not be positioned directly against the back.

■ Waist Pack

Another option for carrying lighter equipment is a waist pack, which is available in various sizes. Carrying a waist pack decreases the amount of weight and space necessary on the bicycle, and keeps the equipment with the rider at all times, even when away from the bike. Waist packs are a practical solution to maintaining the security of controlled substances and other valuable items. This option can be used alone if needs are minimal or in conjunction with a pannier system. Medical field vests can also be used in collaboration with utility belts and pouches. Some EMS departments require body armor, which can offer many pockets and pouches.

■ Trailers

While a trailer is not typically considered an option for carrying EMS equipment, it might be practical in some situations. Trailers may be impractical for special events because they typically sit low to the ground and could be hazardous in crowded areas; however, they can be ideal for search-and-rescue operations. Many trailers can carry up to 70 pounds of equipment, which translates into several gallons of water, blankets, and other necessary items. A trailer tracks behind a bike very well. Since they sit so low to the ground, their center of gravity is much lower, which improves balance.

■ Organization and Care of Medical Equipment

It is easier to work as a bike medic if your medical equipment is grouped in a logical order. One way to do this is to divide your gear in relation to the ABCs of medical care: Airway, Breathing, and Circulation. One of the most effective ways to keep these items together is the use of resealable freezer bags. These come in a variety of sizes, and they are transparent, disposable, waterproof, and cost-effective. A quart-size bag can carry a nasal cannula, nonrebreather and a nebulizer to keep with your portable oxygen. Your IV supplies can be grouped and kept in a gallon-size or larger bag. You may group all your bandaging to fit into one bag. Keeping these items together also helps protect them from moisture and damage from rolling around loosely in your panniers or backpack.

■ Medication

Medication is best kept in its original packaging for protection. The original packaging quickly identifies the drug, dose, and expiration date. However, this may not always be convenient. For example, small glass ampules of epinephrine 1:1000 can be wrapped in 4 × 4s and placed in a 35 mm film capsule or a properly labeled empty medicine bottle. You may choose to tape a syringe with a needle to the packaged medicine or keep them together in a single sealable storage bag.

The bike medic needs to carry the necessary medication and equipment to treat severe allergic reactions caused by insect stings and foods. A convenient and easily accessible way to do so is to construct an anaphylaxis kit containing the following items: 1 disposable sharps shuttle, 1 TB syringe, 1 3-mL syringe with 21-gauge needle, 1 Epi 1:1000, 1 50 mg/L mL benadryl (diphenhydramine). These items, with the exception of the 3 mL syringe, can be placed in the sharps shuttle for easy access. The 3 mL syringe can be taped to the outside of the sharps container. Local protocols should dictate actual drug choices, quantities, and deployment schemes.

■ AEDs and Cardiac Monitors/ Defibrillators

One of the biggest investments of an EMS bike team is the AED or cardiac monitor/defibrillator. Advances in technology have made both of these devices smaller, lighter, and more cost-effective.

Bike teams usually choose AEDs for a number of reasons. First, they can be used by civilians, first responders, EMTs, and paramedics. This makes them highly adaptable for bike teams that may not always have personnel available to deliver advanced cardiac care. AEDs are significantly lighter and more compact than cardiac monitor/defibrillators. They can easily fit into a pannier bag or backpack. AEDs are designed to be rugged, and some are even waterproof. However, AEDs are limited to defibrillation and passive monitoring of the heart. When buying an AED, a bike team must consider their needs and select an appropriate model.

Considerations when buying an AED include cost, biphasic current, multi-lead capability, diagnostic screen, manual override for ALS care, infant and child capability, compatibility of defibrillator pads with ambulance's monitor/defibrillator, internal memory data storage, infrared or USB data downloads, and capacity for future upgrades.

Cardiac monitors/defibrillators require advanced life support training to interpret the cardiac rhythm and initiate appropriate care. They can defibrillate, cardiovert, and pace the heart. Some include features such as 3-, 4-, and 12-lead capabilities, pulse oximetry, blood pressure monitoring, end tidal CO2 monitoring, and GPS clock synchronization with dispatch and wireless technology. Cardiac monitors/defibrillators tend to be heavier and bulkier than AEDs, and, because of their functionality, cost considerably more. The primary reasons why some bike teams choose the monitor/defibrillator are to perform a 12-lead ECG and to have the ability to cardiovert or pace the heart. This can be useful if the bike team is to be ALS-enabled at all times.

■ Portable Oxygen

There are several factors to consider in selecting a portable oxygen tank for a bike team. Oxygen cylinders come in many sizes. As the size of oxygen cylinders increases, so does the weight and volume. Oxygen bottles are made from aluminum, steel, and such composite materials as epoxy, fiberglass, and carbon fiber, but aluminum is the most common. Aluminum is 50% lighter than steel. The composite materials are 70% lighter than steel oxygen tanks and have a higher working pressure, but are the most expensive. The most commonly used portable oxygen cylinder in the pre-hospital setting is the size D cylinder, which is 16.5 inches tall and holds 425 liters of oxygen. They range in weight from 10

FIGURE 23-5 Oxygen is available in bike-friendly sizes, like the cylinder on the right.

pounds (steel) to 3 pounds (carbon fiber); aluminum cylinders weigh 5 pounds. Some bike teams use the D cylinder because it is the same size as the cylinders used on their ambulance or fire apparatus. This may not be the best choice because of the size and weight.

There are a variety of smaller oxygen cylinders available to bike medics. The aluminum M6 (6 cubic feet) is less than 11.5 inches long, weighs 3 pounds, and holds 164 liters of oxygen (**FIGURE 23-5**). Smaller size cylinders such as the M2 (2 cubic feet), which hold only 34 liters of oxygen, may not last long enough for another oxygen source to arrive if you need to use a non-rebreather mask at 10 L/per minute flow. For this reason, many bike teams have found the M6 cylinder to be the best choice. In addition, some trunk bags are designed to carry the M6 bottle.

Sometimes bicycle riding conditions or a fall can damage an oxygen cylinder. Oxygen cylinders are under high pressure, and although they are equipped with a safety valve, they can become a missile or explosive if severely damaged. Check the oxygen tank and regulator for bulges, dents, or gouges before each assignment and after any falls or crashes.

Calculating the Duration of Supply of Oxygen

It is important to be able to calculate the duration of supply of oxygen especially if you do not have a spare oxygen cylinder or if you work with different size tanks during different assignments. It would be potentially life threatening for the patient if the oxygen ran out prior to an ambulance arrival on scene. Refer to your department's standard operating procedures and guidelines. It may be beneficial to create a chart listing all possible flow rate and capacity scenarios that provides you with duration of time.

Typical EMS Bike Team Equipment

TABLE 23-1 lists examples of medical gear for two bikes, both of which use a trunk bag and panniers to carry equipment. One of the bikes is set up for BLS; the other for ALS. They are set up to operate as a team. The weight of the rear rack bag and panniers with the BLS equipment is approximately 13 pounds. The weight of the rear rack bag and panniers with the ALS equipment is approximately 24 pounds. This is just an example; each medical bike team must assess its own situation and determine how to equip its bike medics to best serve its constituency. Decisions about the equipment, drugs, and other supplies to be carried should be made in conjunction with the agency medical director.

■ Other Examples

Toronto EMS (panniers)

- Laerdal 911 defibrillator with spare pads, battery, and MCM.
- Oxygen (mini tank) with regulator and flow gauge.
- Trauma kit: adult and child bag valve mask and reservoir bag; blood pressure cuff; antiseptic hand cleaner; adult and child oxygen masks and tubing; nasal cannula; oral airways; portable suction (V-Vac); spare ventolin nebulas; saline solution; sharps container; disposable gloves.

- Symptom relief kit: glucagons; epinephrine 1:1000; ASA, nitrolingual spray; ventolin nebules, 1.25 mg and 2.5 mg; 1-mL syringes with 28 gauge needle; 3-mL syringes with 21-gauge needle; 25-gauge needles; alcohol wipes; gauze; glucometer with glucose test strip; Band-aids.
- First Aid Kit (carried on the rider): adhesive tape; CIDA rinse antiseptic hand rinse; nasal airways; oral airways; triangular bandages; emergency blanket; motion sickness bags; gauze (4 X 4); kling bandage (various sizes); pressure dressings large and small; quick splint; Band-aids.

London Ambulance Service (trunk-style panniers)

Medical kit: defibrillator; one liter oxygen/entonox and one liter pulse oximeter monitor; automatic blood pressure monitor; adult/child bag and mask resuscitators; nasal/oropharangeal airways; maternity kit; adult/child oxygen masks; adrenaline; aspirin; glucagon; GTN; hypostop; salbutamol; watergel; bandages; dressings; clinical waste sharps bin/yellow bags; rubber gloves and cleanser. The paramedic carries an additional extended skills drug and equipment pack, and a bike tool kit.

Williamson Medical Center (backpack)

Willamson Medical Center's EMS cyclists operate in teams of two. The team members are typically equipped to split the weight of the equipment.

Rider 1: IV supplies (saline, IV catheter, etc.); oxygen; nasal/oropharangeal airways; nasal cannula; high-flow mask; combi-tube or endotracheal tube (depending on rider's licensure); bandages; antibacterial ointment; castile soap; anaphylaxis kit; hot packs; cold packs; assorted Band-aids; basic and advanced pharmacology as determined by the medical director

Rider 2: AED; bandages; elastic bandages; gauze (rolls and 4 X 4 squares, sterile & nonsterile); castile soap; antibacterial ointment; anaphylaxis kit; stethoscope; blood pressure cuff; assorted Band-aids; basic and advanced pharmacology as determined by the medical director.

Conclusion

Although they are deployed in a wide variety of circumstances, all EMS cyclists share one thing in common: their primary purpose is to respond to the emergency medical needs of their communities.

TABLE 23-1 EMS Bike Team Equipment

Basic Life Support Bike (BLS)

Rack Bag (contains the lightest, most readily used and accessible equipment)

6–10 sets of exam gloves

1 disposable mask with fluid shield

1 heavy trauma dressing

2 ABD Pads (absorbent wound dressing)

5–10 sterile 4 × 4s

Assorted band-aids, antibiotic ointment and cleansing wipes

1 roll of 2-inch tape

3 triangular bandages

1 roll of gauze

1 elastic bandage

1 SAM splint (moldable splint)

1 blood pressure cuff and stethoscope

1 biohazard red bag

Anaphylaxis kit

　1 TB (tuberculin) 1-mL syringe

　1 3-mL syringe with 21-gauge needle

　1 ampule epinephrine 1:1000

　1 50-mg in 1 mL vial of benadryl (diphenhydramine)

　2 alcohol preps

　1 disposable sharps shuttle

Bike tools

Patch kit

Tire levers

Multipurpose tool

Non-Drive Side Pannier

Bag valve mask (BVM)

100 mm, 90-mm oral pharyngeal airway

Combitube or PTL

Drive Side Pannier

1 500-mL normal saline

1 10-gtt (drops per ml) tubing, primary IV line

2 each 22-, 20-, 18-, and 16-gauge IV catheters

1 sharps shuttle

Advanced Life Support Bike (ALS)

Trunk Rear Rack Bag

1 glucometer with test strips and finger-stick devices

1 amp of D50 (50% dextrose)

1 1-mg dose of glucagon

2 epinephrine 1:10,000

1 atropine

2 lidocaine

1 150-mg solu-medrol

1 nitroglycerine spray

1 bottle of low-dose chewable aspirin

Drive Side Pannier

AED or cardiac monitor

Non-Drive Side Pannier

M6 O_2 cylinder and regulator

Intubation roll

1 nasal cannula

1 non-rebreather

1 nebulizer with 2 albuterol

Some EMS bike teams operate only during special events while others operate full-time. Regardless of the frequency and circumstances of deployment, EMS cyclists must ensure that they carry the appropriate medical equipment and supplies in the most readily accessible manner possible. This requires ongoing needs assessment and adjustment to ensure that the bike team responds to advances in medical technology as well as the changing needs of those whom it serves.

References

Lynch, Tom (2004). Medical Pannier Bags for EMS Bike Use. *IPMBA News*, Winter, pg 10.

Toronto EMS. http://www.toronto.ca/ems/operations/bikes.htm, January 21, 2007.

Scene Management and Safety

Introduction

One of the most difficult tasks of EMS cycling is that of scene management and safety. This guide cannot fully prepare you for the endless variety of conditions you will face in the performance of your duties. Patients, suspects, bystanders, family members, weather, terrain, and other man-made and natural circumstances provide an endless array of challenges. However, this chapter can and does provide an overview of scene management and safety.

In a typical emergency call, the dispatch information provides clues as to the circumstances that can be expected when approaching or arriving at a scene. However, because many EMS cyclists work events rather than answer calls, the cyclist often receives requests for assistance from a bystander or the complainant. There may be no dispatch information to review. Therefore, getting as much accurate information as possible about the emergency call is vitally important, as is communicating that information to dispatch or the command center.

Approaching the Scene

Many conditions dictate how quickly a bike medic can respond to a scene, such as crowd density, ter-

rain and obstacles, cycling ability, adequacy of lighting equipment at night, and level of fitness. Negotiating a crowd via bicycle to get to a scene can be as frustrating as driving an ambulance or fire apparatus. Use of a whistle, vocalization, or siren may be necessary to clear pedestrians from your path. The goal is to arrive on scene quickly, safely, and prepared to control the situation while administering patient care.

■ Scene Assessment

Just as EMS personnel in motor vehicles conduct a "windshield survey" of the scene to ensure safe staging, bike medics should begin their approach with a "handlebar survey" (**FIGURE 24-1**). On a bicycle, you are in a vulnerable position. You can be physically constrained by your environment, and you may not be able to resist threats as you straddle the bike. Retreat becomes difficult once you commit to the area around the scene. While your main concern is with the immediate scene, resist the urge to focus solely on it. A scene assessment will reveal the urgency of the situation and potential hazards.

Slow as you near the scene to evaluate the situation. Ride a large circle around it, surveying the entire area. Look for safety issues first. Are the police present? If not, do you need to call them? Hostile patients, suspects, and bystanders are not the only potential hazards. Physical hazards such as unsafe structures, sharp debris, chemical spills or leaks, and downed power lines may also be present. Plan an escape route in case the scene becomes unsafe, and be prepared to use the mechanical advantage afforded by the bike as necessary. Determine the number of patients and the nature and mechanism of the injury or illness. Request additional resources if necessary. Look for an entry point to the scene for other responding agencies and ambulance crews that may enable them to avoid crowds, blocked roads, or other obstacles. The more familiar you are with the scene, the better prepared you will be to provide assistance without putting yourself at risk.

Establishing Scene Safety

Upon arrival at the scene, identify yourself as an emergency medical care provider so you will not be mistaken for a law enforcement officer. A hostile patient is less likely to exhibit aggression towards medical personnel than toward a police officer, so identifying yourself may be all that is required to keep the situation calm. Communicate your arrival

FIGURE 24-1 A scene assessment will reveal the urgency of the situation and potential hazards.

on scene to dispatch, and indicate if the location differs from the original information conveyed or if it was a non-dispatched incident. Provide very detailed location information, including cross streets and landmarks, in case you need assistance. A bicycle is much more difficult to locate visually than an ambulance.

Place the bike to provide room to work on and around your patient while at the same time preventing bystanders from encroaching onto the scene (**FIGURE 24-2**). The bicycle can provide both a limited physical barrier and a larger psychological one. Place the bike with the drive chain side away from the scene. This will provide some protection if someone pushes against the bike, because the kickstand is on the non-drive train side. It can be helpful to ask a bystander to hold onto the bicycle and keep it upright. Natural or built barriers can also be used to help secure the scene.

The bike should be staged far enough away from

the patient to allow for an adequate work area and reduce the risk of the bike falling onto you or the patient. Night operations may require you to stage your bike so that you can optimize the lighting system on your handlebars to illuminate the scene. For daytime operations, some bike medics mark their location with shockcorded poles topped with flags to enable back-up personnel or transport to find them more easily. These can be carried in a fairly compact space and extended when needed. A small piece of suction tubing may be attached to the rear rack to serve as a mount for the pole, which requires a minimal amount of space and weight. Strobes can be useful for this purpose at night.

In a crowded situation, theft from the bicycle is a possibility. Developing a protocol to protect controlled substances is the responsibility of the medical director; many require that these items be carried on the body rather than on the bike. Valuable medical equipment should be secured in the panniers.

Administering Patient Care

When the scene is secure and you are reasonably certain that both you and the patient are safe, begin administering patient care according to agency protocol. If back-up or transport is needed, provide a patient report and detailed directions to the scene. Request that the ambulance personnel bring any additional equipment, such as spinal immobilization or cardiac monitor, with them if they are not able to bring the vehicle close to the scene. Eliminating unnecessary trips for additional equipment saves time, looks professional, and makes for a smoother transfer of patient care. Bystanders can be asked to meet the ambulance crew and guide them to the scene.

Additional Equipment

Request that the ambulance personnel bring any additional equipment, such as spinal immobilization or cardiac monitor, with them if they are not able to bring the vehicle close to the scene.

Leaving the Scene

After the patient has been removed from the scene, the scene must be dismantled. Many EMS supplies, such as cervical collars, IV catheters,

FIGURE 24-2 Place the bike to provide room to work on and around your patient while at the same time preventing bystanders from encroaching onto the scene.

tubing, oxygen supplies, etc., come in separate packaging that can sometimes become separated from crews who are working scenes, especially when the patient's condition demands quick transport. Trash left on the scene reflects poorly on your department. Take time to make certain that all trash (especially sharps) is accounted for and removed from the scene; each team member should carry a small sharps container and several red bio-hazard bags. These take up very little cargo space and can be placed in the waste receptacle of the responding ambulance for disposal at the hospital.

Cleaning up the scene will likely not attract attention from the public, but failing to do so will, and will be perceived as putting the public at risk. The safety of the public is as much part of your job as the safety of patients and yourself.

Cleaning up the Scene

Trash left on the scene reflects poorly on your department. Take time to make certain that all trash (especially sharps) is accounted for and removed from the scene.

The Hostile Scene

Sometimes an EMS scene may be or become hostile. When a scene becomes unsafe, the bike medic's best approach is to leave the scene until it can be secured by police. If a situation escalates quickly and/or there is no escape route, it may be necessary to take a defensive posture. This means that your

FIGURE 24-3 The bicycle can be used as a barrier between you and a hostile patient or onlooker.

intention is only to protect yourself from the threat, not to subdue a hostile person. In some areas, EMS personnel are issued firearms or pepper spray. Use of these levels of force or any personal safety and conflict management training is regulated by departmental guidelines, not IPMBA standards.

The first line of defense between a hostile individual and yourself is the placement of your bike. Try to create a barrier by placing the bike between you and the hostile patient (**FIGURE 24-3**). If necessary, you can drag the bike while stepping backward to remove yourself from the situation. If the patient charges you, dropping the bike in his or her path may cause the person to trip and fall, giving you time to escape.

Most police cyclists make it a habit to unbuckle their helmets when approaching a suspect, and it is advisable for medics to do the same in a potentially hostile situation. The purpose of a helmet is to protect your head. It will do that whether the protection is needed to avoid injury from an impact with the ground or from an intentional blow to the head. Buckled straps, however, can prove deadly if the helmet is grabbed in a fight.

Conclusion

Scene management and safety are essential for delivering good patient care. Principles for scene management and safety for EMS cyclists are similar to those practiced every day by EMTs, paramedics, and firefighters. Learning and practicing the skills of responding with your bike, staging, and taking defensive measures if necessary are essential to the professional bike medic.

Glossary

Active lighting: A light source that involves a bulb and an energy source in the form of a battery or generator.

Anaerobic threshold: The exercise level at which the body begins to switch from aerobic (oxygen-using) to anaerobic processes to produce energy.

Automatic external defibrillator (AED): A device that delivers a measured electrical shock to the heart in an attempt to restart it.

Backward flip: A fall in which the front wheel "unweights" to the point at which the rider lands on his back.

Bar ends: Any of various-shaped extensions that connect to the ends of mountain bike handlebars.

Barrel adjuster: A threaded bolt with a hole through its center and a special nut designed to be turned by hand, allowing the fine adjustments of cable tension.

Basal metabolic rate: The minimum amount of energy needed by the body to maintain itself at its current level.

Bicycle: A two-wheeled, chain-driven vehicle propelled by pedaling.

Bicycle fit: The art and science of adjusting a bicycle to provide the rider with maximum comfort, efficiency, and injury prevention.

Bicycle lane: A portion of a roadway that has been designated by striping, signing and/or pavement markings for the preferential or exclusive use of bicyclists.

Bicycle path: A bikeway physically separated from motorized vehicular traffic by an open space or barrier and either within the highway right-of-way or an independent right-of-way.

Bicycle Response Team (BRT): A team of police cyclists trained in crowd management techniques.

Bike rodeo: An obstacle or skills course, sponsored or promoted by public safety agencies, which encourages community involvement and bicycle safety.

Bike route: A signed or mapped route whose purpose is to facilitate bike travel.

Bottom bracket: The bearing assembly to which the bicycle's crank arms are attached.

Brakes: Assembly which provides the ability to slow and stop a bicycle.

Brake pads: The rubber blocks attached to the brake cantilever arms on rim brakes which slow and stop the bike.

Braze-on: Any small fitting attached to a bicycle frame (typically by brazing or silver soldering) for guiding brake and shifter cables or for attaching water bottle cages or racks.

Cable guide: A tube, mounted on the frame, that guides a brake or shift cable.

Cable housing: Flexible tubing that contains a brake or shift cable.

Carbohydrate: The primary fuel for physical activity, containing molecules of glucose.

Cassette: The assembly of gears mated to the rear hub, also known as a cogset.

Chain tool: A tool for disconnecting and attaching a chain link.

Chainrings: The gears on the front of the bike, part of the crank set assembly.

Chain elongation: Elongation of a chain beyond the standard .5 inch per link, also known as chain wear or chain stretch.

Chain stays: The tubes that connect the bottom bracket to the rear wheel.

Chromoly: An alloy of steel, chromium, and molybdenum, used for frames.

Cleat: The mechanism on the bottom of a bicycle shoe that locks into a clipless pedal.

Clipless pedal: A pedal designed to lock to a mating device (cleat) on the bottom of the cyclist's shoe by means of a special spring-loaded mechanism.

Cog: A sprocket mounted to the cassette on a multi-speed bike.

Components: The mechanical parts of the bicycle, including the crankset, derailleurs, shifters, and brakes.

Concealment: An object or barrier that hides a person from view but cannot stop projectiles.

Conductive Energy Device (CED): An electronic control device that overrides the central nervous system, causing the muscles to contract and inhibiting the subject's ability to resist or fight.

Cover: An object or barrier that provides protection from projectiles.

CPSC: The Consumer Product Safety Commission, which sets the U.S. standards for bicycle helmets.

Crankarms: The levers that connect the pedals to the bottom bracket spindle and that hold the front chain rings.

Crankset: A group of components that comprise the removeable parts of the bottom bracket, the chainrings, and the crankarms.

Cross-chaining: Allowing the chain to ride on either the longest front chain ring and largest rear cog, or smallest front chain ring and smallest rear cog.

Crossover dismount: A move in which the cyclist crosses one leg over the back wheel, coming to a stop with both legs on the same side of the bike.

Dehydration: A condition in which fluid loss exceeds fluid replenishment.

Derailleur: A gear-changing device that "derails" the chain from one chain ring to another while the bicycle is in motion.

Disc brakes: Brakes consisting of a caliper and rotor and operated by a mechanical or hydraulic internal piston.

Down tube: The frame tube that connects the head tube to the bottom bracket.

Drive train: A system of shifters, cassette, front and rear derailleurs, crank set, and chain that drives a derailleur bike.

Dropouts: The forward-facing slots into which the rear-wheel axle is clamped to mount the wheel. The forward slope allows the wheel to drop out forwards to facilitate changing the tire.

Electrolytes: A substance in solution which transmits an electric current by the formation of ions. Commonly found in sports drinks, electrolytes are used to replenish the body after dehydration caused by exercise, diarrhea, or vomiting.

EMS Cyclist Instructor (EMSCI): A certified EMS cyclist who is certified to conduct the IPMBA EMS Cyclist Certification Course.

Endo: A fall on a bicycle in which the rear end lifts off the ground and the rider goes over the handlebars.

Ferrule: A removable, metal cylinder used to secure the ends of cable housing caps.

Float: The amount of lateral movement afforded to the foot by clipless pedals.

Fork: The pair of tubes (blades) that connect the front wheel to the steerer tube.

Frame: The structure, usually made of tubing, which forms the foundation for a bicycle.

Front suspension: Front shocks or other front fork suspension designed to absorb shock.

Full suspension: A bike equipped with both a front suspension fork and a rear shock or coil spring.

Gauntlet: A training exercise in which a bike officer learns about the vulnerability of his or her weapons while in the riding position.

Glycolysis: The breakdown of carbohydrates to fuel activity.

Good Spin: 75-100 pedal revolutions per minute; maximizes efficiency and conserves energy.

Grips: Rubber or plastic sheaths that cover the handlebars where you place your hands.

Grip shifter: A shifter in which the gear is changed by twisting the handlebar grip.

Handlebar Survey: A scene assessment conducted by public safety cyclists as they approach an incident scene.

Hardtail: A bike with front suspension but no rear suspension.

Headset: The bearings inside the head tube that support the steerer tube.

Head tube: The frame tube that supports the steerer tube, and the fork.

Hook slide: Also known as a power slide, a manuever used to enable the cyclist to change direction quickly.

Hub: The center part of the wheel which is attached to the rim by spokes.

Hydraulic: A type of brakes which use brake fluid to actuate the pads, which offer better modulation even than most high-end side-pull calipers.

Hyponatremia: A condition that results when fluid intake exceeds fluid loss, diluting the body's sodium level.

Index shifters: Shifters that click into distinct positions that correspond with certain cogs and do not require fine-tuning.

International Police Mountain Bike Association (IPMBA): A non-profit organization dedicated to promoting the use of bikes for public safety, providing resources and networking opportunities, and offering the best, most complete training for public safety cyclists.

IPMBA Public Safety Cyclist: A person who has been certified by an IPMBA instructor after completing a standard course of instruction and passing both written and on-bike skills testing.

Jockey wheel: The pulley in a rear derailleur that

guides the chain from cog to cog during a gear shift.

Knobbies: Heavy-duty tires with large knobs spaced far apart to provide traction in wet, muddy conditions.

Lactic threshold: The highest intensity of exercise you can sustain before your body's ability to clear and buffer lactic acid is surpassed by the rate at which it is produced.

Lateral fall: A sideways fall off the bike.

League of American Bicyclists: The oldest and largest bicycle advocacy organization in the United States.

Limit screws: Factory-set screws that control a derailleur's range of motion.

Lockdown: Applying both front and rear brakes with equal force, bringing the bike to a complete stop, used at low speeds.

Lumen: A measurement of the amount of light that falls on an area at a certain distance from the light source.

Master link: A special link on a bicycle chain that can be opened by flexing a plate, removing a screw, or means other than driving out a rivet.

Maximum Braking: A technique used to bring the bike to a stop or reduce its speed when it is traveling too fast for the rider to dismount safely.

Maximum Heart Rate (MHR): The fastest rate at which the heart should pump during physical exertion.

Mountain bike (MTB): A bicycle intended for riding off-road. An MTB usually has a heavy-duty frame, fat (often knobby) tires, upright handlebars, and a longer wheelbase, lower top tube and greater clearances than a road bike.

Moving hazard: Anything that moves that may collide with a cyclist and cause him or her to crash.

Moving maneuvers: Crowd control movements employed by bicycle response teams, including columns, lines, diagonals, wedges, crossbow, and leapfrog.

MyPyramid: A food guidance system developed by the U.S. Department of Agriculture in 2005.

Nutrition panel: A food label required by the U.S. Food & Drug Administration.

One-third of the lane rule: Cyclists should occupy the appropriate one-third portion of the right-most lane leading to their destination.

Operations plan: A document that details all logistics for a special event or other operation.

Overcompensation: The strengthening of muscles during the rest periods of progressive overload.

Panniers: Bags that attach to the sides of a bicycle for carrying supplies.

Passive lighting: Reflective devices that do not provide their own light sources.

Pedal pressure: The amount of force applied to the pedals by the rider.

Pedal retention: A device designed to keep the cyclist's feet on the pedals.

Pinch flat: A flat tire caused by the tube being pinched between the rim and a hard object, usually due to under-inflated tires.

Police Cyclist Instructor (PCI): A certified police cyclist who is certified to conduct the IPMBA Police Cyclist Certification Course.

Presta valve: An air filler valve used on most high-pressure bicycle tires. It is thin, screws shut, and held closed by air pressure.

Preventive maintenance: Ongoing cleaning and care performed to keep a bicycle in good working order and prevent serious repairs.

Progressive overload: A means of improving fitness through alternating cycles of muscle stress and rest.

Public Safety: any public safety service, including law enforcement, security, and emergency medical service.

Quick-release: A lever used on wheel hubs, and sometimes seat posts, which replaces the locknut for easy, no-tool removal or adjustment.

Quick Turn: A collision avoidance technique that results in the rider traveling in a different direction.

Rack: A frame that attaches over the rear wheel for carrying rack bags or attaching panniers.

Rear scan: Glancing backwards over the shoulder to monitor traffic, also known as a shoulder check.

Retro-reflective materials: Passive lighting devices that reflect light back to its source.

R.I.C.E.: Acronym for rest, ice, compression and elevation, a basic treatment regime for strains and sprains.

Rim: The outer part of a bicycle wheel that supports the tube and the tire.

Rim brakes: Brakes that work by applying pressure on both sides of the wheel rim with brake pads.

Rim tape, rim strip: A strip of plastic or cloth placed inside a wheel rim to protect the tube from sharp spoke edges.

Roadway: The portion of the highway, including shoulders, designated for vehicle use.

Rock Dodge: An obstacle avoidance technique that results in the rider continuing straight.

Saddle: A bicycle seat.

Schrader: An air filler valve found on standard passenger vehicles. It is thick and is held shut by a spring.

Seat post: The removable tube onto which the saddle mounts.

Seat stays: The tubes that connect the rear wheel to the top of the seat tube.

Seat tube: The frame tube that connects between the top tube and the bottom bracket. The seat post inserts into the top of the seat tube.

Security Cyclist Instructor (SCI): A certified security cyclist who is certified to conduct the IPMBA Security Cyclist Certification Course.

Shared roadway: A road or street that is open to both bicycle and motor vehicle travel.

Shifter: A lever or other mechanism operated by the rider to shift gears.

Site survey: An in-depth analysis of an event location resulting in a site map and operations plan.

Skewer: The portion of a wheel quick-release mechanism that extends through the hub axle.

Speed Positioning Principle: The slowest vehicles operate in the rightmost lane and the fastest vehicles operate in the leftmost lane.

Spin: Pedaling with a high cadence and low pedal force; the result of proper gear selection.

Sprocket: A disc bearing teeth for driving a chain; applies to both the front chainrings and rear cassette.

Static maneuvers: Employed by Bicycle Response Teams operating in a small geographic area. Examples include the post and barrier techniques.

Steerer tube: The tube that goes through the head tube and connects the fork to the handlebar stem.

Stem: The tube that connects the handlebars to the steerer tube.

Surface hazard: An obstacle on the riding surface that makes the rider lose control and crash.

Suspension fork: A fork equipped with shock absorber(s).

Three R's: Principles to which all training should adhere: realism, recency, and relevance.

Tire bead: The edge of a tire that seats down inside the wheel rim and is held in place by air pressure within a small groove in the wheel rim.

Tire inserts: Puncture-resistant liners placed between the tire and the inner tube.

Tire levers: Little crowbars used to help remove a tire from the rim.

Toe clips: A clip-and-strap system that connects a rider's feet to the pedals.

Top tube: The top, horizontal frame tube connecting the head tube and the seat tube.

Trackstand: The act of balancing a bicycle without apparent motion, by means of small forward-and-backward movements.

Vehicular cycling: The act of operating a bicycle in accordance with the motor vehicle code.

Visual hazard: An obstacle or condition that prevents cyclists and motorists from seeing one another and other road hazards.

VO2 max: Aerobic capacity; the maximum amount of oxygen the body can use during a given time.

Watt: The rate of energy consumption by an electrical device.

Wheel: An assembly comprised of four parts: hub, rim, spokes, and tire.

Workstand: A frame that holds a bicycle off the ground for convenient repair; also known as a repair stand.

Index

Photo Credits

Top left cover image courtesy of Kathleen Vonk.

Section 1
Opener © Jamie Rector/Bloomberg News/Landov.

Chapter 1
Opener courtesy of St. Paul Police Department; 1-1 © Stamford Historical Society; 1-2 Courtesy of Seattle Police Department; 1-3 Courtesy of Greg Johnson; 1-4 Courtesy of British Columbia Ambulance Service; 1-5 Courtesy of Mickey Veich.

Chapter 2
Opener courtesy of Joseph Labolito, Temple University Photographer, Temple University Police Department; 2-1 Courtesy of Kathleen Vonk; 2-2 Courtesy of Christopher Davala; 2-3 Courtesy of Rick McClure, LAFD; 2-5 Courtesy of Jody Reid.

Chapter 3
Opener courtesy of John Brandt; 3-1A-D Courtesy of Trek Bicycle Corporation; 3-2 and 3-4 illustrations by Todd Telander which first appeared in *Zinn & the Art of Mountain Bike Maintenance* (VeloPress, 2005), used here with permission of the publisher.

Chapter 5
Opener courtesy of John Brandt; 5-1A Courtesy of Greg Johnson; 5-1B Courtesy of Christopher Davala; 5-3 Courtesy of Thames Valley Police.

Chapter 6
Opener courtesy of Al Simpson; 6-1 Courtesy of Greg Johnson.

Chapter 7
Opener courtesy of John Brandt; 7-3 Courtesy of David Hildebrand; 7-8 Courtesy of Thomas Moreland; 7-9 and 7-10 Adapted from the 46-page booklet Bicycling Street Smarts, copyright Rodale, Inc., and published by Rubel BikeMaps (www.bicyclingstreetsmarts.com).

Chapter 8
Opener courtesy of Kathleen Vonk; 8-1, 8-2, and 8-4 Courtesy of British Columbia Bike Sense and the Oregon Department of Transportation, Pedestrian and Bicycle Program; 8-3, 8-5, 8-6, 8-7, and 8-8 Adapted from the 46-page booklet Bicycling Street Smarts, copyright Rodale, Inc., and published by Rubel BikeMaps (www.bicyclingstreetsmarts.com).

Chapter 9
Opener © photobar/ShutterStock, Inc.; 9-1 and 9-2 Adapted from the 46-page booklet Bicycling Street Smarts, copyright Rodale, Inc., and published by Rubel BikeMaps (www.bicyclingstreetsmarts.com); 9-3 Courtesy of British Columbia Bike Sense and the Oregon Department of Transportation, Pedestrian and Bicycle Program.

Chapter 10
Opener courtesy of Matt Crenko, Bethlehem Police Department; 10-1 Courtesy of John Brandt; 10-2 Courtesy of Thames Valley Police.

Chapter 11
Opener courtesy of Rich Bahret, People Places and Things Photography.

Chapter 12
Opener courtesy of John Brandt; 12-5 through 12-13 and 12-15 through 12-26 illustrations by Todd Telander which first appeared in *Zinn & the Art of Mountain Bike Maintenance* (VeloPress, 2005), used here with permission of the publisher.
Selected text by Lennard Zinn (pp. 115-133) first appeared in *Zinn & the Art of Mountain Bike Maintenance* (VeloPress, 2005), used here with permission of the publisher.

Chapter 13
Opener courtesy of National Cancer Institute; 13-1 Courtesy of USDA; 13-2 © Tom Oliveira/ShutterStock, Inc.

Chapter 14
Opener courtesy of Jon Pesesko, Bethlehem Police Department; 14-1A-F Courtesy of Jim Bowell; 14-2 Courtesy of Al Simpson; 14-3 © E. M. Singletary, M.D. Used with permission.

Chapter 15
Opener, 15-1, and 15-2 courtesy of Bethlehem Police Department.

Chapter 16
Opener, 16-1, 16-2, and 16-3 courtesy of Jim Bowell.

Section 2
Opener © Alan Diaz/AP Photos.

Chapter 17
17-2 Courtesy of Thames Valley Police.

Chapter 19
Opener, 19-2A and C, 19-3, and 19-5 courtesy of Kathleen Vonk; 19-2B and D Courtesy of John Brandt.

Chapter 20
Opener, 20-1, and 20-2 Courtesy of Tony Valdes; 20-3 Courtesy of John Brandt; 20-4 Courtesy of Steve Reid.

Chapter 21
Opener courtesy of Kathleen Vonk; 21-2 and 21-3 Courtesy of Jody Reid.

Section 3
Opener courtesy East Baton Rouge EMS.

Chapter 22
Opener courtesy of Gerard Robinson; 22-1 Courtesy of Thomas Lynch, MBE; 22-2 and 22-4 Courtesy of Greg Johnson; 22-3 Courtesy of Steve Bardens.

Chapter 23
23-1 and 23-4 Courtesy of Greg Johnson; 23-2 Courtesy of Jim Bowell; 23-3 Courtesy of Thomas Lynch, MBE.

Chapter 24
Opener courtesy of Kathleen Vonk; 24-1 Courtesy of Greg Johnson.

Unless otherwise indicated, photographs are under copyright of Jones and Bartlett Publishers, courtesy of the Maryland Institute of Emergency Medical Service Systems.